D0927483

WITHDRAWN

THE STORY-SHAPED WORLD

The Story-Shaped World

Fiction and Metaphysics:
Some Variations on a Theme

BRIAN WICKER

UNIVERSITY OF NOTRE DAME PRESS
Notre Dame, Indiana 46556

American edition 1975
University of Notre Dame Press
Notre Dame, Indiana 46556

First published 1975 by
The Athlone Press
University of London
at 4 Gower Street London WCI

Library of Congress Cataloging in Publication Data

Wicker, Brian, 1929–
    The story-shaped world.

    Bibliography: p.
    Includes index.
    1. Fiction—20th century—History and criticism.
2. Fiction—Technique. I. Title.
PN3503.W46 1975   808.3   74–27889
ISBN 0–268–01669–0

Printed in the United States of America

*For Teresa, especially
and for Mary, Philip and Lucy as well*

Preface

We have been saying for a long time now that literature is an indispensable witness in the courts of the philosopher and the theologian; and conversely that the literary critic can no longer afford to be a mere visitor in the territory of the speculative thinker. In this book I have tried to bear witness in two places at once, by discussing some common themes from both points of view. In Part One I have tried to explore the philosophical and theological implications of two main ideas: the idea that metaphor, especially as understood by linguists, is endemic in all communication since it is simply one of the two 'poles' of language itself; and the idea that metaphor is never an 'innocent' figure but always implies a subterranean metaphysic. In Part Two I try to show how the conclusions drawn from these provocative and sometimes unwelcome thoughts illuminate the work of various modern writers of fiction.

I should perhaps indicate briefly how the material of the book is organised. I have subtitled it 'some variations on a theme' to suggest how each chapter, while retaining a measure of self-sufficiency and unity of purpose, contributes from a particular viewpoint to a common set of preoccupations. After an introduction in which I introduce some basic elements of my theme, I try in Chapter 1 to show the hidden connections between modern theories of language and the traditional concepts of 'analogy' and 'metaphor'. Chapter 2 pursues this investigation further by considering the concept of narrative, in which the related dimensions of analogy and metaphor play a crucial role. Chapters 3 and 4 explore two concepts that have arisen in the preceding discussion: those of 'Nature' and 'God'. These four chapters constitute the 'theoretical' aspect of my enquiry. In Part Two I approach my theme from the critical end, by essays on three pairs of contrasting masters of fiction in the present century: Lawrence and Joyce, Waugh and Beckett, Robbe-Grillet and Mailer. In each case some aspect of what has already been discussed in a theoretical way is as it were tested out in the practice of narrative art.

Thus the various sections of the book circle around a set of related notions that constitute its central preoccupation. But the theme as such I do not attempt to 'state' directly, though I hope it emerges with increasing clarity from the juxtaposition of different approaches. For it is not a thesis but rather an exploration of the relations that hold, I believe, between apparently disparate concepts drawn from a variety of disciplines: linguistics, literary criticism, the philosophy of language, speculative theology. I shall be satisfied if a few new connections between these disciplines have been made and not too many wires have become crossed in the process.

My thanks are due to many people with whom I have discussed the content and form of this book, but especially to Ian Gregor, David Lodge and Walter Stein who have all made important suggestions and saved me from many mistakes, although they are in no sense responsible for those that remain. I must also thank the editors of *New Blackfriars* (Herbert McCabe) and *The Journal of Narrative Technique* (George Perkins) for accepting parts of the book for publication as articles. The poem *Myxomatosis* by Philip Larkin is reprinted from *The Less Deceived* by permission of Mr Larkin and The Marvell Press, England. Finally, I must thank my sister, Mrs Shirley Edwards for drawing a diagram, Mrs Sylvia Buchanan for help with the bibliography and index, and especially my wife and family for putting up with me while the work was written.

Department of Extramural Studies   B.W.
University of Birmingham
1974

Contents

Note

In addition to the numbered footnotes, notes of a more extended and discursive character are to be found at the end of each part, on pages 107–13 and 208–12 respectively. Asterisks are used to refer the reader to these notes.

Introduction: Metaphor and Metaphysics in Fiction

The novel has always been the most comprehensive and ill-defined of literary forms. But today the novelist is faced with an unprecedented number of mutually incompatible choices, not merely of subject-matter and style, but between basic conceptions of what a novel is and indeed of what kind of world the novelist himself is living in and trying to depict. Not only do critics debate among themselves the 'poetics' of fiction, but novelists too are often involved in the critical argument.[1] Among the strands within the current discussion, and among the various kinds of works that offer themselves to the reader under the general rubric of 'novels' one particular disagreement seems to me to be especially significant. It can be illustrated by reference to two well-known names in the world of the contemporary novel: Alain Robbe-Grillet and Norman Mailer. At the level of style, the disagreement between the two may be seen in their differing attitudes to the use of metaphor in fiction. For Mailer, a rich metaphorical diet is a necessity for the would-be novelist of today. As he himself puts it, reporting his own thoughts as those of a character in one of his own 'non-fiction novels',

> technology had penetrated the modern mind to such a depth that voyages in space had become the last way to investigate the meta-physical pits of that world of technique which choked the pores of modern consciousness—yes, we would have to go out into space until the breadth and mystery of new discovery would force us to comprehend the world once again as poets, comprehend as savages

[1] See the series of articles on 'Towards a Poetics of Fiction' in *Novel*, beginning in Vol. i (Fall 1967); also Lodge, *The Novelist at the Crossroads*, Josipovici, *The World and the Book*, Bergonzi, *The Situation of the Novel*.

who knew that if the universe was a lock, its key was a metaphor rather than measure.[2]

Mailer's plea for a return to an older poetic and metaphorical way of looking at and describing the world is incarnated in the very style of the plea itself: a 'savage' poetry in which metaphors proliferate and mingle in the effort to encompass the problem of the novelist confronted by the mystery of a new discovery; which is also the rediscovery of an ancient wisdom. Robbe-Grillet on the other hand, sees it as the job of the modern novelist to get rid of all metaphors, to cleanse his linguistic palate of the taste of what he calls this 'never innocent figure of speech'. To use metaphors, for example to speak of 'capricious' weather, 'majestic' mountains or the 'merciless' sun, is to taint a mere object with an illicitly anthropomorphic and moral meaning. Such attribution is never disinterested, for it stems from a dangerous yearning for reassurance that the world I inhabit is conformable to my designs upon it, that it has the meaning I want it to have. And furthermore, the price I necessarily pay for this reassurance is extortionate: for it is nothing less than the sacrifice of my personal liberty.

> If I . . . confuse my own sadness with the sadness I attribute to the landscape, if I claim that this is no superficial relationship, I am thereby recognising that my present life is to some extent predestined. The landscape existed *before* me; if it is really *it* that is sad, it was sad *before* I was, and the harmony I feel today between its form and my mood was waiting for me long before my birth; I have always been destined for this sadness. . .[3]

But such a subjection of man to nature is not in fact inescapable. Today, Robbe-Grillet believes, we can see how to escape the 'metaphysical pact' that other men made in days gone by.

Despite their contradictory conclusions about the value of metaphor, the impulse from which the arguments of the two novelists spring is the same: a search for freedom. They differ because they have different conceptions of what enslaves them and their fellow-men. For Robbe-Grillet, the apparent despot is 'Nature':

[2] *A Fire on the Moon*, pp. 379–80.
[3] *Snapshots and Towards a New Novel*, p. 80.

... it is precisely Nature—animal, vegetable and mineral—that is the first to be tainted with our anthropomorphical vocabulary. This Nature, whether mountain, sea, forest, desert or valley, is both our model and our heart. She is in us and in front of us at the same time. She is neither temporary nor contingent. She petrifies us, judges us, and assures our salvation ... [Therefore] to reject our alleged 'nature' and the vocabulary that perpetuates its myth, to treat objects as purely external and superficial, is not—as people have claimed—to deny man, but to refuse to accept the 'pan-anthropic' content of traditional, and probably every other, humanism. In the final analysis it is merely to carry my claim to personal liberty to its logical conclusion.[4]

But the real despot, as Robbe-Grillet goes on to show in discussing nineteenth-century romantic fiction, is a bourgeois ideology which presents its particular mode of interpreting the world—the 'humanist' mode, the romantic mode, a metaphorical mode—as if it were ultimate and unchallengeable. In Mailer's case, however, the immediate cause of man's subjection is technology, the denaturing transformation of the human habitat by a seemingly irresistible historical force which oppresses the modern individual's soul. But behind that immediate diagnosis Mailer arraigns what he calls 'corporation-land', that is to say American super-power capitalism and all its cultural spawnings. For example, the ultimate significance of the Apollo II moon-voyage was that 'it could yet prove a revelation of the nature of the men who governed the world and the men who might take that rule away from them'.[5] Thus, in a sense, Mailer's tyrant also, like Robbe-Grillet's, is the enslaving power of a bourgeois ideology.

Allowing then for the profound differences of historical background between the Frenchman and the American, the Parisian and the New Yorker, it is possible to see beneath the apparent conflict about vocabulary, or 'style' a certain consensus about the fundamental determinants of contemporary life. Each of them in his own way admits the truth underlying Robbe-Grillet's affirmation that in humanistic and romantic fiction 'anthropomorphic analogies [i.e. metaphors] are too insistently, too coherently, repeated not to reveal a whole metaphysical system'.[6]

[4] Ibid., p. 81.   [5] Loc. cit.
[6] *Snapshots*, p. 78. On the distinction between analogies and metaphors, which Robbe-Grillet here fails to acknowledge, see below Chap. 1 passim.

That is to say, they both admit that to adopt a metaphorical 'style' is to adopt a metaphysical world-view. What divides them is the question whether the adoption of such a view helps or hinders men's search for freedom. If Robbe-Grillet maintains, as the basic tenet of his philosophy that 'Man looks at the world, but the world doesn't look back at him',[7] and that the recognition of this fact is a pre-condition of freedom, Mailer holds just the opposite: the universe is a 'lock' to which man has the key, and freedom lies in just this intimate reciprocity between Man and Nature. (That the key must be metaphor is of course obvious from the fact that even to state the principle it is necessary to speak by way of metaphor.)

It is not my concern here to explain *why* these two novelists, both strongly individualistic but also remarkably representative of general trends, should stand philosophically on such opposed sides of a fundamental divide. But it *is* to my purpose to draw attention to a remarkable parallel between the current literary debate about the vocabulary appropriate to fiction and a corresponding debate about the appropriate language for describing religious experience. For it is my contention, as I hope to show in subsequent chapters of this book, that the arguments in each case are ultimately about the same problem; and that the solution, if there is one, to the apparent contradictions is equally applicable to each area of concern. Indeed, I want to maintain that neither is fully intelligible without reference to the other: for the relation of fact to fiction, of the real world to the world of story, is itself a kind of 'metaphysical pact', a secret to which the narrator's art is the metaphorical key.

We may establish the parallel, to begin with, by noting that the difference between those who think like Robbe-Grillet and those who think like Norman Mailer is remarkably like the difference diagnosed three hundred years ago, by Pascal—'the first modern man'[8]—between the mode of thinking of the philosophers and that of the poets or story-tellers. Pascal's famous opposition between the God of the Philosophers and the God of Abraham, Isaac and Jacob is in the first place an opposition between styles of language. But Pascal knew well enough, as we do also, that the choice of a style is also the choice of a whole world-view. When the poets and story-tellers talked of God in the language of Mailer's 'savages', by way of metaphor, they were also

---

[7] Ibid., p. 82.　　　　[8] Goldmann, *The Hidden God*, p. 171.

choosing its accompanying metaphysic. Whereas, when the philosophers, remote ancestors of Robbe-Grillet's liberated man, spoke of Him they did so (if at all) in the sophisticated abstract language of geometrically-defined objects and value-free physical laws. Now the baneful intellectual dissociation which Pascal diagnosed as afflicting Christianity in his own time is far from cured today: indeed its ravages are as evident as ever. Consider for instance the contemporary divergence between the 'savage' poetic language of an all-too-religious counter-culture, with its pop-poetry and its pentecostal speaking with tongues, and the cool calculated understatements of canny philosophers and cautious academics. On the one hand we have language like this:

> we want
> to zap them
> with holiness
>
> we want
> to levitate them
> with joy
>
> we want
> to open them
> with love vessels
>
> we want
> to clothe the wretched
> with linen and light
>
> we want
> to put music and truth
> in our underwear[9]

and on the other hand we have the grim determined probings of academic philosophers, uncertainly picking their way amid treacherous linguistic craters like inexperienced astronauts on their first moonwalk:

> What is the contemporary Christian doing when he uses the word 'God' as he does? . . . the first step toward an answer . . . will [be to]

[9] See Roszak, *The Making of a Counter Culture*, p. 152, quoting a poem by Julian Beck published in *Paradise Now* (*International Times*, London, 12–25 July 1968).

draw attention to, and clarify the idea of, the edges of language. The second step will clarify, in the light of our earlier reflections on language, the linguistic behaviour of speaking at the edges of language, beginning first with some patterns of behaviour more or less closely related to that of religion . . . the third step will show that this initial analysis of religious discourse produces a more adequate description than those which present it as a set of factual propositions . . . etc. etc.[10]

To anyone versed in history there should be nothing surprising about this rift between the 'sophisticated' value-free language of the philosopher and the 'savage' metaphorical language of the poet and story-teller. The times when the two have danced harmoniously together have been very few. If Pascal, the greatest religious mind of the Cartesian revolution, sought a solution of the conflict in the ultimate victory of the poets' metaphors over the philosophers' 'measures', Aquinas—the greatest theologian of the medieval world— could develop his religious philosophical synthesis only by under- valuing the cognitive value of poetry and narrative in theology. From the eighteenth-century onwards anyone who sought to mend the quarrel had to take, as his basic premiss, the fact of this initial separa- tion. For Pascal the new theology of Descartes led to the divorce between God the author of mathematical truths and the order of the universe and God the source of personal love and consolation. This divorce was later made absolute by Laplace. In the nineteenth century the same divorce was recognised by thinkers such as Coleridge and Newman and even Mill (not to mention Dickens) as having been further hardened by the new morality of Benthamism, which was given per- verted expression in the commerical utilitarian calculus of Victorian hard times. Against this they placed the demands of a sensitive moral conscience, the internal culture of the individual's feelings, an aware- ness of lost community and of the divine as a personal presence within the privacy of the soul.

Today the grounds for the divorce have shifted yet again. If the quarrels among theologians and philosophers are less heated this may be because they feel there is no need to look out for an innocent or a

---

[10] Van Buren, *The Edges of Language*, p. 76. I use Van Buren's example here simply to illustrate a general point, not to suggest that his work is any more 'academic' than many others in the field.

guilty partner. But if this new-found liberalism is to be welcomed for legal or moral reasons, it may well be that it is rooted in a new indifference to the whole idea of a marriage. This certainly seems to be the case with the religious adherents of the 'counter-culture', who see the philosophical treatment of religion as old hat, useless, irrelevant. The relatively modern efforts of thinkers like Teilhard de Chardin to mend the marriage often appear like the work of elderly marriage-counsellors in an age which rejects not only the marriage but the whole family of concepts that surrounds it. Yet if the theological debate is less heated, the corresponding literary argument seems today to be more intense. It is as though the issues have not been resolved, only transferred to another arena, in which the conceptual weapons used appear more up-to-date and relevant.

The fact that tends to be forgotten amid the current literary quarrel between—to use very crude labels—the 'Americans' led by Mailer and the 'French' led by Robbe-Grillet is that both regard their task as helping to free the individual from a system of emotional and cultural constraints which they see rooted in the inherited ideology of their respective societies. How then is it that they come to such mutually incompatible conclusions at the level of fictional expression? It can only be because the one sees the possibility of such freedom as lying in the recovery of a liberating metaphysic long ago disastrously abandoned, while the other sees any such metaphysic as historically and necessarily part of the oppressive ideology itself. It is impossible not to sympathise with both views, for each contains a large measure of truth. The problem then is not to decide between them but to try to discover why they should ever have come to the point of outright conflict. What has happened to make such profound diagnoses incompatible with each other? I think the clue can only lie in the mutual recognition that to admit the validity of metaphor at all is *ipso facto* to admit a whole metaphysical system. This is the common ground. The divergence comes, I want to suggest, when the cognitive role of *metaphor* is misunderstood through the weakening of a necessary counter-balancing force which I shall call—for the time being, risking some misunderstanding which I hope to remedy later—the pull of *analogical* language.

The medieval philosophical synthesis of Aquinas and others, in which a highly developed theory of *analogical* language played a crucial part, was wrought at the expense of underplaying the importance of poetry and story-telling: that is to say, by undervaluing, or even misunderstanding the role of *metaphorical* language. To put it shortly, the medievals had a highly developed sense of the *analogical*, but a correspondingly under-developed sense of the *metaphorical* uses of words. Inevitably, therefore, when the medieval achievement dis-integrated this highly developed theory of analogical language was the first victim of the collapse. Thenceforth thinkers like Pascal could rescue essential imaginative truths only by *substituting* a theory of metaphor for the defunct theory of analogy. And almost all subsequent debate has been conducted (at least until quite recently, with the revival of interest in what the medievals actually said) within the terms set by the dichotomy that faced Pascal. A great deal of the debate about metaphysical language in the tradition of Anglo-Saxon linguistic philosophy, and consequently a great deal of the 'new theology' that has been built upon it, is to my mind vitiated by pre-supposing, as a starting point, the futility of the medieval (i.e. thomist) account of analogical predication; and this has happened just at the time when there might have been the possibility of a new kind of synthesis based upon a marriage of the two partners, *metaphor* and *analogy*. The promotion of such a courtship is a basic purpose of this book.

Part One: Theoretical

I

Metaphor and 'Analogy'

In this chapter I want to explore the idea that the use of metaphorical language necessarily involves what Robbe-Grillet calls a 'whole metaphysical system'. In particular I shall try to show what such an assertion might mean by discussing the implications of contemporary ideas of 'metaphor' and 'analogy' and kindred terms.

i

The classical theorists looked on the use of metaphor with a certain lofty disdain. 'All such arts are fanciful and meant to charm the hearer. Nobody uses fine language when teaching geometry', said Aristotle; and Aquinas seems to have shared something of the same outlook.[1] Metaphor in the classical scheme then was simply a device of 'style', a rhetorical instrument. A different view of metaphor could only be formulated, perhaps, when theorists of language began to recognise the role that language had in forming and not just expressing, the contents of the mind. From the time of Giambattista Vico the truth has been emerging that metaphor is not just a way of describing things but is a way of *experiencing* them. The neo-classical idea of 'mathematical plainness' espoused by Thomas Sprat in the seventeenth century gave way eventually to Coleridge's heady enthusiasm: 'I would endeavour to destroy the old antithesis of Words and Things; elevating, as it were Words into Things and living Things too'.[2]

The basis for this change was the recognition that metaphor is a lamp, not just a mirror, held up to nature. This is why Shakespeare's

---

[1] *Rhetoric*, III 1404a; Aquinas, *Summa Theologiae*, I, Q. 1, Art. 9. See also Hawkes, *Metaphor*, pp. 6–11, and for a more positive view of Aristotle's theory of metaphor see Burrell, *Analogy and Philosophical Language*, pp. 71–5. Also See below p. 112, note to p. 95.

[2] Letter to Godwin, Sept. 1800 in *Collected Letters*, p. 626.

poetry had the effect, as Coleridge said, of making the reader himself into a kind of poet, an 'active creative being'. To make and to understand a metaphor are alike acts of the creative imagination. And furthermore, such acts are social as well as individual: for the language by which we see the world is itself a social reality. Thus insofar as language is incurably metaphorical, and what I. A. Richards called the 'omnipresent principle'[3] is embedded in every utterance we make, every metaphor is a co-operative endeavour. It not only joins us to things, it joins us to each other.

But if the Romantic tradition supports the thesis of some contemporary writers (Mailer is the obvious example) that metaphor is necessary even for understanding, let alone describing, the findings of modern consciousness, the dangers inherent in it must be recognised and credit be given to other modern writers, like Robbe-Grillet, for alerting us to them. The recurring temptation to self-indulgence and even dishonesty that goes with a dedication to metaphorical language is far from conquered today. Yet there is a deeper danger even than this: namely that language itself may become a barrier between ourselves and the world, instead of a lamp held up to illuminate it. If all language is metaphorical, as I. A. Richards seems to suggest, then all things automatically tend to become humanised and the world is delivered up to the not always tender mercies of man's own thirst for meaning. We need the corrective presence of the not-human, of the other, of that which is impervious to linguistic manipulation, if we are not to be led astray by what Robbe-Grillet calls our 'grandiose aspirations'. Ruskin's demand that we should repudiate the pathetic fallacy was not only a timely reminder to his contemporaries: it is also timely for us. In the world of fabulations and allegories, when our storytellers are only too anxious to tell us about 'hidden persuaders, hidden dimensions, plots, secret organisations, evil systems, all kinds of conspiracies against spontaneity of consciousness, even cosmic takeover',[4] we need vigilantly to maintain a countervailing respect for things as they are. As Frank Kermode has put it, 'there is a recurring need for adjustments in the interest of reality as well as of control'.[5]

---

[3] *The Philosophy of Rhetoric*, p. 92. Richards voices the 'modern' theory in a notably clear and persuasive way in the last two chapters of this book, taking as his starting point the view that 'not until Coleridge do we get any adequate setting of these chief problems of language' (p. 103).

[4] Tanner, *City of Words*, p. 16.   [5] *The Sense of an Ending*, p. 17.

Now I think the value of certain modern ideas about language is that for the first time they provide us with a counterweight to the dangerous pull of metaphor without denying its cognitive importance. They do so by placing metaphor in opposition, not to some supposedly literal language (Sprat's 'mathematical plainness') but to *metonymic* language. That is, they admit, one might say, that metaphor is an 'omnipresent principle' but they deny that it is the only, or over-riding principle. On the contrary, it is only one aspect, or axis of language and has to be constantly seen in partnership with another aspect or axis to which it is always complementary, namely the metonymic axis.

In order to show what this assertion means we must first of all go back to the work of Saussure, the 'father' of modern linguistics. Saussure showed that any actual utterance always involves two distinct kinds of act: (a) the act of choosing certain particular linguistic items (e.g. phonemes, words) rather than others of the same kind, and (b) the act of combining the chosen items in *this* way rather than in some other possible way. To take an obvious, if over-simplified example, the sentence 'you may stay today' may be regarded as the unique utterance it is because (a) out of all possible personal pronouns, only *you* is chosen, out of all possible auxiliary verbs only *may* is chosen, out of all main verbs only *stay* is chosen and out of all possible adverbs only *today* is chosen: and (b) because out of all the various possible orders, or functional arrangements, between these particular words which English grammar allows, the speaker has arranged his items in *this* particular order. Any alteration, whether in the choice of an item *or* in its functional position or role would result in a different sentence, with a different meaning. Thus, to substitute another personal pronoun— say 'he' for *you*—would produce a different sentence. But similarly to change the order of the words—say by placing *may* before *you* and thus changing the sentence into a question—would equally alter the sentence and its meaning.

Now Jakobson, following Saussure, has further pointed out that these two different kinds of act—the act of *selecting* items from a range on the one hand and the act of *combining* the chosen items in a certain way on the other— rest upon different, but complementary principles.[6] For the act of selection always implies the possible *substitution* of a

---

[6] Jakobson and Halle, *Fundamentals of Language*, pp. 58–62.

different but similar item, in place of the item chosen, without disturbance of the functional arrangement, or 'context' as a whole. Whereas the act of *combination* always sets up a functional arrangement or structure such that this arrangement could take a number of different forms without affecting the actual choice of the items included in it. In other words, the same items can be arranged in different ways just as different items can be arranged in the same way. Thus we have two sets of linked principles, each set constituting one side of a binary opposition:

Selection	v.	Combination
Similarity	v.	Contiguity
Substitution	v.	Context

Of these principles, only *contiguity* remains so far undefined. *Contiguity* is Jakobson's term for the relation of each item to the items next to it in the 'context'. That is to say, if (as we have already established) the relation of a chosen item to another item of the same kind which has *not* been chosen is one of 'similarity', the relation of that item to those others of different kinds which *have* been chosen must be the functional one of 'contiguity'. Thus, to pursue our exemplary sentence further, whereas we may say that e.g. all the personal pronouns which could be chosen as its subject are 'similar' to each other in the sense that they are items of the same kind, and can undertake the same function in the context, the four separate words themselves (you-may-stay-today) constitute a 'chain', each link of which is *contiguous*, that is *connected* by its particular role, to the next.

A number of other terms are commonly used to denote certain aspects of Saussure's distinction, and some of these are important for the present argument. The most important of these are the terms *syntagmatic* and *paradigmatic*. Syntagmatic, of course, is just another term for Jakobson's 'combination': for it denotes functional arrangement. But the term paradigmatic draws our attention to the 'selection' and 'substitution' features of the opposite principle, since an item chosen from a range of similar items may obviously be regarded as a 'paradigm' of all items of that kind. Now the terms *syntagmatic* and *paradigmatic* go back to Saussure and are clearly related to his distinction between *la langue* ('the language') and *la parole* ('speech'). 'The language' is that treasury of linguistic units and rules which exist independently of the individual speaker, and into which he is born as he learns to talk. 'Speech' on the other hand refers to the individual's drawing upon this treasury for the purpose of actual utterance. All utterance involves both 'langue' and 'parole'. But in Saussure's sense it seems clear that 'the language' is to be placed on the 'paradigmatic' side and 'speech' on the syntagmatic: for 'the language' is the treasury of items, or paradigms, from which the user selects, and 'speech' is the act of linking them into a significant chain, or syntagm. (A closely related pair of terms, used particularly by theorists such as Barthes, when speaking of non-verbal 'languages', or communication systems, is 'code' (paradigmatic) and 'message' (syntagmatic).)

Another pair of commonly used terms, and one more directly to our purpose, is that of *metaphor* and *metonymy*. These are clearly related to the contrasting concepts of 'similarity' on the one hand and of 'context' on the other. A metaphor after all is the verbal recognition of a similarity between the apparently dissimilar: whereas a *metonymy*— that is the use of a part, attribute or symbolic object for a whole or thing signified—is clearly a case of the contextual principle. As Jakobson puts it, 'any linguistic unit at one and the same time serves as a context for simpler units and/or finds its own context in a more complex linguistic unit',[7] and this is clearly the principle at work in the case of a *metonymy*. Consider the dictionary examples of 'sceptre', 'crown' or 'White House' used to indicate the sovereign authority of the state. Here the smaller unit (sceptre, crown, White House) has its context in the larger unit (sovereignty) and finds its significance in precisely that relationship.

Thus a larger list of the terms necessary to describe the structure of any actual utterance would have to include the following:

Language	Speech
Code	Message
Paradigmatic relation	Syntagmatic relation
Selection	Combination
Substitution	Context
Metaphor	Metonymy

Such a multiplicity of terms may well seem exasperating. In introducing yet another ingredient into this already rich mixture, therefore, I want to make it clear that I do so in order to clarify, and perhaps simplify, what is already there. My new ingredient is the term *analogy*.

[7] Ibid.

Now it should be made plain at the outset that I am not using this word in its common-or-garden sense: the sense in which, for example, Robbe-Grillet can speak of 'anthropomorphic analogies' when he means metaphors. *Analogy* in the sense I intend is not a genus of which metaphor is just one species. I am speaking of analogy in the sense in which it was used, as part of a theory of language, by e.g. Aquinas. In this sense analogy is more like metonymy than it is like metaphor. Thus Aquinas's simplest illustration of what is meant by an analogy is the application of the word 'healthy' to a person and to his 'urine'. (A modern medical equivalent might be *complexion*, in that we regard a healthy complexion as a sign of a healthy man just as medieval opinion regarded healthy urine as a sign of general health.)[8] Now it is obvious that in this example we have a part, or attribute that 'stands for' the whole: a metonymy. But it is also important to note the kind of relation that holds between a healthy complexion and a healthy man: namely that one is an *effect* of the other as *cause*. This underlying causal relationship is fundamental to the scholastic conception of analogy. For analogical language is concerned with a system of *reliable* signs. This is why, for example, a healthy bank balance (unlike a healthy complexion) is not a true 'analogue' of a healthy man.[9*]

Now, if *analogy* always has a causal basis, it seems a worthwhile hypothesis to suggest that perhaps all genuine metonymies have a causal basis. Or, to put it another way, that *analogy* in the scholastic sense is just another term for what is meant, in the structuralist schema, by the metonymic, or syntagmatic (contextural) relation. So far from being just another word for metaphor, analogy then becomes a necessary opposing principle to metaphor: and the two terms refer to the two 'poles' (Jakobson) or 'axes' of communication, and as such are interchangeable with such other binary oppositions as syntagm/paradigm and combination/selection. Now clearly the question whether all metonymies have a causal basis can hardly be decided by examining every possible example. But it is at least clear that the standard dictionary examples of metonymy fit into my hypothesis. The relations of 'crown' and 'sovereign', 'sceptre' and 'authority', 'White House' and 'President' etc. are clearly explicable in causal (historical) terms. Each is a reliable sign, or symbol, of the other only for that reason. Without the underlying causal historical link we could not reliably assume that,

[8] See Herbert McCabe, in *Summa Theologiae*, iii, p. xvii.
[9] *Summa Theologiae*, I, Q. 13, Art. 5.

for example, statements that emanate from the White House have the authority of the President, or that prosecutions undertaken under the aegis of the crown have the weight of government backing behind them. In the absence of some such explanation for the linking of the two elements in these metonymies, we would surely find ourselves confronted with nothing but an arbitrary juxtaposition of disparate elements, not a system of meaningful signs. To put the point in another way, a metonymy which lacked causal explicability would constitute a breach of the 'grammar' of the communications system itself.

However, it is necessary to my hypothesis to be able to show that a causal connection underlies *all* the items on the 'syntagmatic' side of the equation (see above p. 15), and not merely those which we can clearly label metonymy. For it is an essential feature of the schema itself that all the terms on each side refer to the same general principle. True, the various words used are designed to emphasise, or bring out, particular aspects: but these are aspects of a single idea. Thus even if the term *syntagmatic* emphasises the aspect of functional arrangement, and the term *contiguity* emphasises the aspect of contextual 'closeness', of the various elements, nevertheless these two are to be understood as aspects only, of a single principle. Therefore, if my hypothesis is to hold, it is necessary to show that there is a causal nexus present, in some form or other, within *any* syntagm, *any* combination, *any* context, *any* contiguity, *any* message. But surely it is not plausible to say that, for example, the different words in a sentence are necessarily related to each other causally? Or that the different elements that go to make up a single context are causally connected with each other? Well, let us consider the implications of the fact that another term for the syntagmatic, or contextual relation is *contiguity*. This term draws attention to the fact that the relation between, say, 'John' and 'hits' in the sentence 'John hits Joe' is akin to the relation of two links in a chain, or two patches of colour in a picture. Were it not for the contiguity between them, the chain could not be continuous, the assorted patches of colour would not constitute a unified picture. So perhaps the old-style grammar books which spoke of, say, transitive verbs 'requiring' an object to complete their sense were not far wrong. For even if the particular rules they proposed were far from accurate, it remains true that any system of communications will have to include some rules whereby it is possible to distinguish valid from invalid 'combinations', continuous from discontinuous 'chains', contexts which are unified from mere juxtapositions of disparate elements. In other words, there will have to be rules governing the way in which one element may be said to 'require' another. And this is only another way of saying that one thing's presence within the chain or context will *cause* another thing to be present also. For example, by being introduced *as subject*, the word 'John' in the sentence 'John hits Joe' *causes* some contiguous word to be its verb and another to be that verb's object: the grammar of the whole system in which the sentence 'John hits Joe' exists ensures this.

I think such a way of speaking only sounds far-fetched because we have an associationist prejudice about causality itself. That is to say, we tend—as post-Humean empiricists—to suppose that the causal relation is a matter of external association of two or more entitities and that it must therefore present itself as a temporal process. Cause, we feel, must precede effect. And clearly, in the case of a simultaneously co-existing structure such as a sentence or a picture, there is no question of one part preceding another in time. (Of course, a sentence will take time to utter or write or read; and a picture will take time to paint or to scan fully: but once there it is a simultaneous whole, a 'gestalt' that exists in a comprehensive present.) What we have in a sentence or a picture, or other kind of complex artificial sign, is a form of internal causal relation that may best be called mutual contextual determination. That is to say, it is *because* element A of the total 'context' has such and such function, that elements B, C, D etc. have their particular functions, and *vice versa*. Contiguity in this sense implies causality.

Now it might be retorted that such contextual determination cannot, strictly speaking, be a cause/effect relation because it is a symmetrical relation. But this is simply the result of Humean prejudice, whereby we tend to think that if A is a cause of which the effect is B, then B cannot at the same time be a cause of which the effect is A. The mistake is to suppose that the only way of speaking of causality is to speak of it as a relation *between* two or more distinct entities: a relation which must of its nature be asymmetrical. But we regularly use the word *because* in cases where nothing of the sort applies.[10] Thus, in a two-party political system, we may well want to say that party A is the opposition party *because* the party B is at present the government, and

[10] See below, Chap. 3, pp. 50–1.

also to say that party B is the government *because* party A is the opposition. Given the two-party system, both propositions are true, although in the Humean sense, neither can be said to be either 'effect' or 'cause'. If we want to find 'the cause' of the situation which allows us to affirm simultaneously these two 'because' propositions, we must look for it in the nature and effects of the two-party-system itself. It is the system which brings it about that these two propositions can both be truly affirmed.

In the same way, underlying the mutual contextual determination which allows us to say at one and the same time (a) that it is because *John* is grammatical subject that *hits* is verb, and because *hits* is transitive *Joe* is object, and (b) that it is because *Joe* is grammatical object that *hits* is verb, and because *hits* is verb *John* is grammatical subject, there is the causal agency of the language itself. If, following Saussure, we say that the utterance (*la parole*) 'John hits Joe' exists as a significant utterance only *because* it draws upon the treasury of rules and signs that exists, in solution as it were, in the language itself (*la langue*), then it becomes clear that beneath the level of mutual contextual determination governing the relation of various words in the sentence there is a fundamental and one-directional causal relation linking that particular utterance to something that might be called its creative source: namely the language itself.

Now this suggests that the language is itself an agent: not an inert treasury of linguistic units and rules, but an active ingredient in the business of communicating in words. Chomsky has distinguished himself from Saussure by explicitly recognising this point. Although his term linguistic *competence* is related to Saussure's concept of 'the language', Chomsky insists that it is necessary to reject the view of 'the language' as merely a systematic inventory of items, and to return to what he calls the Humboldtian conception of underlying competence as a system of generative processes.[11] In other words, Chomsky goes beyond even Saussure's admission that 'the language' is a feature of human brains and not just an abstraction; for him it is an active influence or agency in the production of speech. Whether we say that competence, or the linguistic faculty, is to be located in the brain of every human individual, or is simply a structural feature of human nature in some less 'materialistic' sense, is unimportant for the present purpose.

[11] Chomsky, *Aspects of the Theory of Syntax*, pp. 3–4. See also Crystal, *Linguistics*, p. 162.

What does matter is that in either case we are here dealing with an active factor in the production of speech.

It seems to follow then that my original hypothesis, namely that there is an underlying causal relation implied in all the differing ways of stating the distinction-within-unity listed above (p. 15) is so far confirmed. Now, this was precisely the purpose of introducing the term *analogy* (in the scholastic sense) into the discussion. Just as structuralism speaks of the syntagmatic and the paradigmatic as complementary axes, or 'poles' of a communications system, so I have referred to the *metaphorical* and the *analogical* to indicate just the same distinction. But using this terminology also serves to emphasise a point which is easily overlooked if we keep to the usual linguists' vocabulary: namely that the whole scheme of distinctions depends ultimately upon a non-Humean concept of causality. Now this fact has particular philosophical, indeed, ideological implications. Thus a cause, it might be said, is not a relationship but a thing: an agent that brings about some effect by the exercise of what can only be called its own 'natural tendency' to behave in a certain way.[12] *Pace* Hume, and empiricists and associationists generally, causality therefore involves a metaphysical notion of *Nature*; for according to this theory, agents behave regularly in certain ways according to what can only be called their 'nature'. This concept of a natural order made up of the sum of the natural tendencies of agents underlies all those commonsense inferences which exemplify at every turn the principles of analogical reasoning. Thus, a healthy complexion is a *reliable* sign, or analogue, of a healthy man only because we believe there is a natural order, or bond between the two things. And if, *per impossible* such a bond did not exist, it would have to be invented. This seems so obvious a point that its importance may easily be missed: which is that, if true, it rules out from the start the whole farrago of post-Humean associationist thought about causality. It further suggests that the discoveries of structuralism in linguistics and elsewhere are not the neutral, value-free or un-metaphysical propositions they may sometimes seem to be. On the contrary, they imply a whole philosophy of 'Nature'[13] without which the structuralist schema itself would fall apart.

However, it should not be overlooked that a re-instatement of

[12] 'A cause is . . . a thing exerting itself, having its influence or imposing its character on the world' (McCabe, in *Summa Theologiae*, iii, Appendix 2, 'Causes').
[13] See below, Chap. 3.

'analogy' in the scholastic sense of the term would also open up the possibility (far from universally welcome) of re-instating the theological uses of analogical language. For many of the metaphors on which we commonly rely and indeed on which officially or unofficially much of the world-view of any society is built, rest upon the common recognition of some basic analogies. Thus, as Lévi-Strauss points out, much of men's sense of cultural identity comes from the transference of facts observed in nature to the human situation. To take just one example, it is not only the 'savage mind' which raises the contrast between, say, the edible and the inedible into a social fact, distinguishing 'us' from 'them' according to the kinds of food each regards as edible. Even in modern Europe, the English regard the French as 'frogs' and the Germans as 'krauts' because they go in for foods which 'we' regard as relatively inedible. On the basis of such analogies, or metonymies, many of our metaphors are constructed. Terence Hawkes, in his book on metaphor, gives three excellent examples from Shakespeare:[14]

> . . . the gallant monarch is in arms,
> And like an eagle o'er his aery towers
> To souse annoyance that comes near his nest.
>
> *(King John)*

> Yet looks he like a King, behold his eye,
> As bright as is the eagle's lightens forth
> Controlling majesty.
>
> *(Richard II)*

> Then the whining schoolboy with his satchel
> And shining face, creeping like snail
> Unwillingly to school.
>
> *(As You Like It)*

From these illustrations we can readily see how the metaphorical similarities between the monarch and the eagle (both are 'high' in their respective spheres) and between the schoolboy and the snail (both 'low') are available only because of an underlying analogical chain, or vertical syntagm which stands to the particular metaphors as language

[14] p. 86.

stands to speech. In the case of Shakespeare, of course, this syntagmatic chain was the 'Great Chain of Being' whereby, as A. O. Lovejoy
comprehensively showed, all the various levels of reality in the medieval and renaissance world were linked together to form a continuous
hierarchy of 'contiguous' levels binding earth to heaven, and man to
the animals below and to God above him.   *

Now this medieval picture of the universe was built-up on the
analogical principle in the strict sense. That is to say, by virtue of its
particular place in the hierarchy, a particular species or kind could truly
serve the philosopher or the poet as a reliable sign, or natural symbol
of some other level in the hierarchy. (For instance, the sun was chief
among the planets, the lion was chief of the animals, the head was the
chief organ of the body etc.) For this reason a huge repertoire of
natural symbols, or analogies was available not only for exploitation
by the poet—whose eye, 'in a fine frenzy rolling doth glance from
heaven to earth, from earth to heaven'—but also by the philosopher,
the scientist and the theologian. (The sacramental theology of medieval
Christendom was rooted in such a system of natural symbols.) But
what was true in the medieval period is still in principle true for our
own time: the analogies themselves may have changed, and the
repertoire of metaphors with them, but the analogical principle itself,
and its capacity for generating metaphors, has not. For underlying the
medieval 'Great Chain of Being' was a causal conception—that of
creation—which was simply another application of the relationship
we have already encountered, between language and speech, between
competence and performance, code and message, system and syntagm
in the structure of human communication itself. Thus, the argumenta-
tive structure of Aquinas's 'Five Ways' involves the notion that God's
existence can be established from the existence of causal chains such as
motion, or the coming-into-being and passing-away of things, by
just the same sort of analogical reasoning which tells us that the
utterance of a sentence, or the employment of a gesture *requires*
the existence of a language, or a code of gestures. This is because
the structuralist principle too involves a *hierarchy of causes* just as the
medieval world picture did: and while the exact form of the hierarchy
is different, the consequences of this fact are fundamentally the
same.

ii

Perhaps it would be as well to illustrate the points so far made by means of some examples. An examination of a couple of short poems may help to explain the necessary connection, as I see it, between the metaphorical and the analogical axes of language, and the metaphysical basis of the connection itself. First of all, to take a fairly obvious, indeed overtly theological case, consider the following sonnet of Gerard Manley Hopkins:

God's Grandeur

The world is charged with the grandeur of God.
   It will flame out, like shining from shook foil;
   It gathers to a greatness, like the ooze of oil
Crushed. Why do men then now not reck his rod?
Generations have trod, have trod, have trod;
   And all is seared with trade; bleared, smeared with toil;
   And wears man's smudge and shares man's smell: the soil
Is bare now, nor can foot feel, being shod.

And all for this, nature is never spent;
   There lives the dearest freshness deep down things;
And though the last lights off the black West went
   Oh, morning, at the brown brink eastward, springs—
Because the Holy Ghost over the bent
   World broods with warm breast and with ah! bright
      wings.[15]

The most important metaphors in this poem come in the first line and the last two. In them we find, not a mere comparison of specific attributes, but the apparently unlimited attribution of one kind of life to a being which in reality has life of another kind. In the first line, Hopkins does not just *liken* God's grandeur to an electrical storm: he says, to quote Gardner's commentary, that 'the world *is* [my italics] a thundercloud charged with beauty and menace, with the electricity of God's creative love and potential wrath'.[16]* Hopkins himself made clear the basis of his metaphor: 'All things are charged with love, are charged

[15] *Collected Poems*, p. 70.
[16] Gardner, *Gerard Manley Hopkins*, ii, p. 230.

with God and if we know how to touch them give off sparks and take fire, yield drops and flow, ring and tell of him'.[17] The metaphor, then, consists in the quite unqualified assertion that God *is* an electric charge in the world. This is not an assertion of likeness in some particular respect or respects: the extent of the comparison is indeterminate. Its basis is a kind of identity, or at least a kind of mutual participation. How it is possible to make a meaningful assertion of this kind I shall have to discuss later. It is in any case a kind of mystery.

Now one of the features of any metaphor that is rooted in a commonly accepted framework of analogies is that if, in some sense, the metaphor holds, then we can draw from it ideas which perhaps the writer himself had no thought of when he wrote it. Hopkins, in his comment quoted above, has drawn some of the implications for us, but there may well be others just as valid. For example, despite the modernity of the electrical image it is possible to see it as merely a way of extending a very traditional idea. Perhaps it is only a modern way of asserting God's unpredictable and shockingly lethal power—the power that, for instance, killed Uzzah when he put out his hand to steady the ark on its way to Jerusalem (2 Sam. 6:6) or which caused hinds to calve prematurely in a thunderstorm (Psalm 29). But there are other things one might draw from the metaphor that could have theological implications for the future as well as for the past. For instance, one might consider the fact that since man has begun to harness electricity for his own use, a new dimension has been added to the way he thinks about God. We can now make an electrical discharge at will, we can charge our batteries, we can measure the strength of electrical charges by means of the gold-leaf electroscope (from which, no doubt, Hopkins first got his metaphor). Does this mean that the significance of the metaphor has changed beyond all recognition? Must we now think of God as somehow within our control? Or has the metaphor simply become inappropriate? If so what shall we replace it with? These are difficult questions, but whatever our reply, we can certainly say that the metaphor is not only in continuity with a traditional idea, but that it has added something to it, linking the past tradition with modern thought and culture. It has developed theologically.*

A different kind of metaphorical example is to be found in the last

---

[17] *Notebooks and Papers*, p. 342 and note.

two lines of the poem, in which the Holy Ghost 'broods' over the world. This metaphor, I suppose, comes ultimately from the first verse of Genesis, but it is mediated to us, as Gardner points out, via *Paradise Lost* (I, 19–22):

> Thou from the first
> Wast present, and with mighty wings outspread
> Dove-like satst brooding on the vast Abyss
> And mad'st it pregnant.

Now in the original Genesis image, 'God's spirit hovered over the water', and the reader was supposed to recall Deuteronomy (32:11) in which Yahweh is said to be

> Like an eagle watching its nest,
> Hovering over its young,
> He spreads his wings out to hold him
> He supports him on his pinions.[18]

But when we read the Genesis lines in the context of Deuteronomy, we see that what has happened is that the Genesis poet has made the Deuteronomy simile into a metaphor.* But as a metaphor for creation *ex nihilo* of course it is philosophically unsatisfactory.[19] For the waters of Genesis are already created—they are the offspring of God's Spirit, which now hovers over them with watchful care. Naturally, the Genesis metaphor is unsatisfactory to Milton on philosophical grounds, because it does not exactly square with creation *ex nihilo*. Yet it is obviously not simply a creation myth of the pagan type. It would be better to say that here is a metaphor struggling to express something that can only be stated in *analogical* terms. But Milton does not follow that path. It would hardly make for great poetry. Instead, he takes up the metaphor and re-interprets it magnificently in terms of 'impregnation' and 'hatching out'. But of course properly speaking, such a metaphor can only apply to a process within the world. It can hardly help to express the idea of original creation as such. So finally Hopkins, no doubt recognising this, and appropriating also the image of the Holy Spirit as a dove, transforms the metaphor into one appropriate to

---

[18] *Jerusalem Bible* version. All Biblical quotations are from this version (henceforth *J.B.*). See also *J.B.* note on Gen. 1:2.

[19] Creation *ex nihilo* only becomes explicit in 2 Mac. 7:28.

the Holy Spirit and his role in overseeing the world-process. It has become a metaphor for that continuously creative energy within the world that is the presence of the Holy Spirit. Thus the metaphor has organically developed over a period of time and in the hands of several authors.[20]

One of the most important and characteristic features of any metaphor is that we can, indeed we must, deny its literal truth if we are to understand its metaphorical significance. Whatever Milton or Hopkins may say, God is not a broody bird, even though they want to say that metaphorically speaking he is. It is at this point that we can bring out one of the crucial differences between metaphor and analogy. For in analogical talk about God, we do not have to deny before we can affirm; we simply affirm that the statement is only true as long as we remember that it is no more than analogical. When we say that God is the cause of the existence of the world, for example, the word *cause* is being used analogically. But this does not mean that (as with metaphor) we want to deny the literal truth of the statement. On the contrary, the point of such analogical language is that, if the theory of analogy is true, we can stretch the meaning of the word in question to cover things which, in everyday talk, we do not have in mind. Of course, such 'stretching' is possible only in the case of words which are sufficiently open-ended to be stretched without breaking. To take an example from the Hopkins poem, the word *bird* is not very elastic, in that only a fairly restricted, and well-established range of entities can legitimately be called birds. This is why we can only call God a bird by way of metaphor: that is, by a means which involves the denial of the literal truth of the expression in order to make the metaphorical point. On the other hand, the word *cause* is very elastic indeed, in the sense that there is no prior, established limit to the range of things that can be causes. It is in virtue of this fact that it is possible to say that God is a cause without necessarily stretching the word to breaking point. In fact, we don't know what its breaking point is. Remembering this distinction, we can now look for the analogical language (if any) that is to be found in the Hopkins sonnet. It is not far to seek. There is only one truly analogical statement in the poem, and this centres in the word *because*. It is *because* the Holy Ghost broods over the world

[20] On the capacity of a metaphor to grow in this way, see below p. 107, note to p. 24.

that, even in the darkest moment of gloom, dawn begins to spring. God, Hopkins suggests, is in some sense the cause even of the most permanent and unchanging rhythms of nature, like the movements of the planets. Behind all the secondary causes—the electrical storm, the industrial factory, the desolation of the countryside by man's activity, the slow revolution of the earth—'broods' the perpetual creative causality of God the Holy Ghost. Implicit in the word *because* is the idea of God as a cause of all the changes in creation; and it is this attribution of causality to God that is the fundamental analogical statement in the poem.

One might summarise the general sense of this poem by saying that the sestet, which is mainly an analogical statement centring on the word *because*, gives the answer to the question posed in the primarily *metaphorical* octave. Indeed, at a deeper level still it might even be suggested that what the poem is saying *is* simply that metaphorical language is itself incomplete without an analogical underpinning. Metaphor (the octave) raises questions that only analogy (the sestet) can answer, while conversely analogy can only answer questions that are raised in a metaphorical form. In the octave a metaphoric relationship is established between God and the world. God is present in the world as thunder and lightning, as the dynamism of the human industrial process. In this sense God has been brought down to the level of the world's concerns, he has become 'like' the world. But he is put on the world's level partly by a kind of positive absence. The world's concerns have blotted God out, for 'all is seared with trade' and 'the soil is bare now'—bare of the growth-processes that were once the true signs of God's creative power. He is both in the world and not in the world, he is embodied in it (the storm, the oil-crushing plant) and absent from it (the bare soil, the commercialism). The world both accommodates and banishes him at the same time. It is because of this paradox that the question arises: why do men now not reck his rod? Men cannot obey God unless he is sufficiently embodied in the world to be recognisable, but they cannot refuse to do so unless he is banished effectively enough for men to be able to forget or ignore him. The octave of the sonnet is designed to generate this problem. It does so by creating a single metaphorical relationship between God and the world which makes the question inevitable. The answer that the sestet gives is the assertion of an underlying causal relationship between God and the world. God is not only the cause of the planetary revolution that ensures that every dusk is followed by a new dawn. He is also the cause of the perpetual 'freshness deep down things' and the fact that 'nature is never spent'. He *is* still available. This second part of the poem is therefore one single, complex causal proposition, corresponding to the single metaphorical proposition of the octave. But whereas the effect of the metaphors in the octave is to bring God down on to the horizontal level of the world by identifying him as the inner dynamism of the world's ongoing process, the effect of the analogy, with its unmistakably vertical implications (God is above the world, penetrating it 'deep down' with a causal energy, or presence, that comes from the abode of a bird that lives on high) is to separate God from the world, to maintain him at a different level from the plane of finite worldly experience. Considered as a whole therefore, the poem embodies in its very structure the inter-twining of two 'axes'.

However, each of the two parts does contain some elements of the other. Within the metaphorical relationship of the octave, we find an analogical relationship embedded. This is the implicit 'because' which underlies the whole metaphorical argument of the octave. God is being ignored and forgotten by the world *because* man's is preoccupied with trade, toil and technology. In this sense, the relation of man to the world, which has been so 'bleared' that it can no longer descry God's presence, is one of analogy. That is to say, the 'seared', 'smudged' world is a fit analogue, a reliable sign of man's own materialism, just as a man's complexion is a reliable sign of his health. The spoiled world reveals man's natural tendency to ruin his environment by forgetting God's creative and recreative power. An exactly corresponding point can be made about the sestet of the poem. Within its primarily analogical emphasis on the causal relationship between God and the world we find buried metaphors of which the most obvious is the 'brooding' metaphor itself. This metaphor is simply the imaginative embodiment of what is at stake logically in the analogical word *because*. The meta-phor fills out the analogy, by adding a new dimension to it, a dimension of significance that can only come from the metaphorical 'axis'.

Now it would be easy to say at this point that, by choosing an overtly theological poem, I have twisted the evidence to suit my own case. Perhaps therefore a second, very different poem may be introduced to make the same fundamental point. I choose a poem by Philip Larkin.

Myxomatosis

Caught in the centre of a soundless field
While hot inexplicable hours go by
What trap is this? Where were its teeth concealed?
You seem to ask.
            I make a sharp reply
Then clean my stick. I'm glad I can't explain
Just in what jaws you were to suppurate:
You may have thought things would come right again
If you could only keep quite still and wait.[21]

In this case the metaphorical and the analogical dimensions each penetrate the whole poem: yet it is clear that the poem's meaning still depends upon their distinction-within-unity, as well as upon the causal underpinning implicit in the analogical foundation of the whole. I think the rabbit, sprawling helplessly on the ground instead of leaping up and down in its normal healthy way is an image of a more general condition, of pain and entrapment. This seems to me implicit in the suggestion of intelligible communication between animal and man: 'What trap is this? . . . you seem to ask'. For men, like trapped animals, are in a state of disorientation, ignorance and helplessness; 'I'm glad I can't explain. . .' Yet to the rabbit the poet, with his natural physical height and superiority, must appear as a God. Indeed he has—and uses—his God-like power over life and death to deny life to the animal 'beneath' him. Nevertheless the disastrous course of events that has led up to the rabbit's torture and pain is parallel to man's own predicament only because, cutting across the 'horizontal' dimension of temporal calamity is a vertical axis of analogy, a sustaining natural bond between the animal and human species. It is only because of this vertical, analogical dimension that the rabbit's catastrophe is a reliable sign, or natural symbol of man's own. Thus, despite the sardonic agnosticism of the last couplet, with its denial of any hope of cure, the essential vertical structure of natural hierarchy is still discernible beneath the apparent 'flatness' of the poem's surface message. The poet may be obscurely assimilating human beings to animals lying on the ground in the throes of agony, but it appears that he can do so only by (inadvertently?) introducing exactly the opposite idea, namely man's

[21] *The Less Deceived*, p. 31.

natural superiority in the hierarchy. Without this, the metaphorical similarity between the epidemic of myxomatosis among rabbits and the epidemic of universal sickness among men which seems to be the core of the poem's meaning would be literally unstateable. The metaphor could not be put into action without the analogical (causal) underpinning.

But just because of man's superiority to the animal, he appears and behaves towards the rabbit like a God. Of course that this God is one who 'can't explain/Just in what jaws you were to suppurate', one whose ignorance and inability to relieve suffering are the principal attributes of his person, is the leading idea of this very black poem. Yet this very idea is in a sense counteracted by the fact that the order of Nature in the poem, with its analogical hierarchy of the two species, nevertheless preserves a capacity for breeding new metaphors—of which a human 'myxomatosis' is, of course, a notable example. Thus the poet who claims to be an ignorant and impotent God ruling over the rabbit turns out, in a paradoxical way, to be still potent after all; still creative, still able to renew the world by the creation of just such new metaphors as this poem itself. In short, even in this act of stating the world's unintelligibility, the world's intelligibility—its natural ordering—shines through. Indeed we might go so far as to say that the poem seems to confirm the view, well expressed by Norman Mailer, that the universe is a lock to which the key is a metaphor.

iii

I have suggested that there is an implicit (if unacknowledged) ideological undercurrent to the structuralist principles with which this essay has dealt. This comes out in the incompatibility of the causal theory that we have found in the analogical/metonymic/syntagmatic dimension with the prevailing associationist concepts that still tend to surround 'scientific' thought. Historically, such associationism and such concepts of 'science' can be traced to the Enlightenment; in England, to the period of Locke, Hartley and Hume. It is not surprising therefore that today it should be widely rejected as just part of an oppressive and outworn bourgeois ideology. For the fundamentally arbitrary and unintelligible character of associationist thinking lends itself very easily to the creation of a false ideology. Once the metaphysical idea of Nature, as an order which exists independently of human thought, has been rejected, it is perhaps inevitable that people should turn for their sense of intelligibility and meaning to what they can create for themselves, and to call this 'Nature'. A good deal of Romantic thinking can be traced in this way to associationist influences even when their results—say the extremer manifestations of Benthamism—are the object of explicit rejection.* From such a 'Nature' formed by men in their own image, the overwhelming urge to manipulate both Nature and other men for the sake of a 'meaningful' existence easily follows. Man's 'grandiose aspirations', to use Robbe-Grillet's phrase, are soon satisfied once external reality, or Nature in the pre-Enlightenment sense, ceases to stand in our way. For example, the height of a mountain means nothing to the romantic devotee of such a 'Nature', as Robbe-Grillet points out, if it doesn't present the moral spectacle of 'majesty'. And from such associations, all kinds of undesirable moral attitudes tend inevitably to follow:

> the things that surround him are like the fairies in fairy stories each one of whom brings the new-born child one of the traits of his future character as a present. Thus the mountain would perhaps have been the first to communicate the feeling of majesty to me . . . this feeling would then . . . in its turn breed others—magnificence, prestige, heroism, nobility, pride. And in my turn I would apply them to other objects . . . and the world would become the depository of all my grandiose aspirations and at the same time be their image and their justification for all eternity.[22]

Given such results of the associationist ideology, it is not surprising that men like Robbe-Grillet should try to find some alternative. But neither is it surprising to find that they reject—if my argument is correct—the only true alternative, namely a genuinely analogical 'Nature'. For such a conception is frankly metaphysical, and indeed potentially theological. Hence the attempt by anti-metaphysical thinkers to find an answer in some theory of value-free objectivity, a world in which there is a choice of meanings based on the primacy of mere phenomena; on surfaces rather than depths. Such a one-dimensional universe will consist according to Robbe-Grillet of objects and gestures, pictures and novels which 'will be *there*, before they are *something*; and will still be there afterwards, hard, unalterable, everpresent, and apparently quite indifferent to their own meaning'.[23] That

---

[22] *Snapshots*, p. 79. [23] Ibid., pp. 54–5.

talk about 'things which are simply there before they are something', that is to say about things which are not things of any *kind* and to which no category-terms can be applied, is incoherent should not blind us to the moral force of this appeal or the legitimacy of its motives. For surely we must admit that once a chain of associations of the kind Robbe-Grillet describes has been established with the force of a prevailing ideology, it is indeed very hard to break: so hard that only a radical reappraisal of fundamental positions can enable us to be liberated from it.

2

Metaphor and 'Fiction'

This chapter is concerned to demonstrate the necessity of making up 'fictions' if we are to understand and explain our own experience. In the first section I discuss how the relation of paradigm and syntagm in language is paralleled by a similar relation that is perceived in the external world. The distinction between metaphors and analogies exists not only in words but in the living things around us. But the metaphorical similarities that we recognise between ourselves and other species, and which traditional societies have understood and used over the ages as means for explaining their own social relations, cannot be put to effective use without the telling of stories. Myths and mythologies are necessary for the activation of the perceived metaphors in nature, and thus for any useful explanation of man's own predicament within it.[1] In the second section of the chapter, I go on to consider another kind of narrative explanation which I take to be complementary to that of the traditional myth: namely the fairytale. By a fairytale I mean a story that uses the idea of magic: and I argue that magic in narrative is complementary to the perception of natural metaphors, since it is essentially a kind of contiguity, the syntagmatic relation in its purest form. But what fairytales explain is a metaphysical rather than a social relation: that is to say, men's relationship to the superior world, that of the 'gods' or God, rather than their relationship to each other. As such they are complementary to myths in their explanatory power. Finally I discuss briefly another aspect of narrative explanation: namely the kind of narrative we have to tell about our own personal experience in order to understand it. Autobiographical narrative too is a necessary part of human understanding.

[1] By 'fictions' here I mean any story that tells of something that has not in fact happened or in a way markedly different from the way it happened. It thus includes myths, legends, fairy-tales and even some autobiographies, as well as novels. For an interesting study of the reasons why the telling of stories is necessary even for the philosopher, see the discussion of the role of myths in Plato's theory of analogical language in Burrell, pp. 58–60.

i

It is not an accident that in books on linguistics the section on the paradigmatic/syntagmatic distinction is often graced with a table or diagram. And this diagram is usually drawn up, like a graph, about two axes, vertical and horizontal, at right angles to each other. David Crystal in his *Linguistics* (p. 166) provides the following typical example:

he	can	go	tomorrow	syntagmatic relationships
she	may	come	soon	
I	will	ask	next	
you	could	sleep	now	

paradigmatic relationships

In this table, what is said is that *he* stands to the other words in the first column (*she, I, you* etc.) as a *paradigm* of personal pronouns; *can* stands to *may, will, could* etc. as a paradigm of auxiliary verbs; and so on. Whereas *he* stands to *can, go,* and *tomorrow* in the top line of the diagram in a syntagmatic relationship; in the second line *she* stands to *may, come* and *soon* in another *syntagmatic* relationship; and so on. Now two things need first of all to be noted about this diagram. One is that sentences are formed as it were by drawing a graph through the square of words. Thus a graph of the form

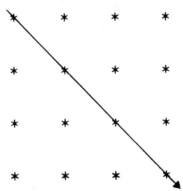

would give the sentence 'he may ask now' while a graph of the form

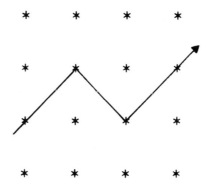

would give the sentence 'I may ask soon' and so on. Only in this two-dimensional matrix can a sentence be properly formed; for as I argued in the previous chapter utterance always consists of two kinds of act: *selection* of paradigm and *combination* into a syntagm. Each dimension of the diagram represents one of these two acts. The second point to note is that there is nothing sacrosanct about the way the diagram is drawn: it could just as well be given the other way round, thus:

he	she	I	you	paradigmatic relations
can	may	will	could	syntagmatic relations
go	come	ask	sleep	
tomorrow	soon	next	now	

In other words, it is only a matter of convention, not a fact of 'nature' that we tend to think of the syntagmatic as the horizontal and of the paradigmatic as the vertical dimension. (In a language such as Chinese, for example, in which the letters are read vertically rather than horizontally, just the opposite might seem the more 'natural' way of presenting the case.)

However, 'conventional' differences such as these tend to be rooted in very deep cultural soil: and if structural anthropologists like Lévi-Strauss are correct, there is always some relation between cultural conventions such as those governing language, which have important social functions, and common observation of what occurs in the natural world. Differing cultural conventions are signs of differing ways of experiencing the world of living things. Thus it seems obvious to the simplest societies that the various species within the biosphere occupy different 'levels' or 'niches' within the environment. Birds fly in the air above, snakes wriggle on the ground below, fishes swim in the deeps, men can walk on the earth or ride above it and so on. Furthermore, within each of these various kinds, some are more equal as it were than others. Flat fish live deeper in the sea than round fish, kangaroos can jump higher than rabbits, hawks fly higher than sparrows. And there are some anomalous kinds, such as ostriches, that 'ought' to be able to fly but can't. Thus the living world of nature itself, we may say, has its own two-dimensional (vertical/horizontal) structure. For individuals of the same species, or kind, governed as they are by a relation of similarity, all occupy the same natural level. Similarity, it might seem, is a horizontal relation in nature. Whereas the relationship that governs the connections between the different kinds, or species may be understood as a vertical, or hierarchical relation: a syntagmatic relation between the various 'levels' or ecological 'niches' of the biosphere. (Indeed it may be literally thought of as a relation of contiguity, as when one species preys upon, or invades the territory of another.)

Yet this cannot be the whole truth. For there is another sense in which men commonly perceive a similarity, or metaphorical relationship *between* the different species on their different levels, and use this perceived similarity as a way of explaining their own situation. Storytellers the world over, from anonymous myth-makers to modern novelists, employ a vast repertoire of vertically-organised metaphors drawn from the similarities they perceive between men and the other species, to explain or enrich the 'horizontal' chain of events, or plot, which they are concerned to unfold to their hearers or readers. Thus Shakespeare will liken the king, who is at the top of the social hierarchy, to an eagle and the whining schoolboy who is at the bottom to a snail, in order to express his Elizabethan concept of the social order; and Evelyn Waugh will use animals that have been dragged out of their natural environment to express his vision of modern social chaos.[2] What this shows is that metaphor is more than the simple perception of similarity: it is always perception of a likeness within a larger dis-similarity. The initial dis-similarity is just as important as the similarity itself. This is why we have to deny the literal truth of a metaphor if we are to grasp its meaning. (To call the king 'lion-hearted' or God a 'rock' only helps us to understand the truth as long as we recognise that kings are not really lions and that rocks are not really divine.) Another way of putting this point is to note that 'substitution' is an essential part of the similarity in metaphor: that is to say, the point of a metaphor is that we can *substitute* things that in nature exist on one level for things that exist on another.

Now it is by working on the basis of this 'natural' way of thinking about metaphor that modern anthropologists studying the stories current in traditional societies have been able to explain social phenomena that baffled earlier generations. For example, Lévi-Strauss's work on Australian totemism, founded on the earlier researches of Evans-Pritchard and Radcliffe-Brown, shows how men use the 'natural' organisation of things to explain their own social structure. The importance of such studies for the present discussion of the place of metaphor in narrative is that they show how inextricable is the connection between the perception of similarities in nature and the telling of stories to bring these similarities to life.

Lévi-Strauss's theory strikingly illustrates the fact that the whole structure of a totemic society is governed by a set of gigantic metaphors. In a society organised on this principle, the divisions and tensions within the human community are expressed in terms of divisions within the animal kingdom. If Lévi-Strauss is right, the purpose of doing this is to make intelligible and tolerable the tensions that exist between different groups within the human community; tensions that arise largely from the nature of the social structure, its kinship pattern etc. By looking at the tensions between human beings under the guise of conflicts between animal species, it is possible for the society to confront those tensions more objectively than would be possible by head-on

[2] Waugh's most systematic use of animal imagery is to be found in *A Handful of Dust*. See also above, p. 21.

assault. To take one example, any society is liable to generate tensions between females and males, parents and children, fathers-in-law and sons-in-law etc. By identifying such opposed pairs with pairs of supposedly 'similar' animal species, the society can understand its own problems more clearly. The basis for such a natural procedure is that man, after all, has his roots in the animal world, and animals need to divide up their world into certain pairs of opposites in order to survive. They need to distinguish the friendly from the hostile, the edible from the inedible, the male from the female etc., so it is not really surprising that men should do the same by using the animal species for their own more complex purposes.[3] By interpreting the resemblances and differences between species within the animal world in terms of friendship and conflict, solidarity and opposition, 'the world of animal life is represented in terms of social relations similar to those of human society'.[4] But conversely, by seeing the social relations of human society in animal terms, the human problems of friendship and solidarity within a community that has tensions built into it, may be clarified and solved.

However, problems of social conflict cannot be solved merely by identifying the human participants with equivalent animal species. We need more than a simple ratio, or proportion between the human group and the animal species. We need an equation between two sets of such ratios or proportions. The mere identification of, say the males of a tribe with the bat and the females with the night owl or the father-in-law with the eaglehawk and the son-sin-law with the crow,[5] tells us nothing about the relations *between* these various pairs. What is required is some link, or common characteristic that joins the members of each pair together. It is not enough to say, *men* are to *bats* as *women* are to *nightowls*: what we need to know is how bats are to nightowls. Only then can we solve the equation. Similarly, it is not enough to say that *fathers-in-law* are to *sons-in-law* as the *eaglehawk* is to the *crow*. We need to know something of the relation that holds between eagle-hawks and crows. Now, since the whole point of this system is to cope with tension and conflict within a community, the relation that is necessary for the system to have any explanatory force must be a double one. That is to say, there must be something *in common*

---

[3] Leach, *Lévi-Strauss*, pp. 39–40.

[4] Lévi-Strauss, *Totemism*, p. 160.

[5] Ibid., pp. 158–161.

between the bat and the nightowl, or between the eaglehawk and the crow, in virtue of which they can be compared, or recognised as members of a community: but there must also be some tension or *difference* between them despite this common bond. The anthropologist must therefore look, firstly at any elements that might be taken as bonds of community between these species: and secondly, he must find the basis for a difference between them that persists despite these bonds.

Following Radcliffe-Brown, Lévi-Strauss holds that, in the case of the bat and the nightowl what is common to the two species is that they both live in trees, and in the case of the eaglehawk and the crow, the common bond is that they are both carnivores. But though the bat and the nightowl both live in trees and eaglehawks and crows are both carnivorous birds, there is plenty of material for conflict between them. For example, eaglehawks are 'hunters', crows merely 'thieves': hence a natural source of competitive tension. But there is only one way of presenting this conflict and that is by means of a myth: for example, a story about a legendary, primordial fight between the two species, the dénouement of which is seen as applicable to the 'equivalent' relationship between the human groups that are identified with the two species in question. Thus the myth of the conflict between the carnivorous species eaglehawk and crow ends with the submission of the crow, who is for ever after condemned to be a mere stealer of game, not a true hunter. This myth not only 'explains' why crows are carrion-eaters and eaglehawks are birds of prey. It also 'explains to the Darling River tribes where this myth operates, why fathers-in-law, who are identified with the eaglehawk, are entitled to exact presents of food from potential sons-in-law, who are identified with the crow.

Now it will be clear, from what I have said already, that the birds of the 'above' are related by a kind of 'contiguity' to the human situation 'here below'. But this vertical relation would be inert without the horizontal axis of the myth which activates the conflict between the two species of bird. That is to say, the vertical paradigmatic relation is useless without a corresponding horizontal, syntagmatic one. Both axes are required for men to be able to 'think with' and thus gain understanding of themselves from the identification with natural species. And according to Lévi-Strauss what holds for totemism in this simple way holds for all communications systems, since these always embody pairs of opposites that express distinction within unity, opposition within solidarity. What we have seen in totemism is a manifestation of a general characteristic of human thought.[6]

Now, in the totemic case it is clear that the paradigmatic relation is conceived in the vertical dimension. This seems natural because the explanation consists in conceiving the relation between man and the other species as one of different levels. In some cases of totemism, indeed, the paradigmatic relation is vertical for quite literal reasons. This is so, for example, in the case of the Nuer, whose explanation of the status of twins (always mysterious in such a society) as quasi-divine beings involves a complex comparison between different species of birds. The birds of the 'above', that is the birds which can fly, are contrasted with the birds of the 'below', who can't (e.g. the guinea-fowl, francolin etc). Yet relative to man even the birds of the 'below' are creatures of the 'above' simply by being birds. Hence the quasi-divine human beings, twins, are assimilated to the *relatively* superior species, namely the non-flying birds, the guinea fowl, francolin etc.[7] But few explanations are as 'natural' as this, even though there is a certain inevitability in the idea that man occupies a midway place in a hierarchy, or chain of being, between the world of spirits who are 'above' him and the world of animals, plants and non-living matter 'below' him. But this does not mean there is any *necessary* connection between the vertical dimension and the paradigmatic relation, as we have already seen.[8] Exactly corresponding connections can still be made when the directions of the two 'axes' are reversed. *This is just what happens when we employ analogy to complement a mythical, or narrative explanation.* Thus, if the myths of totemism emphasise the differences of levels between men and animals, in order to assert a metaphoric similarity between them that gives insight into the human situation, it is equally possible to emphasise what is common between men and animals, i.e. to insist that men and animals are *all* of the 'here below' by comparison with the higher world of superior spiritual beings, in order to show that the relation of the whole of the 'here below' to the superior world is a syntagmatic one. The verbal links that would be necessary to join these levels together would then have to be analogies, not metaphors. 'Natural theology' would have arrived to complete a sociology.

However, such an analogical linking of the world here below to the

---

[6] Ibid., p. 163 and Chap. 5.   [7] Ibid., pp. 151–3.
[8] See above, p. 35.

world above would still be inert without a corresponding paradigmatic dimension. Hence the need for a story to be told of the upper world and its inhabitants, and their relation to the here below, in order to activate the otherwise inert analogical relations set up by the syntagmatic axis. In other words, a horizontal, or narrative dimension is necessary in order to give flesh and bones to the analogical structure, and to give the *whole* totality any explanatory power. The difference between such a structure and the totemic structure, in terms of their explanatory roles, would then be this. Whereas the totemic story is designed primarily to explain the true nature of human *social* relations, that is, relations on the horizontal level of history, the 'theological' story is designed primarily to explain a metaphysical relation: the relation that holds between nature (including man) and the gods, or God, who are above nature. This is why Pascal was right to see that the God of love and consolation, the God who features as a character in the stories of Abraham, Isaac and Jacob, had to be prepared to humble himself sufficiently to become a real character in a story told by men.

ii

One reason for introducing mythologies into the discussion at this point has been to make a further connection between the syntagmatic dimension of narrative and the concept of causality already mentioned in an earlier chapter. Now in much mythological thinking, the typical form of causality at work is *magic*. And the analysis of the idea of magic is valuable for any consideration of causality as it appears in narrative. Edmund Leach has pointed out that there is an almost exact parallel between the metaphor/metonymic distinction, based on the similarity/contiguity dichotomy, and the two sorts of magic described by Frazer at the beginning of *The Golden Bough*.[9] 'Homeopathic' magic was based on the idea of bringing about an effect in A by doing the same thing to a similar object B in a similar situation. The *similarity* of B to A would then somehow ensure the magical influence was carried from B to A. 'Contagious' magic, on the other hand, depended upon actual contact between B and A; in this case, the magical power present in A reaches right out to touch, and thereby affect B. Whereas in the first case the working of the magic seems to involve a causal *process*, in

[9] Leach, *Lévi-Strauss*, p. 49.

the latter case it operates simply by bringing the two entities concerned into the same '*context*'. In fact the magic *is* this context. This comes out in the fact that whereas the first sort of magic would have to be formulated as a proposition in the form of: 'A brought about F in B', the second can only be formulated by a proposition of the form: 'B because A', or 'because A, B'.[10] Now, in this second case A and B stand not for objects but for *clauses*. And this helps us to see why in such a case the 'magic' itself can only be inserted, as it were, into the relation at the point indicated by the 'because'. For the events which are described in each of the clauses (say, '*Cinderella's pumpkin turned into a golden coach* because *the fairy godmother waved her wand*') are in themselves quite intelligible. We can 'visualise' them without raising any questions as to their explanation. What is not intelligible is precisely their connection, that is to say the relation denoted by 'because'. 'Magic' goes proxy, as it were, for an intelligible connection here. It simply indicates that we do not know the rationale of 'because' in such a case as this. But in a proposition of the other sort (say 'the fairy godmother brought about the form of a golden coach in the pumpkin') the *whole* of what is being described is strictly speaking unintelligible. That is to say the actual *process* whereby the effect is (magically) transferred remains wholly indescribable. This is precisely because it *is* magic: and that means, not that it is a very difficult process to observe or analyse, but simply that it is not a discernible process at all. It is a sheer 'contiguity'. (It is worth noting, in passing, that just the same objection can be levelled at associationist theories of causality in general: the associative process itself always turns out to be too elusive for detection because, in fact, it is reducible in the end to a contiguity).

Propositions describing homeopathic magic, then, are always reducible at their critical points to propositions about contagious magic: and such propositions are themselves simply propositions that combine two clauses in a single context, the special feature of which is that the contextual relation signified by 'because' is in principle wholly beyond explanation. But 'magic' is not the only case of this kind: the *creatio ex nihilo* whereby, theologians say, God brought the world into existence (and indeed whereby he keeps it in existence too) is another instance of the same principle of sheer 'contiguity'. This is of course why the

[10] See above p. 20 and below pp. 50 ff.

Genesis story describes God's creative act in terms appropriate to those of a middle-eastern magician. Creation is a kind of magic: or perhaps it would be better to say, magic is a metaphor for creation.

Now it is important to notice that it seems possible to speak of a magical act or transformation only within the context of a *story*. That is to say a magic event can never be observed, it can only be told. And this is also why stories, and especially stories which tell of magical events, have a unique and necessary role in the description and, in a sense, the explanation of otherwise indescribable, inexplicable events. Fairy tales, for example, like myths, often suggest explanations of why things happen, or why things are as they are, which no other form of utterance could provide. Like the natural species, we may say the characters in fairy tales are 'good to think with'. Because they deal in final causes they explain things which no amount of science based on 'association' can explain. The job of the fairytale is to show that Why? questions cannot be answered except in one way: by telling stories. The story does not *contain* the answer, it *is* the answer. The answer cannot be translated into factual, that is non-narrative form, for the answer *is* the narrative form. G. K. Chesterton grasped this, though his example is open to dispute, when he said that if we want to know why, for example, an egg can turn into a chicken—for no egg *suggests* a chicken—then 'it is essential that we should regard (this question) in the philosophic manner of fairy tales, not in the unphilosophic manner of science'. In other words, science cannot deal with the question since the question assumes an inner synthesis which we do not possess. This is why 'the ordinary scientific man is strictly a sentimentalist . . . in this essential sense, that he is soaked and swept away by mere associations. He has so often seen birds fly and lay eggs that he feels as if there must be some dreamy, tender connection between the two ideas, whereas there is none.' This being so there is no scientific reason why, for instance, apple trees should not grow crimson tulips rather than apples. The 'cool rationalist from fairy land' understands this fact, and is therefore appropriately astonished when he finds that apple trees go on year after year for some mysterious reason, producing apples rather than tulips, and eggs continually turn into chickens rather than bananas. Whereas Chesterton's sentimental 'materialist professor' although he is strictly a mystic in the sense that he talks about a law even though he has no means of penetrating its nature, finds nothing astonishing in what is, after all, a perpetual mystery.[11]* (Is this what Wittgenstein really meant when he said that it is not *how* things are in the world, but *that* they are as they are, that is the 'mystical' thing about them?)[12]

Now what kind of answer do we find in fairy tales to this question Why? Chesterton's thesis seems to me exactly right, even though its special applicability to biological cases is an instance of Chestertonian special pleading: 'When we are asked why eggs turn to birds, or fruits fall in autumn, we must answer exactly as the fairy godmother would answer if Cinderella asked her why mice turned to horses or her clothes fell from her at twelve o'clock. We must answer that it is *magic*'.[13] What Chesterton means by magic here is just that un-analysable contiguity which we ascribe to the relation between cause and effect even though we cannot strictly observe it or finally verify it because it lies behind, and is presupposed by, every process of scientific experimentation. But the point I want to make here, and which Chester-ton does not make, is that the *only* way in which this kind of connection between cause and effect, this axiomatic 'magic', can be displayed is by way of stories. That is to say, the only way such an axiom can be incorporated into an account of an event, is for the teller to construct an account which has this axiom, this principle of 'magic', explicitly built into it from the very start.

But fairytales tend to concentrate on the metaphysical rather than the social problems men have to face. That is to say, what the totemic myth does for the 'mystery' of apparently unalterable social condi-tions, the fairytale is able to do for apparently unalterable metaphysical conditions. It helps us to understand the fundamental laws of existence even when we cannot penetrate them. The fairytale is 'good to think with' for that reason.

If we want to see how a story such as the tale of Cinderella helps to explain a metaphysical point, we must begin by considering the story of Cinderella as a metaphor for the relation between human beings and the upper world. That is to say the one is a metaphor for the other, related to it by a similarity of structure. But whereas the one is only a fairy tale, the other is 'for real'. Now the relation of Cinderella, here below, to her fairy-godmother from the upper world, is a magical one, for it is magic that brings the fairy-godmother to Cinderella, and it is

---

[11] *Orthodoxy*, pp. 90–3.   [12] *Tractatus Logico-Philosophicus*, 6.44.
[13] *Orthodoxy*, p. 91.

magic which brings Cinderella herself out of her misery into the lime-light. Magic then, is the essential *syntagmatic* (causal) link in the structure of the story: it is what makes it a fairystory. Similarly, on the other side of the equation, there is a corresponding syntagmatic structural relation in 'reality', namely the causal link between human beings and the divine powers. But although, as a relation of creative causal dependence this relation is strictly unimaginable, the 'image' of it which is found in the story reveals, by its sheer contiguity, the equally 'contiguous' nature of the relation between creator and creature.

Now the horizontal relation of the two sides of the equation to each other is a metaphorical one. The story is a metaphor for the reality. Here then we have just the opposite case from that of totemism. Here the metaphorical dimension is the horizontal one, asserting a similarity of structure between the fairy story as a whole and the creation-story as a whole which it explains precisely being a metaphor for it. Mean-while the vertical dimension is the syntagmatic, or causal dimension, suggesting the way the levels on each side are related to each other. However, the fairy story is not in competition with the totemic myth, but complements it. For in presenting the contrast thus sharply, I have oversimplified the matter. It would be possible, both in the totemic myth and in the fairy story to reverse the paradigmatic/syntagmatic axes: and thus to produce a correspondingly different, but complementary result in each case. It would be possible to extract a metaphysical meaning from the myth (an affirmation of man's solidarity with the rest of creation perhaps). And it would be possible to affirm a sociological meaning in the Cinderella fairystory: emphasising per-haps the contrasting fortunes of rich and poor, ugly and beautiful, in the society in which the characters live. In fact it is always possible to interpret the two-dimensional structure of a story in two ways according to the direction of the axes. But equally, in all cases, there can be no question of conflict between the two interpretations thus arrived at. There is a metaphysical *and* a sociological interpretation for every tale.

As I have said, the magical connection between the fairy godmother and Cinderella is itself a metaphor for the mystery of causality. Two things need to be said about this connection. Firstly, magic, as Chester-ton says, is far from haphazard or unintelligible. On the contrary, there are very clear, even rigid rules governing the operation of magic in fairytales. 'The note of the fairy utterance is, "you may live in a place of gold and sapphire, if you do not say the word 'cow' ", or "you may live happily with the King's daughter, if you do not show her an onion" '.[14] It is a highly rational system in the sense that, given the initial premiss, everything follows logically, even inexorably. Secondly, the fairy godmother's power e.g. to make Cinderella's clothes fall from her at exactly twelve o'clock, is totally and unambiguously manifested *in* the very falling-off of these clothes. If we want to know in what the magic consists, we can do no more than point to its effects. The clothes are actually touched by it. The magic reaches right out to them. There is no process that could possibly be open to analysis or investigation here; only simple contact, sheer 'contiguity'. This sheer contiguity may be regarded as a fairytale metaphor for God's causal activity in the world: that too is sheer contiguity; whatever is touched by it just happens. This is the meaning of creation. It is the syntagmatic relationship in its most complete and unambiguous form.

iii

It is worth noting finally, in this discussion of the explanatory powers of stories that narrative is not only a unique instrument for describing certain kinds of truths about the external world, it is also, for similar reasons, uniquely important in explaining what happens inside oneself. Thus the autobiographer is one who is trying to make sense of himself in relation to the world by recollecting his past in a narrative. For he knows that it is only in the retelling of his own story that he can put his life into order and shore up the fragments of his past against his ruin. As Evelyn Waugh's Charles Ryder remarks, his theme is memory. For his memories are his life as he knows it now, and as Rousseau pointed out in his own autobiography, 'to know me in my latter years it is necessary to have known me well in my youth.[15]

Now the autobiographer's deliberate recollection of his memories is more than a search for a subjective inner reality, the self: it is also a search for the world that the self inhabits. And the commerce of the self and the world is a *story* that the autobiographer has to tell. This is why there is no getting away from the need to tell stories in order to

[14] Ibid., p. 97.
[15] *Confessions*, Book 4, p. 169. See also Waugh, *Brideshead Revisited*, III, Chap. 1.

explain ourselves as well as to describe the world. As Barbara Hardy has put it, narrative is not just

> an aesthetic invention used by artists to control, manipulate and order experience, but [it is] a primary act of mind transferred to art from life itself... For we dream in narrative, daydream in narrative, remember, anticipate, hope, despair, believe, doubt, plan, revise, criticise, construct, gossip, learn, hate and love by narrative. In order really to live, we make up stories about ourselves and others, about the personal as well as the social past and future...[16]

In saying this, Barbara Hardy is surely echoing the reflections upon memory and anticipation pondered by St Augustine in Books X and XI of the *Confessions*: reflections which led him to formulate his theory that time past and time future are not so much objective modalities of things themselves as modalities of our experience of things. Thus memory is more than just a field or 'spacious palace' containing, higgledy-piggledy, 'the treasures of innumerable images, brought into it from things of all sorts perceived by the senses', for, as Augustine himself recognised, we can measure the temporal lengths of different memories against each other,[17] and this proves that there is a certain temporal order even among the miscellaneous images that the memory stores up. So to recall something from the memory, in however simple a fashion, is already to recall it as part of a temporal sequence. Memory itself furnishes us with the beginnings of a narrative order—and of course, the same goes for our anticipations of the future too. In this sense, then, there is a primitive, potential narrative lodged in the very faculty that enables us to experience the world as temporal at all. But *mere* remembering is a rarity: we are seldom so innocent as merely to recall the order of things which memory provides. When I try to re-trace the sequence of movements I made five minutes ago in order to find the pencil that I now want to use, and which I absent-mindedly misplaced, I am trying, of course, simply to recall. But the task is made difficult by my own temptation to reshuffle those memories according to some order which I would like to impose on the past. I refuse to

[16] 'Towards a Poetics of Fiction: An Approach through Narrative', *Novel*, 2 (Fall 1968), p. 5. Cf. George Orwell, 'Why I Write', *Collected Essays*, i, p. 2.

[17] In this paragraph I am indebted to Stephen Crites, 'The Narrative Quality of Experience' in *Journal of the American Academy of Religion*, 39 (1971), pp. 291–311.

believe I was so stupid as merely to have dropped the pencil behind a pile of papers: so I try to remember the facts differently—perhaps in order to be able to blame someone else for the loss. In other words, I am caught between telling the story as it actually happened and re-telling it as I would like it to have happened. Or perhaps—to take a more serious case—I may retell it according to some artistic instinct for embellishment, or because of some new perspective that I have acquired from intervening experiences, and which now sheds a different light upon the facts. In other words, in any possible autobiography I might write, I shall not be merely recalling, I shall be *re-collecting* the past: that is to say, I shall be refashioning it into a new kind of order—an order dependent of course, upon the actual order of past events for its materials, but independent of it insofar as autobiography inevitably becomes a narrative with an *end* in view.

Frank Kermode has drawn attention to the dangers inherent in the ambiguity of this word 'end'. For a story is always liable to be shaped unduly by the 'end' that is projected by it: an end which is both a purpose and a terminus:

> Men in the middest make considerable imaginative investments in coherent patterns which, by the provision of an end, make possible a satisfying consonance with the origins and the middle. That is why the image of the end can never be *permanently* falsified. But they also, when awake and sane, feel the need to show a marked respect for things as they are; so that there is a recurring need for adjustments in the interest of reality as well as of control.[18]

The danger comes when stories that are essentially *fictions*—that is, narratives with ends which we recognise to be consciously and explicitly chosen for specific and limited purposes—regress to the status of narratives whose ends are taken to be really, not just fictionally operative: i.e. myths. For Kermode it is one of the most insidious of contemporary temptations to turn what should be regarded as fiction into myth: and the pressure underlying this temptation is what he calls our sense of an ending, our special urge to read the end into the beginning, to divine a purpose in everything—perhaps because today the world that awaits us outside our narrative windowframe is so manifestly lacking in purpose. Another way of describing this pressure

[18] *The Sense of an Ending*, p. 17.

towards 'myth' would be to say that we have an over-developed sense of the horizontal dimension of narrative. Over against this we need to cultivate a special understanding of the vertical aspects: and in particular the awareness that the story is *only* a story, a 'fiction', something devised and controlled from 'above' by a narrative voice, which is itself open to criticism, to inspection, to judgement by *us*: and a kind of *art* in which metaphoric 'overtones' and poetic resonances hover above or lurk below the level of mere plot to give the story a depth and richness of texture sufficient to counteract our dangerous temptation to read or listen simply in order to find out at all costs what happened 'in the end'.

3
Metaphor and 'Nature'

In this chapter I first of all consider the implications of the concept of 'natural tendencies' which lies at the root of the causal relation. An analysis of this relation leads to the conclusion that not only are terms like 'natural tendencies' unavoidable in commonsense, but that they are implicit in scientific language too. But such terms are irreducibly *metaphorical*, since they entail the systematic use of similarities between animate and inanimate things: and hence they also imply a 'whole metaphysical system'. In the second section I go on to draw out the implications of this conclusion for the contemporary debate about the forces currently threatening Nature and suggest that in order to cope with them we may have to revitalise the ancient notion of the angels as 'powers of Nature'. Certain trends in contemporary fiction suggest that this might be a very relevant development to pursue.

i

As I have already noted, the use of analogy begins with very mundane things. The paradigm case of the analogical stretching of words is that whereby we say, for example, that not only the man but his complexion or his diet are 'healthy'. It is crucial to the use of 'healthy' in such cases that the healthiness of the diet should be a cause of the health of the man, and the health of the man be the cause of the health of his complexion. But the theory of analogy does more than presuppose a causal relationship: it presupposes a 'transitive' view of causality itself. That is to say, the term *cause* denotes, not an association or regularity between things but (as we have seen) an agent, a 'thing exerting itself, having its influence or imposing its character on the world'.[1] Or, to put it another way, it is a thing that is exerting itself according to its *natural tendencies*.

[1] See above p. 20, note 12.

Now it is this notion of active causal agencies which exert themselves according to their own 'natures' which distinguished the transitive concept of causality, prevalent in the pre-Enlightenment world, from the intransitive Enlightenment notion most clearly expressed by Hume. According to Hume, to look for a cause is to look, not for a thing that is 'exerting itself' according to its own nature, but for a 'necessary connection' between two or more things (*Treatise of Human Nature*, I, iii, 2). And what leads us (on Hume's view) to affirm the existence of such a necessary relationship, say between a lighted cigarette-end and a cinema fire, is some regularly observed association between lighted cigarette-ends and cinema fires, such that a fire always occurs when a lighted cigarette-end is dropped in a cinema, and never occurs without the dropping of a lighted cigarette-end. From the observation of such a regular sequence we are led to conclude that there must be a 'necessary connection' between the two things. This 'necessary connection' itself is what we mean by causality.

Of course, it will immediately be objected that this is a preposterous notion: we know perfectly well that cinema fires can occur without being caused by cigarette-ends, and also that quite often people drop lighted cigarette-ends and no fire results. As a comprehensive definition of causality the intrasitive theory seems plainly absurd. But the fact that we can think of so many exceptions to it is, surely, just the virtue of the intransitive theory. It leads us to *question* the obvious answer; to enquire whether contributory factors other than the cigarette-end itself may have been involved, whether the fire started before or after the cigarette-end was dropped etc. etc. Nevertheless it fails to account for what we actually do when we investigate the fire. For the fact is that we are not looking for *the* cause of the fire: we are trying to isolate the factors that brought it about. And what brought it about will be an enormous number of connected factors of various kinds. The cigarette-end will have played one role in the event: but other roles will have been played by such factors as staff negligence, the inflammability of the carpets, the poor lighting, the draft under the door, the absence of adequate warning signs, the high temperature of the room, etc. etc. So to investigate what brought about the fire is not to look for something called *the* cause: it is to isolate the factors that, by their natural tendencies, played a part in the bringing about of the fire. Yet it is obvious that, out of the host of factors involved, only some can be said to have natural tendencies to bring about fires. These would obviously include the lighted cigarette-end, but not (for example) the absence of warning signs. An *absence* obviously cannot be an agent which has natural tendencies of any kind. Nevertheless it remains true that if we had known all the natural tendencies of the things involved we would have been able to predict with certainty that the fire would have happened exactly as it did. It is the object of empirical investigation to get as near as possible to this state of knowledge.

Now it is tempting to think that, because the intransitive view of causality historically has had the virtue of stimulating empirical investigation, its virtues can somehow be combined with those of the transitive theory. But the two theories are mutually exclusive, and were designed to be so. Nevertheless, attempts *have* been made to combine elements of both, and one of them—that of Mill—is instructive for a particular reason: namely that it shows that you cannot help using metaphorical language in the statement of the transitive theory.

Mill's Humean starting point is clear:

> Between the phenomena . . . which exist at any instant, and the phenomena which exist at the succeeding instant there is an invariable order of succession . . . this collective order is made up of particular sequences, obtaining invariably among the separate parts . . . The invariable antecedent is termed the cause, the invariable consequent, the effect.

However, Mill realises that such invariable sequence seldom subsists between a single antecedent and a single consequent. There is rather a 'sum of antecedents' to which the effect is consequent: and it is the sum of the antecedents which is the 'real cause' (*System of Logic*, III, 5§2). Further Mill sees that from no particular sum of antecedents can we be sure that a particular consequent will necessarily follow. For very often what would follow, if this sum of the antecedents were allowed to exert itself unimpeded, does not happen because its exertions *are* impeded. We may say, for example, that the sum of antecedents enumerated above[2] would cause a fire in the cinema if unimpeded: but of course very often something else interferes—a person steps on the cigarette-end, the cigarette-end drops on the stonework instead of the carpet, etc. etc. So the fire that would otherwise have happened

---

[2] See above p. 51.

doesn't happen. Of course, whatever does happen only happens because of a sum of antecedents: but then this sum includes the unexpected interfering agencies as well as the agencies in the original sum. Thus Mill's analysis of causality can only tell us what *tends* to happen, not what must happen:

> To accommodate the expression of the law to the real phenomena we must say, not that [an] object moves (i.e. in the direction the sum of antecedents would, if unimpeded, have pushed it) but that it *tends* to move in the direction and with the velocity specified. (*System of Logic*, x, 10§5).

In going so far, Mill has already gone beyond anything that an intransitive view of causality could logically accommodate. He has already modified the notion of an invariable sequence between a particular sum of antecedents and the necessary consequent since he has admitted that we can never be sure that we have included in this sum of antecedents everything that might be involved. In fact, the 'necessary connection' which is of the essence of causality on the intransitive theory can now exist only (a) between the whole universe of causes at one instant and the whole order of the universe at the next (only in this way could we be sure that we had included *all* the relevant antecedents): or (b) between a particular sum of antecedents and what it will *tend* to produce.

However, Mill goes further. He insists that not only does e.g. the body that is subject to a certain force move in the predicted manner unless counteracted: he also says that it tends to do so even if it is counteracted. That is to say,

> it still exerts, in the original direction, the same energy of movement as if its first impulse had been undisturbed, and produces, by that energy, an exactly equivalent quantity of effect.

For example, even if a force of one ton fails to raise a three-ton object, so that nothing actually happens at all, according to Mill the one ton force is still exerting itself. We can be sure of this because if we add a further force of two tons from another source, then the object will rise and this shows that the original force was exerting itself all the time (*System of Logic*, loc. cit.).* In other words, the absence of anything happening may be the sum of the effects of two forces working against each other.

Now it is easy to see that there must be something wrong with this picture. How can two forces, both actually at work (i.e. the three-ton weight of the object that *tends* to stay on the ground and the one-ton force that is *tending* to raise it) produce a 'sum' that is precisely nothing? Mill is here surely muddling up two incompatible pictures; one is the notion that the sum of a negative and a positive number may be zero, the other is the fact that the result of two opposing forces in action against each other may produce a state of rest. In the case of the first picture Mill's trouble is that the two forces in question are not respectively positive and negative: the idea does not make sense. A *negative* force can no more be an agent than an absence of warning signs. On the other hand, in the case of the second picture, the notion of an object *tending* to produce an effect even in the absence of any actual result can only be equivalent to *trying*. But what sense does it make to say that the three-ton object is trying to stay on the ground, and the one-ton force is trying to raise it?

One answer is that it makes no sense at all. This seems to be Geach's view, when he dismisses Mill's idea of the sum of effects as a mere muddle.[3] But even if it is a muddle, it is not a mere muddle. There is a reason why Mill was led to his conclusion, and even if it was wrong it was significant as the unwitting expression of a continuing trend in human thinking. For the fact, as even Jacques Monod admits, is that the history of human civilisation shows how, in the course of the encounter between man and the inanimate world, man has started with the idea that things are somehow alive, and are therefore 'trying' to do what they naturally tend to do.* Only later do men come to understand the difference between living things, about which it is legitimate to say that they 'try' to do such and such, and inanimate things which, having no capacity for forming purposes or intentions, cannot be properly spoken of as 'trying' to do anything.

Now it may well be that 'primitive' man was simply wrong in ascribing intentionality to inanimate things. But even if he was, the fact remains that there is still a residually metaphorical character to our ascription of tendencies to any inanimate object, arising from the fact that such ascription of tendencies proceeds from cases of intentional behaviour to those of non-intentional behaviour. And this residually metaphorical character is never altogether eliminated. (Norman

[3] *Three Philosophers*, p. 103.

Mailer's talk about the 'thrust' of the Saturn rocket's engines is a characteristic example of this fact.) Mill's problem was that in order to make sense of his causality theory, he had to use the metaphorical language of 'trying' even at the very moment when he wanted to employ the purely mathematical language of a sum of positive and negative numbers.

It might be objected that the use of metaphorical language in the case of inanimate, and therefore non-intentional behaviour, is simply a confusion of categories, and if a theory requires such a confusion it must itself be confused. Certainly there is a genuine danger of confusing categories when we speak of the natural tendences of inanimate objects. Pascal was right to point out that

> Nearly all philosophers confuse their ideas of things, and speak spiritually of corporeal things, and corporeally of spiritual ones, for they boldly assert that bodies tend to fall, that they aspire towards their centres, that they flee from destruction, that they fear a void, that they have inclinations, sympathies, antipathies, all things pertaining only to spirit. (*Pensées*, 199)

But he was surely wrong to lump together all ascriptions of tendencies and call them simple confusion of thought. It is a *fact* that bodies tend to fall, for example, even if it is an illicit metaphor to say that they flee from destruction. So the problem is how to distinguish the legitimate language from the illegitimate—a problem that Pascal's Cartesian contemporaries did not wholly solve. For example, the Cartesian conception of inertia—a crucial concept in Cartesian physics—is that of a *tendency* of bodies to stay in the same state: an ascription of a teleological property to corporeal objects that clearly offends against Pascal's all-too-inclusive strictures about conceptual confusion.[4] Descartes's theory breaks down at this point precisely because he cannot do without the very notion that he is trying to eliminate: namely the notion that even inanimate objects have natural tendencies. As Mill's example shows, the language of 'tendencies' cannot be wholly freed from the teleological language of 'trying' and therefore of purposes and final causes.* In short, for all its metaphorical overtones and metaphorical implications, the idea of natural tendencies in things is not a piece of outworn superstition, but a necessary part of scientific

---

[4] Kenny, *Descartes*, pp. 213–14.

reasoning as to the causes of phenomena, as well as being simple common sense.[5]

But there is more to be said in support of the transitive theory than that. It is not only very old (as one would expect from a piece of commonsense): at least as old as the theory of Thales of Miletus that a magnet had a 'soul' which attracted iron,[6] or, to put it more generally, that 'all things are full of gods'. It is also very modern. Cybernetics for example involves the notion that change consists in the turning of a thing-in-potency to a thing-in-act by the 'influence'—that is to say, natural tendency, or power—of a mover, or 'cause'.[7] W. Ross Ashby, in his *Introduction to Cybernetics*,[8] refers to such a change as the browning of the skin through sunshine as the 'influence' of an 'operator' (i.e. the sunshine) upon an 'operand' (i.e. the thing-in-potency) by turning it into a 'transform' (i.e. thing-in-act). I doubt if the cybernetician is fully aware of the implications of his 'metaphor' (if such it be) concerning the influence of the sun, but it certainly resounds with Aquinas's Aristotelean dictum: *causa importat influxum quemdam ad esse causati.*[9] Or, as Gilson puts it, 'something of the being of the cause passes into the being of that which undergoes the effect'.[10] That is to say, there is something of the sunshine in the brown skin that is not present in the unbrowned skin, just as for Thales, when water is heated something of the fire (namely, 'the hot') passes into the water to make it hot.[11]* Of course, this power is not a 'god' who has taken up residence in the thing, though that may be the 'primitive' way of understanding the matter.[12] But neither is it a mere word, a periphrastic study in a worn-out philosophical fashion. On the contrary, it is real in so far as its exercise tells us something about the nature of the thing that has it. As Ruskin put it, in his polemic against the empiricism of his nineteenth-century opponents:

---

[5] On the unavoidable use of metaphors in science see Max Black, *Models and Metaphors* and D. Berggren, 'The Use and Abuse of Metaphor' in *The Review of Metaphysics,* 16 (December 1962 and March 1963), pp. 237–58 and 450–72.

[6] Aristotle, *de Anima,* 405 a 19.

[7] I owe this point to Hugo Meynell, pp. 13–15.   [8] p. 10.

[9] *In Metaphysics,* Lib. V, Lect. 1.

[10] *Spirit of Mediaeval Philosophy,* p. 86.

[11] A. H. Armstrong, *Introduction to Ancient Philosophy,* p. 4.

[12] 'Primitive' here should not be thought to imply any evaluative judgement, or any assertion (à la Lévy-Bruhl, Monod *et al.*) of the necessary logical or scientific superiority of allegedly 'modern' concepts.

the word 'blue' does *not* mean the *sensation* caused by a gentian on the human eye; but it means the *power* of producing that sensation; and this power is always there, in the thing, whether we are there to experience it or not, and would remain there though there were not left a man on the face of the earth. Precisely in the same way gunpowder has a power of exploding. It will not explode if you put no match to it. But it always has the power of so exploding, and is therefore called an explosive compound, which it very positively and assuredly is, whatever philosophy may say to the contrary. (*Modern Painters*, IV, 12§2)

If it were not for the inferences that are made, by scientists and common men alike, from the supposition that such things as gunpowder have natural tendencies to behave in certain ways, a good many facts, such as the existence of hitherto unknown planets, substances and properties, would never have become known. This is itself a refutation of Descartes's thesis that the only things we can predicate of corporeal objects are those which 'can be derived from indubitable true axioms with the sort of self-evidence which belongs to mathematical proof'.[13] But it is also a refutation of the desperate remedy taken by some of Descartes's followers (notably Geulincx and Malebranche[14]) that, since we cannot ascribe natural tendencies to corporeal things, corporeal things cannot exercise causality at all. For them only God is a true cause: everything else is simply organised coincidence on a gigantic scale.

To sum up: *Pace* thinkers like Monod, the belief in natural tendencies does not imply any sort of Bergsonian vitalism, let alone that 'all things are full of gods' in the sense that Thales intended, but simply that the metaphorical language that is needed to formulate causal connections must inevitably contain metaphysical overtones. When the cybernetician talks about the influence of the sun upon skin, for instance, he is simply unpacking an altogether unavoidable expression, which is more fully articulated in the Thomist dictum already quoted. If it is a metaphor, it is certainly not a dead one. Similarly, Descartes's failure to rid the term *inertia* of its—to him unwelcome—associations with natural tendencies, is not due to any failure on his part to translate his language fully into mathematical terms. On the contrary, the term 'inertia' just *is* a term for a natural tendency, despite its being basic to

[13] *Principles of Philosophy*, quoted in Kenny, *Descartes*, p. 203.
[14] See Copleston, *History of Philosophy*, IV, pp. 177–9 and 188–90.

his physics. The same goes for a huge mass of metaphorical language which lies buried beneath the apparently innocent, or neutral talk of scientists even today. Appearances not withstanding, 'tendency' terms such as energy, inertia, attraction, repulsion, thrust and many others which are the common coin of physics or engineering remain, often buried and lacking their original 'textural overtones' but still active, in the formulation of the models and hypotheses of contemporary science; and all of these go back to the commonsense supposition that things have natural tendencies: a supposition that is expressible only in language which is radically metaphorical. As Max Black tersely puts it: 'Perhaps every science must start with metaphor and end with algebra; and perhaps without the metaphor there would never have been any algebra.'[15]

ii

The argument of this chapter so far has been that 'natural tendencies' language is indispensable both for science and commonsense and that metaphor is a necessary element in such language. A consequence has emerged, namely that there is no avoiding metaphysical involvements once this premiss is granted, since a metaphysic is implied by the very fact of metaphor itself. For metaphor asserts a relation between man and a world which is properly called 'Nature'; that is to say, a world ordered and intelligible and subject to discernible 'natural tendencies' inherent in things themselves.

But if the epistemological conclusion is philosophically compelling, as I think it is, the social and political implications are nevertheless dangerous. Precedents set by many of the novelists and poets of this century who have acknowledged such a 'metaphysical' role for metaphor are hardly reassuring. As Denis Donoghue has said, the imperial role given since Coleridge to the poet's metaphorically-orientated imagination provides the basis for an ordering of human experience, on behalf of the supposedly unimaginative majority, by a self-selected élite: the men of imagination.[16] And this élitist claim is not just a charter for minority rule in the arts: it has unmistakable political implications. Conrad's dealings with the mysterious powers of darkness inside the human psyche were inseparable from his dealings with darkness in the political sphere, and always tempted him to confuse a sense of mystery

[15] *Models and Metaphors*, p. 242.   [16] *Yeats*, p. 121.

with the business of mystification, to confound profundity with portentousness. Lawrence's 'unseen presences' easily turned into dark and perverse gods. Yeats's heterodox and nationalistic religiosity proved fertile soil for fascist ideas. Against such precedents, to which we were alerted, if in a somewhat wooden way, by C. P. Snow more than a decade ago, the anti-metaphysical case presented by Robbe-Grillet and others seems eminently appropriate. If you want to remove the potentially fascist implications of a romantic, imperial theory of the imagination then you must root out its cause (the metaphysical itch, the grandiose aspiration of man to find an ultimate meaning in life) and you must eliminate the modes of its expression—that is, the poetic metaphors, the heart-searching romantic tragic fictions, the collaboration with big plots being hatched by something called 'nature', to which all writers are tempted even now. As a political corrective, then, the anti-metaphysical impulse of much 'new-novel' writing has much to commend it. It perhaps represents the one democratic aesthetic we have, abolishing the need for an élite of poets or madmen, adepts of secret disciplines or practitioners of psychological speleology. Yet, as we have seen, by reducing language and the imaginative creativity it embodies, to a merely instrumental role, this anti-metaphysical stance itself risks creating, like all revolutions, a new imperialism of its own. It implies a 'narrowing of the range of human consciousness', to use Orwell's phrase,[17] which is as drastic in its implications for the manipulation of human beings as is the indiscriminate expansion of consciousness involved in Yeats's cabbalistic mysticism. Can we find a role for the concept of 'Nature' which does not arise from an alienating ideology masquerading as an objective force beyond human control, but which respects man's freedom as well as his itch to find, at all costs, an ultimate meaning in his life?

Modern fiction is not particularly reassuring in the answers it gives. The disappearance of Nature is one of its central themes. Among those novelists who tend to see the banishment of Nature as an accomplished fact, two responses seem to prevail. The first is typified by Robbe-Grillet's verdict that modern man feels no deprivation at the loss of

[17] 'Lear, Tolstoy and the Fool' in *Collected Essays etc.* iv, p. 294. Orwell's point is that the 'narrowing' in Tolstoy's case resulted from his unconscious authoritarianism. It was this which made it impossible for Tolstoy—himself a great landowner who had given away his inheritance—to appreciate the truths enshrined in *King Lear*.

Nature, for Nature was never more than bourgeois illusion, comforting perhaps in a meaningless world but no less illusory for all that. To be rid of Nature is to be at last free. The second response is typified by Beckett's verdict: there is no more Nature, and the loss is tragic and the deprivation catastrophic. To be rid of Nature is to be in the realm of 'the lost ones', in a world of sheer 'lessness'. A third response however has to be considered. This is latent in Mailer's identification of the source of our troubles about Nature with the triumph of what he calls corporation-land: that combination of technology, materialism and exploitative brutality towards the environment which is most evident in the cities of America. However, in Mailer's case there is also a certain fascination for, as well as hatred of, this massive agglomeration of brutalities: there is pride, energy, vitality in it, as well as regimentation, pollution and despair. Mailer's ambivalence is characteristic of a general uncertainty about 'the big plot being hatched out by nature'.[18]

This uncertainty is evident enough elsewhere, in the utterance of people speaking from many different viewpoints. Thus Harvey Cox in his plea for a matter-of-fact acceptance of the positive Christian values of the 'secular city' admitted in the early nineteen sixties that modern man's attitude to what he called (after Max Weber) 'disenchanted nature' was essentially childish: 'Like a child suddenly released from parental constraints, he takes savage pride in smashing nature and brutalising it'. But everything would come out right in the end: the brutality was only a passing phase. 'The mature secular man neither reverences nor ravages nature . . . Nature is neither his brother nor his god'.[19]

The trouble with this view was that it was far from clear how modern man could avoid the dilemma of either reverencing or ravaging the world. Cox pleaded for an attitude that would treat Nature matter-of-factly, since man is not an expression of Nature but a subject facing it, even a monarch surveying it. But the very facts seemed to be against this so-called matter-of-factness, as Rachel Carson saw:

> The balance of nature is not the same as in Pleistocene times, but it is still there: a complex, precise, and highly integrated system of relationships between living things which cannot be safely ignored any more than the law of gravity can be defied with impunity by a man perched on the edge of a cliff. The balance is not a *status quo*:

[18] Tanner, *City of Words*, p. 148.   [19] Cox, *The Secular City*, p. 23.

it is fluid, ever shifting, in a constant state of adjustment. Man, too, is part of this balance.

Because man is part of Nature, a crucial element in its 'balance', he must take up an attitude towards it which can only be called a kind of reverence. He must develop a reverential sensibility because this is necessary to his very understanding of the facts:

> We see with understanding eye only if we have walked in the garden at night and here and there with a flashlight have glimpsed the mantis stealthily creeping upon her prey. Then we sense something of the drama of the hunter and the hunted. Then we begin to feel something of the relentless pressing force by which nature controls her own.[20]

Rachel Carson's plea for reverence clashes not only with Harvey Cox's secular theology, but also with the optimism of some of her opponents in the debate about the environment. Thus, for John Maddox, her plea for a reverential sensibility is little more than a 'literary trick'.[21] Yet it seems to be generally agreed—though the limits of the agreement are far from clear—that Rachel Carson's main point is valid: man *is* part of the balance. As the generally middle-of-the-road report by Barbara Ward and René Dubos for the United Nations conference on the environment, called *Only One Earth* puts it, in a chapter entitled 'A Delicate Balance',

> the lessons learnt in piecing together the infinite history of our universe and of Planet Earth . . . teach us surely one thing above all—a need for extreme caution, a sense of the appalling vastness and complexity of the forces than can be unleashed and of the egg-shell delicacy of the arrangements that can be upset.[22]

But the delicate balance that has to be respected is not just an ecological problem: it is also a human problem. If the 'balance of Nature' compels us to adopt the ethical attitude which Albert Schweitzer called 'reverence for life', for the sake of our own biological survival, the balance of justice in the world seems to compel us to be ready, if necessary, to ravage nature for the sake of our survival as civilised human beings. *Only One Earth* presents the dilemma very clearly:

[20] *Silent Spring*, pp. 215ff. [21] *The Doomsday Syndrome*, p. 15.
[22] p. 85.

The astonishing thing about our deepened understanding of reality over the last four or five decades is the degree to which it confirms and reinforces so many of the older moral insights of man. The philosophers told us we were one, part of a greater unity which transcends our local drives and needs. They told us that all living things are held together in a most intricate web of interdependence. They told us that aggression and violence, blindly breaking down the delicate relationships of existence, could lead to destruction and death. These were, if you like, intuitions drawn in the main from the study of human societies and behaviour. What we now learn is that they are factual descriptions of the way the universe actually works.[23]

Yet despite this new understanding of the 'delicate balance',

most developed peoples are still affected with one type of 'tunnel vision'. Although they make up no more than a third of the human race, they find it exceptionally difficult to focus their minds on the two-thirds of humanity with whom they share the biosphere. Like the elephants round the water hole, they do not notice the other thirsty animals. It hardly crosses their minds that they may be trampling the place to ruins. . .[24]

In short, without a balance of human justice between the haves and the have-nots in the world, there may come a catastrophic imbalance in Nature itself. Nature may then be forced to unleash its own vast and complex forces, to 'fight back' against human aggression for its own survival, by terrifying 'ecological invasions' of its own.* We may come full circle to that point in ancient tragic thinking at which the Furies, present as the forces in Nature itself, turn upon mankind and pursue him relentlessly until he has atoned for his vile offences and the balance of things has been restored.

The reference to ancient tragic thinking here is far from incidental. For if it is true that modern discoveries have brought back into focus the older moral insights of man, they have also resurrected the older conceptions of the tragic consequences that follow from disturbing the 'delicate balance'. If the modern problem is that of maintaining, at one and the same time and by one and the same means, the balance of forces in Nature and the balance of human justice among nations, then the problem is not really modern at all. It is simply a restatement of the

[23] Ibid., p. 85.   [24] Ibid., p. 205.

ancient wisdom which refused to drive a wedge between Man and Nature. To take just one expression of this wisdon, the ancient Greek notion of *Dikē* implied both the business of maintaining a balance in Nature and the business of restoring justice between men. *Dikē* operated, without essential distinction both in 'Nature' and in human affairs. It signified what was simply natural in the sense that, for example, rivers flowed downhill because of it, but it also signified a logic in human behaviour: thus if you killed someone, *Dikē* would ensure that someone else killed you. That was how the world went.[25] It followed of course that a man's task was first of all to find his place (his *moira*, or portion) in this universal and self-adjusting system and to keep to it. If he did not, then the Furies, that is the process of *Dikē*, would come to see that he was brought to book. But exactly the same went for the natural order. It was because of *Dikē* that the sun had to keep its place in the heavens, just as a man had to keep his place in the society: and if it did not, the Furies would come and put it right, too. The Furies not only policed mankind: they policed Nature as well.

However, there is one element in the modern situation that was not available to the ancient Greek tragedians: this is the feeling, very apparent as we have seen in much modern fiction, that in any case the fight for a maintanance of the balance is hopeless. The iron laws of entropy will ensure that. Nature is not in balance but in decline. We live in a world that is on the wane. At best, human civilisation is a temporary regrouping of the forces that are trying, against impossible odds, to form a rearguard against the onset of chaos. At worst, it is actually hastening the catastrophe.* Is there anything in the 'older moral insights' of man to cope with this new form of tragic thinking?

Perhaps the Christian equivalent of the idea of *Dikē* can help us here. There is a parallel in Christian thought to the Greek conception of powers which operate simultaneously in the natural and in the moral spheres: it is to be found in the unfashionable but highly pertinent doctrine of the angels. A brief consideration of the meaning of this doctrine may be of some use in making sense of the contemporary possibility of a radical imbalance in Nature brought about by some kind of conscious choice.

Originally, the angels were scarcely distinguishable, in the Biblical

---

[25] Aylen, *Greek Tragedy*, p. 354. See also Armstrong, p. 4.

writings, from God himself. They are part of God's 'court', and go-
betweens mediating God's thoughts to men.[26] Indeed in the Yahwist
tradition they were simply ways of talking about the holiness or power
of Yahweh.[27] But when it became necessary for the Israelites to find
some means of accommodating their experience of alien nature religions
to their own monotheism, they did so by interpreting the nature gods
of these religions as subordinate powers serving under Yahweh.[28]*
Thus Yahweh's supremacy was preserved while the 'gods' of surrounding cultures became the powers of nature through which he ruled the
world. However, if the angels were responsible for policing nature,
they were also responsible for meting out human justice. Just as they
emerged slowly from God's bosom into separate identities as the
powers of Nature, so too they emerged slowly as separate powers
meting out God's justice to men. (God's accusatory wrath—his
'satan'—became 'Satan', his personal prosecuting counsel).[29] Thus the
inextricable connection between the balance of Nature and the balance
of justice remained perfectly clear.

Nevertheless, the 'balance' as envisaged in Jewish religion was
radically different from that of Greek thought for one overwhelming
reason: man was a 'fallen' creature in a 'fallen' world. And just as the
fallenness of man was the result of an aboriginal calamity that had
distorted the very meaning of human justice, so the fallenness of the
world was the result of an aboriginal calamity that had disorientated
the whole of Nature.* The fall of the angels and the fall of man were
twin aspects of a single gigantic tragedy. Yet if the tragedy was vaster
and more catastrophic than anything that a Greek tragic thinker could
envisage, it was also less final: for it was of the essence of the matter
that somehow the tragedy was the product of free and conscious
choice—a choice that could be reversed.

It is the contention of the New Testament writers that this aboriginal
disorientation of both Nature and justice *has* been reversed. Christ's
defeat of the 'principalities and powers' means that one and the same
redeeming act of love has restored the balance of both Nature and

[26] Job 1:6; Psalm 89:6–7; 1 Kings 22:19. See also Jacob's dream at Bethel,
Gen. 28: 10–12.

[27] Timothy MacDermott, 'The Devil and his Angels' in *New Blackfriars*, xlviii
(October 1966), pp. 16–25.

[28] Caird, *Principalities and Powers*, pp. 1–4.

[29] Ibid. pp. 31ff. See also MacDermott, p. 19.

justice. For it was lack of love which led to the 'fall of the angels': that is, to the collapse of both justice and Nature into chaos. The tragedy of Satan's fall lies in the fact that, as God's prosecuting counsel, he became such a stickler for the divine law that he would go to any lengths to secure a verdict, forgetting altogether the claims of love: 'His tragedy consists in precisely this, that law is not the ultimate truth about God, so that, in defending the honour of God's law, Satan become the enemy of God's true purpose.'[30] Now the divine law which Satan takes to be ultimate and irresistible is precisely the law of *Dikē*. In moral terms this is the law of an 'eye for an eye and a tooth for a tooth'. In religious terms, it is the legalism of a system which thinks of man's dealings with God as a kind of cash-register religion of rewards and punishments. But the law for which Satan is such a stickler is not confined to these human planes. Nature's 'laws' too are misconstrued and distorted by the Satanic powers.[31] People are made physically and psychologically ill by them[32] even the wild animals become their prey.[33] Finally, through such superstitions as astrology the very stars themselves are recruited into the Satanic service for the exercise of evil.[34]

Now the ultimate truth about God which Satan forgot is the law of love: and it is the work of Christ, as the New Testament sees it, to show that it is love, not *Dikē* which makes the world go round. To the apparently invincible law of blind and tragic vengeance, Christ replies with the love of enemies which breaks the vicious circle of unending tragedy (Matt. 5:44, Luke 6:27–35). To the religious legalism of the Pharisaic spirit he replies with the Holy Spirit which blows wherever it will, and leads men into the truth without prior conditions (John 14:17). Against the apparently invincible political powers of the world Christ sets the assertion that all power comes from God, and that without it the political powers are helpless (John 19:11). And to the Satanic grip on Nature itself, Christ replies with the exercise of a power to cast out demons, and to control the elements themselves—the wind,

---

[30] Caird, p. 37 and MacDermott, pp. 21–2.

[31] The powers are deceptive, making men think that laws and processes which are actually the results of God's will are somehow unalterable decrees of fate, that is simply part of the 'human condition'. See Schlier, *Principalities and Powers in the New Testament*, p. 29.

[32] Schlier, pp. 21–2.   [33] Caird, pp. 56–60.

[34] Schlier, p. 23.

the water, the tempest. Even the wild animals are tamed: he rides the unbroken colt (Mark 11:1–7).[35]

Now all of these victories over the fallen powers are represented as victories for love. But what can such talk mean? That the power of love should conquer fear, legalism, political injustice is perhaps understandable: but that it should put right the very balance of Nature itself is hardly intelligible at all. No doubt this is why the 'mature secular man' finds it necessary to de-mythologise the Christian gospel's teaching about the redemption of Nature, and to say that all the talk in the New Testament about Christ's victory over the fallen powers of Nature through love is just—to use Eliot's words in *East Coker*—a 'periphrastic study in a worn-out poetical fashion' or, in Donald Mackinnon's terms, mere 'remote metaphysical chatter'.[36]

But it is just at this point that the findings of the biologists and the environmentalists seem to demand a return to the 'older insights'. We must become 'friends of the earth', they say, and not hurt it.[37] We must pledge loyalty to the vulnerable and fragile planet:

> Alone in space, alone in its life-supporting systems, powered by inconceivable energies, mediating them to us through the most delicate adjustments, wayward, unlikely, unpredictable, but nourishing, enlivening and enriching in the largest degree—is this not a precious home for all of us earthlings? Is it not worth our love?[38]

Or, to put the same point in another way,

> We travel together, passengers on a little space-ship, dependent on its vulnerable supplies of air and soil; all committed for our safety to its security and peace, preserved from annihilation only by the care, the work, and I will say the love, we give our fragile craft.[39]

But, it will be objected, this is not the Christian point at all. It is one thing to say that unless we 'love' our planet it will refuse to go on supporting us: it is quite another to say that it is love which keeps it

[35] Caird, pp. 70ff.   [36] *Borderlands of Theology*, p. 92.
[37] Rattray Taylor, *Doomsday Book*, Chap. 11.
[38] Ward and Dubos, pp. 298–9.
[39] Adlai Stevenson speaking to U.N. Economic and Social Council in 1965 (quoted in Maddox, p. 20).

going. How can we talk of it being love that makes the world go round, when we know that the world is dominated by the DNA molecule and the second law of thermodynamics? It is at this point that the earlier discussion about the concept of causality—a concept radically connected with the transitive notion of the natural tendencies of things—becomes crucially relevant. For at the level of transitive causality, neither Clausius's law nor Jacques Monod's chance and necessity have anything relevant to say. Such men Chesterton called 'sentimental professors' who have been swept away by mere associations, mistaking the empirical generalisations and experimental discoveries of science for 'mere mechanical processes, continuing their course by themselves . . . by fixed laws, self-caused and self-sustained'.[40] For love is not the answer to the question *how* the world goes round, but *why* it exists at all. As we have already seen, the one answer to that question is—'*magic*'.[41] But 'magic' is only another name for the creative causal contiguity continually at work in Nature for which another term is the angelic powers—who are, as Newman said, the powers of Nature, but are also the agents of God's love.*

But of course the Christian gospel is not primarily concerned to assert the power of the angels: it is concerned to reveal the creative power of Christ's love, what D. H. Lawrence called 'the greater morality' of life itself.[42] For the gospel writers see this greater morality incarnated in Christ because he constitutes in his own person *the* centre of tragic (though far from wasted) resistance to the chaos and disintegration of the world: a chaos that they, like novelists today, see in terms of hidden plots, occult influences, arbitrary events, bureaucratic unintelligibilities and the like, and which they sum up as the work of the fallen angels, the 'principalities and powers' of this world. In other words, the Christ of the gospels like the heroes or anti-heroes of many modern novels, is the arch-enemy of the cosmic collapse: the centre of a life-asserting organisation and energy directed towards the defeat of an otherwise inexorable process of disintegration. But, as Camus saw, such defiance of what presents itself as an irresistible decree of fate is the very essence of the tragic: 'Revolt is not enough to make a tragedy. Neither is the affirmation of a divine order. Both revolt and an order

[40] Newman, *Parochial and Plain Sermons*, ii, p. 363.

[41] See above, p. 45. Newman makes the same point, op. cit., pp. 361–2.

[42] *Study of Thomas Hardy* in *D. H. Lawrence, Selected Literary Criticism*, pp. 176–8.

are necessary, the first pushing against the second, and each rein-
forcing the other with its own strength'.[43]

In this sense, we have to see the death of Christ in tragic terms.[44]
He is destroyed because he defied the limits set by the system of political,
social and metaphysical powers which St John calls 'the world'.
Indeed, in his death, the prince of this world seems to have conquered
for good and all. Love seems to have been finally defeated, so that the
process of entropic disorder and corruption can go on unchecked. And
having been apparently destroyed, Christ seems powerless to help
those who try to carry on the struggle. He can do nothing to stop the
inevitable process of *Dikē* by which the world takes its due revenge:

> Because you do not belong to the world, because my choice with-
> draws you from the world, therefore the world hates you . . . indeed
> the hour is coming when anyone who kills you will think he is
> doing a holy duty for God (John 15:19–16:2).

But if the New Testament reveals Christ in death as defeated by the
powers of this world, it also reveals in his resurrection that, ultimately,
it is they who will be finally defeated. That is to say, not only will the
human world be brought to a final justice, but the very cosmos will be
brought into the power of overriding love—a love which will show
that the second law of thermodynamics is not an inexorable and invincible decree of fate, promulgated from the very beginning of the
world, but that even the physical universe is subject to God's mercy
and love (Col. 1:18–20).[45]

Yet the fate of Nature is still bound up with the fate of men. It is
not divine love in some abstract sense, but as manifested in the love of

---

[43] *Selected Essays*, p. 198.
[44] See articles by Mackinnon noted in *Borderlands of Theology*, p. 97 (cf.
below, p. 209, note).
[45] As the *J.B.* puts it:
>   As he is the beginning
>   he was first to be born from the dead
>   so that he should be first in every way;
>   because God wanted all perfection
>   to be found in him
>   and all things to be reconciled through him and for him
>   everything in heaven and everything in earth,
>   when he made peace
>   by his death on the cross.

human beings for one another, that will somehow determine the fate of at least that portion of the cosmos with which human beings have anything to do. What they achieve, in their hungering and thirsting after justice, will radically affect the kind of environment in which they finally find themselves. If this is what the environmentalists are saying in their pleadings for a new kind of love and loyalty to the planet earth, it is also what we learn from the Christian text which best sums up the true dimensions of the contemporary debate about the maintenance of the balance of Nature and the balance of justice: I mean St Matthew's stupendous vision of the solemn court-room scene in which the choice that faces mankind is at last made absolutely plain, and our 'sense of an ending' to the human story completely vindicated, the narrative structure of our consciousness and the 'story-shape' of our world manifested. If men are capable of loving one another enough to satisfy the hunger, and to slake the thirst for justice that they all feel, St Matthew seems to say, then the world which they ultimately inhabit will be a world worthy of the reverence they will have shown towards it: but if they are not, then they will be sentenced, by an inexorable *Dikē* of their own making, to eternal life in an environment appropriately ravaged:

> When the Son of Man comes in his glory, escorted by all the angels, then he will take his seat on his throne of glory. All the nations will be assembled before him and he will separate men one from another as the shepherd separates sheep from goats. He will place the sheep on his right hand and the goats on his left. Then the King will say to those on his right hand, 'Come, you whom my father has blessed, take for your heritage the kingdom prepared for you since the foundation of the world. For I was hungry and you gave me food; I was thirsty and you gave me drink; I was a stranger and you made me welcome; naked and you clothed me, sick and you visited me, in prison and you came to see me.' Then the virtuous will say to him in reply, 'Lord, when did we see you hungry and feed you; or thirsty and give you drink? When did we see you a stranger and make you welcome; naked and clothe you; sick or in prison and go to see you?' And the King will answer, 'I tell you solemnly, in so far as you did this to one of the least of these brothers of mine, you did it to me'. Next he will say to those on his left hand, 'Go away from me, with your curse upon you, to the eternal fire prepared for the devil and

his angels. For I was hungry and you never gave me food; I was thirsty and you never gave me anything to drink; I was a stranger and you never made me welcome, naked and you never clothed me, sick and in prison and you never visited me.' Then, it will be their turn to ask, 'Lord, when did we see you hungry or thirsty, a stranger or naked, sick or in prison, and did not come to your help?' Then he will answer, 'I tell you solemnly, in so far as you neglected to do this to one of the least of these, you neglected to do it to me'. And they will go away to eternal punishment, and the virtuous to eternal life (Matt. 25:31–46).

4
Metaphor and 'God'

In this chapter I try to show how some of the conclusions arrived at in the previous chapters of this book apply specifically to theology. In the first part I discuss very briefly some of the difficulties that arise when philosophers attempt to formulate rules for speaking about God in the absence of the crucial distinction I have already established between the metaphorical and the analogical ways of 'stretching' words to cover things not available in ordinary experience. In the second part I go on to show how the theory of metaphor, and the theory of narrative derived from it, which I have already sketched in Chapters 1 and 2, can help to supply the deficiency. Finally I hint at one way in which the reading of fiction may play an important role in any modern understanding of theological, and especially of Christian claims.

i

For many thinkers today, the 'doctrine of analogy' in all of its various forms, has lost any value it may once have had. I think there are several reasons for this disillusionment:

1. One of the consequences of Bibilical criticism, positivistic or existential philosophy and post-Feuerbachian reductionism has been to encourage the idea that we can speak about ultimate reality, if at all, only in metaphors. Thus Paul Van Buren rejects the analogical theory of God-talk because 'the cognitive approach requires speaking of that which it admits is ineffable. It involves speaking of God by analogy, yet it is granted by its proponents that they cannot say to what extent its analogies are apt and proper'. Van Buren concludes that the choice of a non-cognitive, or 'blik' conception of God is the only rational alternative left.[1] A slightly different reason for rejecting the analogical

[1] *The Secular Meaning of the Gospel*, pp. 97–8. Van Buren has modified his views in his more recent book, *The Edges of Language*, but although he now

theory is given by Leslie Dewart. For him, the fundamental mistake of the analogical theory is to assume that 'a true proposition is one which by virtue of its representative power bridges intentionally the onto-logical gap between object and subject'. Analogical predication is no longer useful, he says, because the ontological gap is itself an obsolete notion. 'God is not an object of thought . . . but he is experienced by us as a reality given *in* empirical intuition . . . This is why experience of God takes on the peculiar character of faith.'[2] In other words we do not need analogy to bridge the gulf between human subject and divine object since God is present to us directly in experience.[3]

2. The writers who reject analogy for reasons such as those just described tend to regard metaphorical language, if valid at all, as only a second-best. The theory of analogical predication, they admit, did after all claim, even if unsuccessfully, to provide a clear, certain and substantial basis for talking about ultimate reality as transcendent, as personal, as infinitely greater than, and beyond, man's capacity. Metaphorical language, on the other hand, suggests to such thinkers, only a vague, poetic and uncertain way of talking, more useful for expressing human feelings and aspirations than for articulating eternal truths or formulating coherent rational arguments. But there are other writers who take exactly the opposite line. They see metaphorical language not only as cognitive, in some important sense, but as en-riching and deepening the prosaic speech of academic philosophers. For such writers, who see themselves primarily as poets or visionaries, metaphorical speech about God, especially that which is couched in mythic or poetic forms, is the most important or even the only possible kind. There are various ways in which this coming-to-terms with metaphor may be achieved. Philip Wheelwright has suggested one in a valuable essay called 'Poetry, Myth and Reality'.[4] He argues that mythical consciousness may be 'a dimension of experience cutting across the empirical dimension as an independent variable', and that metaphor may therefore be an essential ingredient in any comprehesive

---

speaks about 'stretching' language in various ways (pp. 83ff) he does not concede a truly cognitive role to analogical language, nor does he distinguish clearly between analogical and metaphorical predication.

[2] *The Future of Belief*, pp. 178–9 and note. See also the same author's *The Foundation of Belief*.

[3] *The Future of Belief*, pp. 168–9 and note.

[4] In Allen Tate's symposium *The Language of Poetry*, pp. 3–32.

account of language. Similarly, Elizabeth Sewell, following the philosophical path mapped out by Michael Polanyi, has argued that we
cannot profitably separate the poetic from the empirical, the imaginative from the intellectual, the mythic from the scientific, since 'the
human organism which has the gift of thought, does not have the
choice of two kinds of thinking. It has only one, in which the organism
as a whole is engaged all along the line.'[5] Hence metaphorical speech is
not an alternative to analogical speech, but both are parts of a *single*
complex mode of expression.

3. Wheelwright and Sewell are concerned to restore what they conceive to be a lost balance by re-emphasising, in a predominantly
empiricist and scientific age, the value and the necessity of poetic,
mythic consciousness together with the kind of language which is
needed to express it, of which metaphor is a conspicuous ingredient.
However, a third category of writers have occasionally gone even
further, by practically equating metaphor with analogy. They do this
in the mistaken but understandable belief that it is possible to reconcile
the two sides of the argument by a kind of intellectual short-cut.
Dorothy Sayers, for example, in her book *The Mind of the Maker*, uses
the two terms interchangeably. That God created the world, she says,

> is a metaphor like other statements about God . . . all language about
> God must, as St Thomas Aquinas pointed out, necessarily be
> analogical. We need not be surprised at this, still less suppose that
> because it is analogical it is therefore valueless or without relation
> to the truth. The fact is, that all language is analogical, we think in a
> series of metaphors.[6]

From having been philosophically invalid and practically useless,
analogy has now become all-important and unavoidable. But this is
because analogy has been assimilated to metaphor, in such a way that
it has become, not the philosopher's but the poet's way of talking. Miss
Sayers was after all a story-teller and literary critic, and it is not
surprising that she should set more store by metaphorical than by
analogical language. In this respect perhaps she was only following up
a characteristic suggestion of Chesterton's:

> All descriptions of the creating or sustaining principle in things
> must be metaphorical, because they must be verbal. Thus the

---

[5] *The Orphic Voice*, p. 19.   [6] p. 17.

pantheist has to speak of God *in* all things as if he were in a box. Thus the evolutionist has, in his very name, the idea of being un- rolled like a carpet. All terms, religious and irreligious, are open to this charge. The only question is whether all terms are useless, or whether one can, with such a phrase, cover a distinct idea about the origin of things.[7]

Here Chesterton takes to an extreme just the opposite view from that of Van Buren. Metaphor is now endemic in all speech. I. A. Richards's theory is here revealed for the exaggeration it is. All language is metaphorical: the literal level has practically disappeared. Conversely all metaphors are equally alive, even those whose original significance has vanished from view. This is surely as gross a distortion as the other, and just as unprofitable. What is required is not an intellectual short-cut to the reconciliation between poetry and philo- sophy, but a careful study of the complex relationship between meta- phorical and analogical ways of talking.

4. However, there is yet another kind of short-cut, and this is taken by those very sophisticated and very modern people who deny that metaphor has any validity at all. A consistent exponent of this position is Alain Robbe-Grillet, whose pursuit of metaphors in order to elimi- nate them entirely from his own, and perhaps from other people's language, is one of the most remarkable literary endeavours of our time. Robbe-Grillet's basic objection to metaphor is exactly the same as Chesterton's reason for rejoicing in it: namely that the use of meta- phor involves us in a whole metaphysical system.[8] Since for Robbe- Grillet metaphysics represent man's worst snare, a delusion born of a bourgeois ideology, distracting him from the true business of freeing himself from his dependence on mere things, the most important task of a writer is to get rid of all those unwelcome but falsely reassuring metaphors by which he ties himself to objects. For metaphors are ways by which we try to bridge some supposed gap between ourselves and the world: and it is just this 'gap' between man and the world which is the insidious beginning of metaphysical speculation. To believe in such a gap is to be assured of the tragic nature of our predicament; to be for ever cut off, but forever yearning to be united with, the world. Whereas the fact is that there is no such gap, no tragic abyss between ourselves, as conscious beings, and the things which surround us. What

---

[7] *Orthodoxy*, p. 140.   [8] *Snapshots*, p. 78.

divides us from the world is not a yawning abyss (a typical metaphor leading to metaphysical delusions of grandeur) but quite simply a measurable distance, a prosaic difference of kind. To recognise this is to be stripped of a reassuring bourgeois illusion and to face reality: a reality which is constantly masked by the metaphorical habit of mind and by the romantic poet's quest for some bridge whereby to cross the chasm that opens up between himself and his environment. Now I think that Robbe-Grillet's case against metaphor is not only perspicacious, but powerful, since it rests on a profound insight into the metaphysical implications of the kind of language we choose to employ and of its origins in an ideology. For him, as for Chesterton, language is not just the adoption of a form of expression; it is the choice of a whole world-view. The only difference between the two is that what the one believes to be the greatest truth, the other believes to be the most insidious delusion. Between these two views it is hardly possible to decide here. It is perhaps worth mentioning, however, the connection that seems to exist between Robbe-Grillet's rejection of metaphysics and the rejection by his fellow-countryman, Jacques Monod, of what he calls man's 'convenant with nature'. Monod certainly has a solution of a sort to the problem of the language to be used about God: namely that no such language is needed at all, and to pretend otherwise is just 'intellectual spinelessness'.[9] Indeed, God is not just an unnecessary hypothesis, but an impossible one. For we know now, from the findings of molecular biology, that the unchangeable conditions under which life itself has come into the world and has evolved within it are the twin laws of iron necessity and totally unpredictable chance. The old idea of a meaningful, teleological direction, or process, in the universe as a whole is simply dead: for we now know that life arose by chance and once begun continues to develop by the inexorable laws of genetic invariance and the random accidents of mutation. Not only are no other concepts required to explain the 'teleonomy' of living beings, i.e. the transmission in a species of the essential unvarying characteristics of that species from generation to generation; but the principle of scientific objectivity, by which alone genuine knowledge can be obtained about anything in Nature, rules out any consideration of 'purposes' other than those which the teleonomy of a species requires. All ascriptions of subjective purposiveness to Nature itself, whereby

[9] *Chance and Necessity*, p. 39.

the mere teleonomies of species become expressions of some overriding cosmic process, are the products of anti-scientific 'vitalisms' or 'animisms'. Not only is Bergson's 'creative evolution' a false vitalism, but so is Polanyi's personalist philosophy. Not only is Teilhard de Chardin an anti-scientific animist, anxious to restore a lost 'covenant with nature', but so are Herbert Spencer, with his positivism, and even Engels with his dialectical materialism. Now, Monod traces the attempt to restore the old 'covenant with nature' to the persistence, despite the rise of scientific objectivity, of the 'anthropocentric illusion': that is to say, the illusion that we can legitimately read human meanings into the things of the external world. In saying this he is expressing just the same objections to a comforting humanism as Robbe-Grillet. Robbe-Grillet too denounces all 'metaphysical pacts' with nature. But the trouble, as we have seen already, is that science is no more able to do away with them than is the art of poetry. For example, when Monod claims that one of the nails in the coffin of all pre-scientific anthropocentricisms is the Cartesian principle of inertia he overlooks the fact that this very concept contradicts Descartes's own theory of language, precisely because of its residually metaphorical character.[10] And he himself continually uses metaphorical terms in his exposition while pretending to have got rid of their unwelcome anthropocentric overtones by the simple, but less-than-candid device of putting them in inverted commas, as though a punctuation mark could dissolve a philosophical problem.*

I have sketched here, very briefly, four different ways in which writers have tried to grapple with the relation between metaphorical language and the analogical language of philosophy in speaking about ultimates. In my own view, they have all made the same two basic mistakes: firstly of failing to see the radical difference between analogy and metaphor, and secondly of failing to understand that despite this difference, both forms of linguistic stretching are necessary—as necessary to each other as the warp and weft of a fabric, as the melody and harmony of a musical score, as the vertical and horizontal axes of a graph. My thesis is that analogy and metaphor are best regarded— to adapt Jakobson's terminology—as the names of the 'two poles' of any adequate discourse whether about ordinary things or about God. Further I want to suggest that historically the result of failing to

[10] See above, p. 55 and below, p. 111, note to p. 76.

appreciate the true nature of the relationship between analogy and metaphor is the root cause of that profound divorce between the God of the Philosophers and the God of Abraham, Isaac and Jacob which Pascal—in this, at any rate, the 'first modern man'—diagnosed as the fundamental disease of Christianity in his own day.

In recent years many philosophers of religion have tried to cope with the problem of talking about God by positing a duality *in God* where, in the older system, there was rather a duality *in the language* used to talk about him. Perhaps the most obvious examples of this 'solution' are to be found in the writings of the 'process' theologians who have taken their inspirations from the philosophy of Whitehead.*

Whitehead's *Process and Reality* is an attempt to synthesise, at a metaphysical level, the findings of twentieth-century mathematical physics and evolutionary biology. The philosophical inspiration for this endeavour comes from Whitehead's devotion to certain philosophical heroes: Descartes, Newton, Locke, Hume and Kant.[11] Now, one of the results of incurring debts to these particular thinkers is that the distinction between the Creator and his creation, which is to say between the first cause and finite created effect, upon which the traditional edifice of Christian orthodoxy (as expressed for example by Aquinas) rested, has to be abandoned. The fundamental reason for this development is the Enlightenment's abandonment of the traditional concept of causality. According to Aquinas, we can only speak intelligibly about God in analogical language; and it is an essential feature of any 'analogy of attribution' that the secondary term of the analogy should stand in a *causal* relation to the first term. (When we predicate 'healthy' of Fido's bark as well as of Fido himself, we do so only because we believe that the healthiness of Fido's bark is an effect of Fido's general healthiness.) For an aristotelean like Aquinas, causality involves the notion that all the things in the world have natural tendencies to behave in certain determinate and intelligible ways. But this notion was largely lost in the Cartesian and subsequent philosophies. This was in part because of the rise of mathematical models as the norms for philosophical investigation. But it was also the result of the duality of Cartesianism (preceded by that of medieval nominalism), which created a gulf between consciousness and the material world. As early as Nicholas of Autrecourt, causality became an extrinsic bond,

[11] pp. vi–vii.

or perceived regularity which kept things together, instead of being the exercise of one thing's power to affect another. What would be the result of applying such a conception of causality to a universe now seen, not in seventeenth-century terms, but in terms of organisms whose growth and decay were ruled by the internal evolutionary laws of biology and psychology? Whitehead's philosophy provides one answer to that question.

In Whitehead's system what emerges is a world made up of innumerable 'actual entities' which are held together not by mathematical laws or empirical generalisations but by what he calls the eternal 'prehensions' or 'lure of feeling' which each entity has for what lies beyond itself. Each actual entity needs to satisfy this 'lure' by transcending itself and becoming something else. While it is a mistake to think of this universal lure of feeling as any kind of consciousness (for Whitehead insists it need not be so), all the same it is true that there is a continuity without break between the lowest and highest levels of actual entities.

> Actual entities . . . are the final real things of which the world is made up. There is no going beyond actual entities to find anything more real. They differ among themselves: God is an actual entity and so is the most trivial puff of existence in far-off empty space. Though there are gradations of importance, and diversities of functions, yet in the principles which actuality exemplifies all are on the same level. The final facts are all alike, actual entities; and these actual entities are drops of experience, complex and interdependent.[12]

Thus God, as one of these innumerable actual entities, is dependent on the world, and it on him.

But this interdependence operates in two ways. God is both *primordial* and *consequent*. In the primordial aspect, he is 'deficiently actual', because 'his feelings are only conceptual and so lack the fullness of actuality'. In this sense he is not conscious, and is 'untrammelled by any reference to any particular course of things . . . [he] is deflected neither by love nor by hatred, for what in fact comes to pass'. But God is end as well as beginning, and as such 'by reason of the relativity of all things, there is reaction of the world on God . . . [his] conceptual

[12] *Process and Reality*. pp. 24–5.

nature is unchanged, by reason of its final completeness. But his derivative nature is consequent upon the creative advance of the world.' The primordial side of God's nature is 'free, complete, primordial, eternal, actual, deficient and unconscious'. The other side originates with physical experience derived from the temporal world, and then acquires integration with the primordial side. It is determined, incomplete, consequent, 'everlasting', fully actual and conscious.[13]

Frankly, I am not sure exactly what Whitehead means in all this, let alone whether ultimately it means anything at all. But it is clear in one respect. Whitehead is trying to reconcile the God who is the subject of philosophical reflection with the positive notion—an incipiently 'religious' one—that God is capable of personal concern for the world; capable of changing himself, adapting himself one might say, for the sake of the world. The religious possibilities of this conception of God come out clearly enough when Whitehead discusses the problem of evil. If we adopt his idea of God, he claims,

> the revolts of destructive evil, purely self-regarding, are dismissed into their triviality of merely individual facts; and yet the good they did achieve in individual joy, in individual sorrow, in the introduction of needed contrast, is yet saved by its relation to the completed whole. The image—and it is but an image—under which this operative growth of God's nature is best conceived is that of a tender care that nothing be lost. . . We conceive of the patience of God, tenderly saving the turmoil of the intermediate world by the completion of his own nature.[14]

Whitehead's disciple Charles Hartshorne has tried to continue this line of thought further in the same direction. For him God is 'supreme yet indebted to all, absolute yet related to all'[15] and this comes out in the fact that God's love, like ours, involves rejoicing with the joys and sorrowing with the sorrows of others. To love is to be open to change from those who are loved, and this two-way relationship applies, univocally it appears, to God just as surely as to human beings.[16]

To put it bluntly, Whitehead and his followers have tried to reconcile the tension between the God of philosophy and the God of religion by

---

[13] Ibid., pp. 486–9.   [14] Ibid., p. 490.
[15] *The Divine Relativity*, Chaps. 1 and 2 passim.
[16] *A Natural Theology for Our Time*, p. 15.

incorporating the tension into God himself. There are two sides to God, they say, equal but opposite. It is in the reconciliation of the two that 'process theology' is interested. The idea is plausible in one respect. Making God partially dependent on the world seems to solve the problem of conceiving God as being simply 'out there', unrelated to the world. God is not 'out there'; he is 'with' the world, not 'before' it, to use Whitehead's phrase and the course of the world has a direct effect on him. Human wickedness can 'hurt' God and hold up the proper progress of reality to its ultimate conclusion. This belief might easily seem to provide a morally elevated basis for ethics—one that modern man can accept and understand. But unfortunately it also leads inevitably to the view that, in the last analysis, the conscious, change-able, influenceable aspect of God, the God of religion, is the senior partner in the firm.

> The God of religion is personal, the philosophical absolute is im-personal; the two are not idential. There is no such thing as the absolute, the infinite, unmoved aspect of the personal God of religion, whose exaltation above all other individuals is expressed by the principle of 'dual transcendence', being dependent and independent, finite and infinite, changeable and unchangeable, individual and universal, each in a uniquely excellent way. Since the relative side is concrete and the abstract is real only in the concrete, the transcendent relativity of God is his overall property.[17]

Thus there is no way of finally upholding the idea of equal and opposite elements in God without subordinating the one to the other. In effect, Hartshorne's argument reduces Whitehead's primordial side of God to 'mere abstraction'. (Perhaps Whitehead could not escape this conclusion himself, but he did not emphasise it.) The concrete, personal and changeable God is the only actual God. The God of philosophy is then deficient in actuality, thinly 'abstract' and incapable of worthwhile relationship: he is 'less than God'.[18]

This argument is surely muddled. To predicate only abstract terms of a subject does not entail that the subject is itself only an abstraction. Sherlock Holmes might deduce, from the evidence, that the murderer must be someone with such and such abstract characteristics, but this

---

[17] Hartshorne, 'The God of Religion and the God of Philosophy' in *Talk o God* (Royal Institute of Philosophy Lectures for 1967–8), pp. 166–7.
[18] *The Divine Relativity*, p. 83.

does not mean that the murderer himself is an abstraction.[19] Similarly, there is no reason to suppose that the philosopher who is prepared, on the strength of his own rational arguments, to say no more about God than that he is (say) 'living' or 'omniscient' or 'eternal', can have in mind only an abstract God. It is merely that he is not prepared, as a *philosopher*, to say more than this about the concrete personal God he believes in. (It may be a valid objection to the 'Five Ways' that they do not all necessarily point to the same God, but it is no objection at all that they only prove the existence of an abstract God. On the contrary: if the only God that exists is, say, a triune personal God; and if the Five Ways prove the existence of God; then it is the triune personal God whose existence they prove, even though they cannot prove his triunity or his personality.) Of course there is still a problem about how, by faith, we can get to a more concrete idea of God than the philosopher can arrive at by philosophy alone. But this is a problem about how to speak of God, not a problem about the abstractness or otherwise of the God we speak about.

Teilhard de Chardin offers a slightly different solution to the problem of God, but one that is still within the general framework of a process theology. Like Whitehead's, Teilhard's thought could also be described as a 'philosophy of organism'. But he was not a Jesuit trained in the era of neo-Thomism for nothing: and he refused to carry his process-theology so far as to find himself predicating a duality of any kind in the Godhead (except that required, of course, by the revealed doctrine of the trinity, which cannot arise from a purely philosophical consideration of divinity). For Teilhard, the world process is not the completion or actualisation of what is somehow potential in God. It is the completion of what is still unfinished in the redemptive process initiated (and in a sense already completed) in and by the work of Christ. It is the body of Christ, the 'phylum of love' which is the immediate product of that capacity for change, development and intensification which Whitehead's process theology ascribes to the Godhead. Yet there *is* a sense in which Teilhard suggests a certain incompleteness in God which only the evolution of the world he has created can remedy. In saying this, Teilhard is trying to elucidate St Paul, especially Colossians, 1:15–17. The work of Christ did not begin with the annunciation: it began with the creation of the world.

---

[19] I owe this example to Geach, *God and the Soul*, p. 113.

'Before anything was created he existed, and he holds all things in his unity.' Hence the process of Christogenesis by which the universe is becoming ever more united to Christ, ever more *in* Christ, is itself a progressive unification of the world with God. In the incarnation, God has voluntarily submitted to the necessity of his own creatures so that the Pleroma will be a fusion into a totality 'which, without adding anything essential to God, will nevertheless be a sort of triumph and generalisation of being'.[20] Geach has characterised ideas such as this, as God needing 'to create a universe full of creatures in order that they, however inferior to him, might be there to love and be loved by— much as a lonely old woman crowds her house with cats.'[21] But whether Teilhard's idea is good theology or not, it has rather more to it than this. The problem is that Christ's human nature, which is clearly a created nature, seems (according to St Paul) to be also in at the beginning of things. He is not just the first-born of all creation: Christ is he in whom all things in heaven and earth were created. How then are we to conceive of God's creative act *ex nihilo* with regard to Christ? How can Christ be both the first-born of all creation and the one in whom all creation occurs? Perhaps we can't know the answer to this question: no doubt it is partly an exegetical crux, and partly a theological mystery. The point, however, is that Teilhard does at least recognise an apparent paradox here which his theory tries to resolve. Unfortunately the resolution seems to involve an equal or worse difficulty than the paradox itself. For Teilhard's answer seems to require that the 'nothing' out of which creation comes should be regarded as a kind of 'something'.

> At the pole of being there is self-subsistent Unity, and all around the periphery, as a necessary consequence, there is multiplicity: *pure* multiplicity, be it understood, a 'creatable void' which is simply nothing—yet which, because of its passive potency for arrangement (i.e. for union) constitutes a possibility, an appeal for being.[22]

With whatever ingenuity one interprets this, there is here surely an illegitimate playing with the word 'nothing'. Yet the point of saying it

[20] Teilhard de Chardin, *Le Milieu Divin*, p. 122.

[21] *God and the Soul*, p. 114.

[22] *Comment Je Voie*, quoted in Mooney, *Teilhard de Chardin and the Mystery of Christ*, p. 172. I am much indebted to Mooney's work for the discussion of Teilhard de Chardin.

is plain. The creaturely nature of Christ is the first movement of this 'arrangement', the first step in the incipient union of multiplicity with unity which is to end with the Pleroma, or final consummation of all things in God. In this sense, creation is not a mere 'superfluous accessory': everything occurs 'as if God had not been able to resist this appeal'.[23] Is Teilhard here falling victim to the old myth of Chaos opposing God until it is vanquished by the divine act of creation?[24] It seems unlikely. But what does seem clear is that he is struggling between two different modes of speaking about God and creation. The first is that followed by 'philosophy' in the shape of the thomist insistence on creation *ex nihilo* as a rational inference from God's freedom and transcendence (a treatment in which 'nothing' must be resolutely interpreted as simply negative 'not anything').[25] The other is the religious way of speaking, in terms of images, myths and metaphors, of which the first chapter of Genesis is a notable example. Teilhard tries to reconcile the two. If he fails, perhaps this is because, like Whitehead and Hartshorne, he has confused a question about the kind of language we have to use to speak about God, with the kind of God we want to speak about.

Both Whitehead and Teilhard assume that the tension they feel exists between the God of religion and the God of philosophy has to be resolved by a theory about God. Whitehead finds himself postulating a dualistic God, with a primordial nature and a consequent nature. Hartshorne takes this dualism further, arguing that the primordial aspect is but an 'abstraction', distinct from, but subordinate to, the concrete personal God who is the subject of religious worship. Teilhard adds a theological perspective to the argument by suggesting that God is in need of completion by the evolution of the universe into union with himself. I have tried to show that each of these solutions leads to insoluble philosophical problems. The conclusion seems to be clear. The answer must lie, not in any theory about God but in a theory about the way we speak of him.

A short cut that has tempted many people consists in saying that when we speak of God in philosophical terms we are using the word God as a common noun, whereas when as religious persons addressing

[23] Ibid., p. 175.
[24] As Trésmontant has suggested. See Mooney, p. 253.
[25] 'Fit ex nihilo, idest non fit ex aliquo' as Aquinas puts it, *Summa Theologiae*, I, Q. 45, Art. 1 ad 3.

their Lord and Master we speak of him, we use the term as a proper name. According to this view, which has recently been re-stated by Professor Gordon Kaufman[26] the duality is not in God, nor is it in the way we apeak of him, but in the difference between the 'available' God and God 'as he is in himself'. The argument goes like this. The term 'God' is a proper name, like the term 'George Washington'. Now in the case of an historical person, such as George Washington, whose real identity cannot be wholly recovered at this distance of time, we have to distinguish between the 'imaginative construct' of George Washington—that is, the picture of him that we can assemble from the available remaining evidence—and the real personage. Everything we say now about George Washington must necessarily refer, in the first place, to the imaginative construct rather than to the real man. True, the name George Washington refers to the real man: but behind that name, apart from the imaginative construct, there is only an unknowable something, a mere 'X'. The same goes for God. When we talk about God, we talk about our 'imaginative construct' of him, which is only a symbol of the real God. God simply as he is in himself is not just ineffable, but totally indescribable in any terms whatever. He is a mere 'X'. On such a theory, the question of believing in God becomes a purely practical one. Is it good policy to behave as if the imaginative construct were the real thing? Is 'God' merely a term for a sense of meaning and purpose in life? a meaning which can only be verified eschatologically?

Using the term 'God' as a proper name is one of the commonest, but in my opinion one of the most religiously corrupting, of all theological fallacies. For since a proper name is simply a label arbitrarily tied to a person, there is nothing to stop someone from tying it to anybody or anything he likes. It may sound edifying to use the name God for a sense of responsibility and reverence towards others, but there is no logical reason, if God is simply a proper name, why the name should not be given, say, to the pursuit of money. There can be no shorter way out of the dilemma posed by Christ—'you cannot serve God and Mammon'—than to say that 'God' and 'Mammon' are simply two different proper names for the same 'X'. Who is to gainsay such a proposition unless he can point to something in the nature of the divine which precludes us from identifying God with money? But to

---

[26] *God the Problem*, Chap. 5.

speak of the nature of the divine is to use the term 'God' not as a
proper name but as a term for that which possesses the divine attributes. Of course, it also follows from the notion that 'God' is a proper
name that there is nothing to show that polytheism is not as true a
philosophy as monotheism. We can have as many beings called 'God'
as we can have people called George Washington.* Hence, on such a
logic, the disputes of the centuries concerning whether this or that
tribe followed the 'true' God would become not just historically pointless but totally unintelligible. The dilemma of D. H. Lawrence's
woman, who rode away from her 'Christian' family in order to find
the God of the Chilchui tribe, would cease to be a story of someone
searching for the true God and would become instead the trivial story
of a person labouring under the burden of an elementary mistake in
logic. No, the fact is that language must reach right out to God as he
is, albeit by means of concepts or 'imaginative constructs', if God is to
be worth having. It would be better not to worship anything than to
worship our own imaginations. Perhaps it is not suprising, in view of
this fact, to find Professor Kaufman concluding that we ought to talk
not about worshipping God, but only about the kinds of moral
behaviour that would be appropriate if we could worship him.[27]

Kaufman's conclusion has a good deal in common with a number of
other theories about the right way to speak of God that have been
canvassed a great deal in recent years. Recognising that the word 'God'
is not a proper name, and does not refer to an object in the way that
'house' seems to refer to objects, a number of philosophers have tried
to make sense of religious language in a way that avoids making claims
that can easily be falsified by empirical tests. Some of these have em-
ployed the notion that the word 'God' as it appears in *stories* is
significantly different from its use in other contexts, in that the kind of
'truth' a story has is different from the kind of truth we find in statements of ordinary fact. Exactly what the difference is may be hard to
spell out; yet everyone knows that, in some sense or other, stories can
be 'true' even though they are fictions. For example they may offer a
way of looking at life which, when understood, we recognise at once
as true, in the sense that it involves us in certain moral commitments
which we find ourselves obliged to undertake. R. B. Braithwaite's
much-discussed lecture *An Empiricist's View of the Nature of Religious*

[27] A full discussion of the logical objections to using 'God' as a proper name is
to be found in Durrant, *The Logical Status of 'God'*.

Belief is a classic statement of this argument. The story of Christ, according to this theory, is not telling us about any transcendent being, but providing a set of controlling images on which to base certain moral commitments. But, as Van Buren has said,[28] the trouble with this theory is that it fails to take into account the fact that Christians do want to make certain claims of a more than moral kind. They want to hold that what obliges them to behave in the ways indicated in the story is God's authority, as a creating and loving father: and to say this must be to say that God exists independently of the story itself. Perhaps then it is better to say that the story does more than proffer a way of living, in terms of some such controlling image as that of Christ's life and death; it sheds a different kind of light on the whole world which we encounter. This is, in brief, the thesis of John Wisdom[29] and others, who say that a story draws our attention to ways of interpreting the world which we could not arrive at by any other means. The story gives a coherent shape to what would otherwise be a jumble of miscellaneous, unintelligible items: 'Christianity in its sacred stories gives nature a shape, or insists that nature does have a shape: it is cosmos, not chaos.'[30] There is, indeed, a great deal in this idea, which I shall explore later in some detail: but even on this account of religious language, something is being left out. As Van Buren puts it, 'if religion proposes a way of seeing, it cannot also be telling us that there is yet another thing to see, another object for example.' In other words, God may be a controlling image, a fictional figure in a certain way of talking about the world, but he can hardly at the same time be the 'discrete individual' Christianity has taken him to be.[31] Van Buren's solution to the problem is to suggest that in talking about God we are stretching language to the limits of what it is capable of doing, and therefore that many of the entailments that we would normally demand of a piece of language that is playing on its 'home ground', so to speak,[32] are here necessarily cut. This is reasonable enough and links with the theory that what distinguishes poetry from dialectical reasoning is precisely that in the former case certain entailments are cut which, in the latter would necessarily have to be present if the words

---

[28] *The Edges of Language*, pp. 37–9.
[29] *Philosophy and Psycho-Analysis*, pp. 154ff.
[30] Van Buren, p. 41.   [31] Ibid., p. 42.
[32] For this metaphor, see Ian Crombie, in Flew and MacIntyre, *New Essays*, p. 111.

were to have any meaning.[33] But there is more to the 'story' theory of language about God than this. The writers who have taken the line that stories help us to make sense of the world in a certain way by providing 'controlling images', and that the Christian stories do this in a particular way, tend to think of the *content* but to forget the *structure* of such stories. Van Buren seems to do the same, insofar as he criticises such theories on the ground that, by providing us with a way of looking at the world as a whole, they necessarily fail to pick out any features that might be regarded as 'facts' of a new kind. If a story sheds a special kind of light on everything, it can't focus on any one thing in order to pick it out in a special way. Yet without being able to 'pick out' God in some way or other, such a theory amounts only to a kind of pantheism. But this argument leaves out the *structure* of the story, and concentrates only on its *content*. And in doing so, it leaves out just that element in stories which has explanatory force. Philosophical theology in the empiricist tradition needs to be married to a structural understanding of narrative if it is to take full account of the place that stories have in the religious understanding of experience.

To sum up: the divorce between the God of religion and the God of philosophy cannot be mended by positing a tension or duality in God. Nor can it be mended by deploying the term 'God' as a proper name instead of as the term for that which possesses the divine attributes. It seems to follow that we can only solve the problem by positing a duality in the language we have to use to speak about God. This is not, in itself, a very surprising conclusion. After all, behind Pascal's argument against Cartesianism lay the hidden suggestion that there was a distinction between the way philosophers talk about God and the way the poets talk about him. (It was the poets, the story-tellers and mythmakers, who told Pascal everything he knew about the God of Abraham, Isaac and Jacob.) In other words, we have to accommodate in our theology both philosophical speech about God and poetic speech about him, and to bring them into a single unified theory. This may seem obvious but, oddly enough, the task has very seldom been seriously attempted. On the whole, the philosophers have tended to regard the poets as people who use inexact, if exciting language in order to arouse emotional responses rather than to give us knowledge of reality, while the poets and literary critics have tended to dismiss the

[33] On this theory of poetry, see J. M. Cameron, *The Night Battle*, pp. 119–49.

philosophers' prosaic mumblings as nothing but, at best, necessary prolegomena to the real business of discovering the truth, at worst, positive hindrances to a true understanding of the 'love and consolation' which an imaginative and emotionally committed mind requires for its spiritual nourishment. The task, then is to try to see beyond the limitations of both sides, in order to discover whether there is any way of enabling the insights of the one to illuminate the dark places in the thoughts of the other.

ii

I have suggested that the answer to the problem is to return to the traditional distinction between two ways of speaking about God: namely the *analogical* and the *metaphorical* way. But I also want to insist that what is needed in particular is a properly developed theory of the *metaphorical* way, and of its natural cognate, namely *narrative*. The rest of this chapter is an attempt to sketch the outlines of a theory which may help to remedy the deficiency.

I have already suggested that metaphor, especially when it has deep cultural roots, is capable of a kind of organic development. But theological metaphor goes further: it is capable of 'doctrinal development' in something like the sense attached to that term by Newman. Metaphor, or at any rate, theologically fruitful metaphor, is always rooted in a cultural tradition. This means, among other things, that it is not open to the theological writer to invent any metaphor for God that he likes. He can only choose from among the metaphors that are part of a tradition, and have a certain preordained validity for him. But if this is a limitation, it is also an opportunity. For it means that the writer can personally develop the meaning of a metaphor in a fruitful way. Theological metaphors are not chosen; they choose us. They come from the web of the language itself (*la langue* in Saussure's sense) and its stock of available ideas. We can pick and choose from among them, but we can't invent wholly new ones. Or if we do they are likely to turn into mere similes, which have a certain illustrative value but no capacity for organic growth.[34]

As an example to illustrate the relation of metaphor to tradition, let us consider the following story:

[34] See above, p. 26 and below, p. 107, note to p. 25.

Throughout the earth men spoke the same language, with the same vocabulary. Now as they moved eastwards, they found a plain in the land of Shinar where they settled. They said to one another, 'Come, let us make bricks and bake them in the fire'. For stone they used bricks and for mortar they used bitumen. 'Come,' they said, 'let us build a town and a tower with its top reaching heaven. Let us make a name for ourselves so that we may not be scattered about the whole earth.' Now Yahweh came down to see the town and the tower that the sons of men had built. 'So they are all a single people with a single language!' said Yahweh. 'This is but the start of their undertakings! There will be nothing too hard for them to do. Come, let us go down and confuse their language on the spot so that they can no longer understand one another.' Yahweh scattered them thence over the whole face of the earth and they stopped building the town. It was named Babel therefore, because there Yahweh confused the language of the whole earth. It was from there that Yahweh scattered them over the whole earth. (Gen. 11:1–9)

Taken simply by itself this story could be interpreted in two ways. In one way, it could be understood as the story of Yahweh's spiteful interference with, and cruel destruction of a work with which the Babylonian people are legitimately occupied in their ordinary lives. On this view, Yahweh is jealous of man's competition. 'If they get up to tricks like that', he says to himself, implicitly if not in so many words, 'then there is no knowing where it will end. They may even threaten me, in my heaven. I had better go down and destroy their work before it gets too far, and make sure that they won't ever be in a position to compete with me in future.' Accordingly, Yahweh goes down and wantonly destroys the tower and scatters the people.

On the other view, however, the meaning is just the opposite. The people are stupidly trying to compete with Yahweh who after all made them in the first place. They can do nothing at all without him. They deserve to be taught a lesson. Far from being cruel and spiteful, Yahweh is simply showing to the people what happens when they attempt to defy his almighty power. He is really kind, and even compassionate. In other words, what seems to them a cruel outrage is just the far-seeing wisdom of a loving parent.

The apparent difficulty of deciding between these two possible interpretations of the text cannot, of course, be solved merely by the application of modern notions of how the rich possibilities of conscious ambiguity in narrative lead to a variety of equally legitimate interpretations of the written text as it stands. We are dealing, after all, with a piece of traditional lore, part of the Yahwist's primeval history which has its origins in the earliest period of Israel's nationhood and the sources of which lie in the oral epics of that period.* Indeed, if Scholes and Kellogg, in their book *The Nature of Narrative* are right then neither the teller of such epics nor their listeners could possibly be in a position to present any kind of subjective 'interpretation' along with the narrative itself. The possibility of such interpretation depends, after all, upon a certain distinction being permitted between the view of the narrative held by the author, and the narrative itself. But such a distinction is foreign to primitive orally transmitted epic literature. The teller is simply 'the instrument through which the tradition takes on a tangible shape': his voice is authoritative because there can be no other.[35] There are no subtle ironies, no hidden points of view, no crevices of subjectivity into which the concept of an authorial 'interpretation' of the given material could insert itself. Hence we can say that the absence of 'interpretation' in the text does suggest a complete freedom to choose between the two opposing views.[36]

But the Yahwistic primeval history allows us to go further than this. For the Babel story is the last episode of that primeval history: and is followed (after a brief Priestly genealogical link passage) by the beginning of the sacred history, the call of Abram. Thus the Yahwist's primeval history deliberately ends with an open question, which only the subsequent sacred history can answer. Von Rad puts the point succinctly: 'Is God's relationship to the nations now finally broken; is God's gracious forbearance now exhausted; has God rejected the nations in wrath for ever?'[37]

The primeval history seems to break off with this question unanswered, leaving the reader's ears ringing with a 'shrill dissonance'. In every previous case (Adam's fall, Cain's crime, the sins of mankind

[35] Scholes and Kellogg, p. 53.

[36] Admittedly there is some element of 'viewpoint' in the text as we have it, i.e. in the 'literature' which the Yahwist, according to von Rad, has made out of the original material (see below, p. 112, note to p. 90). For example, Yahweh has to come near before he can see the tower, not because he is short-sighted but because to him it seems so puny. Here we have a remarkably satirical comment on man's feeble efforts. But none of this affects my main point.

[37] *Genesis*, p. 149.

that were punished by the flood—each sin, and each punishment, worse than the last) the breach with God has been partly healed by a divine compassion. Yahweh does not utterly desert those he has punished. His will to save mankind remains clear. But with the Tower of Babel story, he leaves mankind scattered, and seemingly helpless. There is no hint here of an ultimate and overarching parental love. The question of Yahweh's future attitude to mankind is left completely open. What will his next move be?

> That is the burdensome question which no thoughtful reader of Ch. 11 can avoid; indeed, one can say that our narrator intended by means of the whole plan of his primeval history to raise precisely this question and to pose it in all its severity. Only then is the reader properly prepared to take up the strangely new thing that now follows the comfortless story about the building of the tower: the election and blessing of Abraham.[38]

Thus, we have to see this story, with its ambiguous moral vision of Yahweh, in the context of the subsequent sacred history if we are to understand it aright. But even so there is plenty of material later in Genesis which would lend support to the idea of Yahweh as capable of hostility, and even spite and cruelty. One might cite, for example, Yahweh's visiting of plagues on Pharaoh because Pharaoh had unwittingly seduced Abraham's wife, thinking she was free to join his harem. What is it then which eventually forces us to see Yahweh in a favourable light? We can only reply, the attitude of the author, or authors, who have so arranged the material of Genesis (and the other Biblical material that belongs with it) that we are prevented, if we read it *as a whole*, sensitively and intelligently, from taking up the 'spiteful' interpretation. For instance, one thing which counts against the 'spiteful' interpretation of Yahweh's action in this case is the fact that there is also in Genesis the story of Sodom (Gen. 18:16–33). On Abraham's protesting to Yahweh that it is wrong to kill the innocent inhabitants along with the guilty ones in Sodom, Yahweh replies 'if at Sodom I find fifty just men in the town I will spare the whole place because of them'. Abraham then proceeds to argue, very correctly, that it is not a matter of fifty, but of *any* just men. Though he does not beat Yahweh down beyond ten, the drift of the argument is plain, as

---

[38] Ibid.

Jeremiah (5:1) and Ezekiel (22:30 f.) realised. Here Yahweh is seen as considerate of the claims of the innocent, and like a reasonable bargainer in an oriental market place recognises a sensible deal when he sees one.

Now the point of examples like this is that they show how the very human and changeable characteristics of Yahweh function as metaphors for the activity of the 'Most High', the creator of heaven and earth. For it is Yahweh's significance that he is a character in a story, and is thus midway between the purely human and the wholly divine worlds. As such he acts as a metaphor by which the creator can manifest himself in an intelligible form. But, as we have seen, not any kind of behaviour on the part of Yahweh the character will count for this purpose: it has to be behaviour that is in keeping with the idea of the creator that the tradition itself enshrines.* And sometimes we have to look beyond a single incident to see what this means.

Within the tradition, however, the metaphorical role of Yahweh can certainly grow and develop. To take one example. There are three versions in Genesis of the story of a patriarch who makes his wife say she is his sister in order to prevent his being killed by a tyrannical king who wants the woman for himself. The argument is that as she is his sister the king will think she is free to join his harem and will not feel it necessary to 'remove' her husband first. But when the king, having seduced the woman (or, in one version, having nearly done so), finds that she is already married, he gives her back to her husband. Now in the first version (Gen. 12:10–20) Yahweh inflicts severe punishment on Pharaoh for having seduced Sarah, the wife of Abraham, despite the fact that Pharaoh had no reason to suspect that she was not free to join his harem. In the second version however (Gen. 20:1–18), this unjust punishment of the subjectively innocent king is avoided. Yahweh tells the king the true facts of the matter in a dream, before he has had time to seduce Sarah, so that the innocent king is not made to suffer for an act he had no reason to think was in any way illicit. In the third version (which is told of Isaac and Rebecca), the trouble is again avoided, this time by making the king discover the truth for himself instead of from a dream (Gen. 26:7–11). Now the commentators agree that these are not three separate stories, but three different versions of the same story.[39] The point of the story is that Yahweh preserves the patriarch, the faithful follower, from being killed by an unscrupulous oriental despot.

[39] See von Rad, pp. 162, 221 and 266, and Vawter, pp. 125ff., 160ff. Also R. de Vaux, pp. 13f.

But, they say, the second and third versions show a more developed moral sense. For whereas in the first case Pharaoh and indeed his whole household suffer severe punishment for having broken a divine law in ignorance, in the second and third versions a dream, or other device, is introduced in order to prevent such an injustice happening. In the progressive development of the 'moral sense' which the three versions of the same story reveal, we can see how Yahweh, as the metaphor for the 'Most High', grows and changes under the pressure of an ongoing cultural tradition. Yahweh is recognisably the same character in each version, but he has been refined and matured during the process of the development of the story. The tradition thus not only sets limits to what can consistently be predicated of Yahweh, but, within those limits, provides the opportunity for a growth of religious and moral awareness through the capacity of the metaphor which enshrines it to grow according to its own internal logic.

A somewhat similar process of development may be noted in the corresponding 'character' of Satan during the Old Testament period. I have referred to this development already[40] but here it may be noted that the growth of the moral sense in the character of Yahweh involves a progressive blackening of Satan, who is made to take on many of the 'bad' qualities that would otherwise have to be given to Yahweh himself. Until the exile Satan had been merely the term for the accusatory and condemnatory aspect of the divine power. As such he was not necessarily an evil being; on the contrary he was part of the divine righteousness. On the other hand, in the later period Satan begins to act on his own account, to take a proper name ('Satan' instead of 'the satan') and even to draw into himself the forces of evil in the universe. For example, whereas in 2 Samuel 24:1 Yahweh in his 'anger' incites David to conduct a census and then punishes him for the act (a census was felt to be impious because it suggested man was thinking of taking over the divine prerogative of supervising the increase of the family or the nation),[41] in the later version of the same story, in 1 Chronicles 21:1, it is Satan, now a character with his own proper name, who is credited with the evil suggestion of the census and with provoking David to undertake it. What in the earlier version was referred to as 'the anger of Yahweh' is now an independent being, with an autonomous will and freedom of action. Yahweh's punishment of David is thus

[40] See above, p. 65.
[41] See *J.B.* editorial note on this verse.

seen as just rather than unjust, for David should have resisted Satan's evil provocation, whereas nothing could be worse than to resist the command of Yahweh himself.[42]

Yahweh then, is a quasi-human character in a story, and this way of treating him is the basic metaphor. The poet, or narrator, has taken upon himself to attribute to Yahweh a kind of life which is not that of God, the Most High, creator of heaven and earth, but of ours. He has done so for the purpose of telling us something about God's 'mighty acts' that could not be told in a non-figurative way. Yet quite clearly this strategy for talking about Yahweh raises acute philosophical problems concerning the divine immutability, omniscience etc. Aquinas discovered this when faced with the story of Noah, in which we are told how Yahweh 'regretted' having made man, his most cherished masterpiece.[43] For *prima facie* this statement entails that Yahweh has changed his mind about man, his creature. Aquinas as a philosopher therefore sees it as an apparent objection to the philosophical doctrine of God's immutability. His solution is characteristic. God knew all along that the creatures he had made would have to be destroyed for their wickedness, but since he knew from the beginning everything he intended to do, this does not argue for any change of mind in God. The 'regret' Yahweh experienced, Aquinas says, is 'only a metaphor'.[44] I don't think we need to reflect on this answer for long to see that, even if it satisfies the philosophical requirement of divine immutability, it makes nonsense of the story by turning Yahweh into a callous, calculating monster. What kind of creator is this, who on Aquinas's premises lovingly makes his masterpiece, man, a free moral agent able to choose his own course, knowing all the while that in a short time he will destroy him again for having exercised the very freedom he has been given? It is far more fitting to think of Yahweh as really regretting his original creative action under the provocation of genuine disappointment with man's performance, than to try to preserve a philosophical point by distorting what is clearly a meta-

[42] See Roy Yates, 'Satan and the Failure of Nerve', in *New Blackfriars* lii (May 1971), pp. 223–8.

[43] *Summa Theologiae*, I, Q. 19, Art. 7 ad 1.

[44] *Summa Theologiae*, loc. cit. It is worth noting that the verses which express Yahweh's 'regret'—i.e. his change of mind—are part of the Yahwist element in the Noah story. The Yahwist tradition of course is much more concrete and down-to-earth in its outlook than the Priestly tradition which is also present in the text as we have it.

phorical description of the divine will into a piece of analogical reasoning.*

This being so, there seems no reason why we should feel a need to excuse the writer of the Noah story for saying, metaphorically that Yahweh 'regretted' having made man. Of course, everyone knows from other passages in Genesis and elsewhere, that Yahweh is not really subject to changes of mind.[45] But for purposes of telling this story, which is basically a story of Yahweh's mercy and fidelity to Noah, it is necessary to say, metaphorically that he is. In other words, Yahweh is a character with quasi-human traits and his function in the Biblical tradition is precisely to exhibit these. However, Yahweh is also the 'Most High, the creator of heaven and earth' (Gen. 14:22). The problem, therefore, is to reconcile what appear to be two irreconcilable aspects of the one divine being. The best way to understand the problem may be to illustrate it with a diagram:

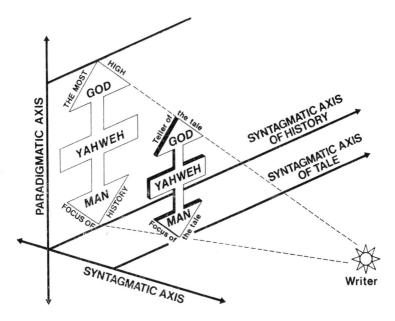

[45] See Mal. 3:6 for a summary of this tradition. See also e.g. Psalm 18:2 where Yahweh is likened to a rock and a fortress, and is therefore totally reliable; and Psalm 34:1 where Yahweh's plans 'hold for ever' and 'the intentions of his heart from age to age'.

The diagram in this case has to be three-dimensional. This is because we want to say that the figure Yahweh is not only a character in the story but also, at the same time, a person who really exists. The complex relation thus involved implies that the structure of the story in which this character appears is projected on to the real world to give *it* a structure which otherwise it would not have. In other words the diagram illustrates the thesis that the sacred story gives 'chaos' a shape, or 'nisus'. For without the story, as the diagram indicates, there would be no shape to reality: it would only be a blank wall. It is not until the structure of the story is projected on to this blank wall that we can recognise that the wall too exhibits the same structure.

Now the structure of the story is similar to the structure of the Cinderella story. It has a vertical dimension in which the top and bottom (God and man) are linked by a causal nexus of dependence. God is at the top of the structure, giving it its existence by his creative narrative voice, and man is at the bottom, at floor level so to speak, where the historical events take place. But in this case we have a third element within this vertical structure: the character of Yahweh who is midway between man, at floor level, and God. (For Yahweh is both God, according to the story, and also characterised by specifically human limitations.) Yahweh is, one might say, a metaphor both for God and for man. In this sense, the vertical dimension of the story is a paradigmatic one, and the floor level is a syntagmatic dimension.

Now, if we see Yahweh as thus related metaphorically to God and to man, then the affirmation of Abram's faith that 'Yahweh *is* God' (Gen. 14:22) will be a piece of metaphorical language. But this will not mean that it is 'only a figure of speech', and not a cognitive statement. For, as usual, corresponding to this metaphorical statement of faith will be a supporting narrative syntagm, a story which will inevitably have to be a story about this one true God. That is to say, from this act of faith, once uttered, it follows that the narratives about Yahweh must be stories of the one true God. If Yahweh is God, then it is not a contingent but a necessary fact that the stories about him will be stories about God: and the information they reveal about God will be reliable for that reason. But, as usual, there is also another possible interpretation, to which just the opposite will apply. Now the act of faith will be in the horizontal dimension, which is the dimension of the narratives. In other words, the act of faith will be the assertion that out of all the stories of gods, only these stories are truly stories of God. It is on this point that faith is focussed: namely that only certain contingent events, out of all the myriad events of history, are genuinely acts of God. It follows, however, from this act of faith that the vertical axis is now an axis of necessity; the axis of the syntagmatic, not of the paradigmatic. (The paradigmatic, it will be recalled, is the axis of choice, in the sense that it is on this axis that we choose *these* words, out of a whole range of eligible words, to make *this* sentence. Similarly, in the present case, faith, being a kind of voluntary commitment, is always a paradigmatic matter. It is the choice, either of *this* god out of all the eligible gods, or of *this* story out of all the eligible stories). On the second interpretation, if the chosen story is a story about the true god, then the god of whom it tells must be God.

Both ways of looking at the matter are equally valid. Nevertheless, each represents a slightly different notion of what faith is. The one starts from a certain conception of the divine and argues to what such a divinity will or will not do. The other starts from a certain sense of what kinds of acts seem to be specially marked with the 'divine' mark, and argues from the stories about these to the existence of the one god who is talked of in those stories. It is I think arguable that one of the ways in which the religion of Israel differed from that of Christianity is that, with the coming of Christianity, the emphasis shifted from the first to the second conception of faith.

But what is the nature of the metaphorical relation between Yahweh, a divine character in a story who is subject to human emotions and the Most High God? Yahweh and God are, quite clearly, not different beings. On the contrary, Yahweh *is* God, as Abram saw when he was confronted by the King of Sodom: 'I raise my hand in the presence of Yahweh, God most High, creator of heaven and earth' (Gen. 14:22). In this reply Abram is explicitly affirming the identity of Israel's divine protector and guardian, Yahweh, and the most high God, El-Elyon. Yet there is certainly a distinction between them, as the difference between the Yahwist and the Elohist traditions makes clear. Yahweh is the name for a humanly approachable figure, whereas in the Elohist tradition God is presented in more remote terms, emphasising the distance between man and himself.[46]* Thus 'Yahweh is God' is by no means a tautology. On the contrary, for Abram and all those coming after him, it is a daring act of faith, indeed the fundamental act of faith.

[46] *J.B.*, Introduction to the Pentateuch, p. 8.

Yahweh, the special protector of the Jewish nation, a god who is far nearer to his people than are the gods who belong to the surrounding nations, (Deut. 4:7) *is* the most high, the creator of heaven and earth, the one whom no man can see and still live (Exod. 33:20). 'Yahweh' and 'Elohim' are therefore different ways of referring to the one true God. They are not the names of two different gods. Now the problem is this. If it is not a tautology to say that Yahweh is God, but a daring affirmation of a not-immediately-obvious identity, where *in the stories in which Yahweh figures as a character*, is the notion of God, in the sense of the Most High, the creator of heaven and earth to be found?

This question needs careful formulation. Of course it is true that constantly in the Old Testament, Yahweh is spoken of as the Creator and the Most High. But this is because the Old Testament is written from within that faith. So the important question is rather this: given that Yahweh is, in the first place, Israel's national protector (one might almost say tribal deity) how is it that anyone, simply reading and hearing the stories in which he figures as a character, would see in those stories the possibility of his being truly God, the Most High? Even here, a qualification must be made. We are not asking this as an historical question, as to how it came about that the Hebrews rose to the idea. We are asking it as a philosophical question, which may be put more formally thus: Yahweh, as the name of a character in a story, is a piece of metaphorical language. Metaphor in theology works by taking for granted that it is possible to affirm certain human characteristics of God. In this way, it brings God into direct contact with the world. It is a kind of incarnation. But it does so only because it presupposes that we already know that these characteristics are not literally true of God. Somehow therefore we have to know already that God is not literally what the metaphor affirms him to be. In a sense Aquinas must be right after all about God's regretting that he made man. For if someone were to suppose that in the Flood story the attribution of regret to Yahweh was literally applicable to God then, according to Aquinas he would not only not obtain a deeper understanding of God's ways with men, he would actually get a far more erroneous, indeed a logically incoherent one.[47] In this sense then, when we read or hear of Yahweh as a character in the story, we must already have at the back of our minds the conception of God as Creator and

---

[47] *Summa Theologiae*, I, Q. 19, Art. 7.

as the Most High. Or, to put it more provocatively, an analogical conception of God must accompany, and even precede any metaphorical speech, and indeed any religious understanding of him.[48] Where is such a conception of God to be found in the stories of Yahweh?

One answer might of course be that the Old Testament is full of hymns and canticles to him, full of prophecies inspired by him, full of references to his attributes—his creativity, omniscience, immutability and so on. Is it not in the light of these references that we are able to recognise the Most High who has to be presupposed in the stories of Yahweh? But this answer will not do. For the *stories* of Yahweh have the theological priority.[49] They are the foundation of the tribal faith that Yahweh *is* God. So it is somehow from these stories themselves that the notion of Yahweh as God has to be extracted. Consider a crucial example, namely the story of the crossing of the 'Red Sea' which is the central episode of the exodus which made Israel into a dedicated nation. In this story Yahweh is pictured as a kind of super-human warrior hero, who is seeking his own glory at Egypt's expense, as a true epic hero should (Exod. 14:18). He is the commanding officer of the whole Israelite army, organising their strategy. But he is also a wonder-worker. He makes the elements obey him so that his army can get through unscathed. He ensures the death of the Egyptian pursuers. As the victory song puts it, 'He has covered himself in glory, horse and rider he has thrown into the sea' (Exod. 15:21). Now the question that faces us is this: how can this story of the mighty deeds of Yahweh, the super-warrior hero be, for the reader or listener, a revelation of the Most High God, Creator of heaven and earth? The question for us is not, how did the Israelites themselves, involved in the events, interpret them? i.e. how did the events become for *them* the revelation of God? For that is a question they would have to answer for themselves. Our question is a different one, stemming from the fact that revelation is something public, and open to others. It implies a tradition that can be appropriated and a community that can be joined, even by those, like ourselves, whose religious and historical suppositions are

[48] See A. Flew, on H. H. Price's *Belief*, in *Mind*, 79 (1970), p. 459, for the argument that a coherent religion cannot do without philosophical belief in God.

[49] I am referring here, of course, to the original orally-transmitted 'sacred stories', not necessarily the written versions we now have. On this distinction see article by S. Crites quoted above, p. 47 note 17.

necessarily different. So the telling of the story, in whatever primitive form, must itself be the beginning of the process whereby the events become available for subsequent assimilation, and so constitute a tradition. And this telling must somehow contain the idea of God, in the light of which the metaphorical talk about Yahweh as a warrior hero can be understood by us *as* talk about God. Yet there seems to be nothing in the story that gives us a basis for any such idea. Of course it is true that the Yahweh in the story is not merely a human warrior; his powers are superhuman. There is no doubt that he is *a* god. But he is described in the story purely and simply in epic hero terms and, taken at face value, the subsequent victory song is just a hymn of praise to this super-warrior. True, it does contain the affirmation 'This is my God, I praise him; the God of my father I extol him' (Exod. 15:21). But by itself this solves nothing, for the question is, how can we recognise the heroic warrior Yahweh *as* God even in the song? The singer of the song himself presupposes an answer to the question we still have to face.

The only answer I can suggest is this. The implicit narrator who is present in the very fact that the story is being told at all, is apparently able to tell a story with Yahweh as a character. Now, it is in this claim to be able to narrate such a story at all that we can find the notion of God somehow contained in the story. Of course, God, the Most High is not contained, or indeed spoken of, in the *events*. But there is more to a story than a series of events. There is the fact that they are being *told*. In a story events are transformed into 'these words in this order' by a process of more or less deliberate selection, including of course a narrative 'point of view'. This point of view is as much part of the story as the events it tells. Or rather, it is not part of it, it is the whole of it, but seen from the angle of narrative technique, or 'rhetoric'. The teller makes implicit claims to know what happened and how it happened, and what the characters involved were like, and so on. This is as true of a folk tale or an epic poem as it is of an historical narrative. Every tale implies a teller: i.e. that voice which makes itself heard whenever the story is told, and which is altered in tone by every change in word or emphasis in the telling. Now in the case of the Yahweh stories, the teller is making the implicit claim to be able to tell us what Yahweh, the divine character said and thought. But is this claim not a piece of gross presumption? Of course, if a god is regarded in a crudely anthropomorphic way, so that accounts of his feelings are regarded as literally true, there is no problem. In so far as the teller thinks his gods are simply men writ large, his claim to be able to tell us what they think or say does not involve anything grossly presumptuous. But if the claim is that the god who is a character in the story is also God, the Most High, and Creator of heaven and earth, and yet the story can report his thoughts and feelings as if they were directly known to the teller, then the claim to be able to tell such a story amounts to the claim to be in the position of God. I might put the point crudely by saying that the only person who is in a position to tell us what Yahweh thought, or said or felt, is God. So God is after all *in* the stories of Yahweh, but not as a character, or as part of what is told, but as the implied teller. The only person who can tell us how Yahweh 'regretted' making man is the God who is beyond all regretting. The only person who can tell us about Yahweh's fighting on Israel's side is the God who is above all fighting.

iii

Every tale implies a teller. But not every tale implies an *author*. In a traditional story of the oral epic kind there can be no distinction between author and teller, because the author is not only anonymous, he is in a sense non-existent. In other words, in such traditional narratives the teller is not an author, but simply 'the instrument through which the tradition takes on a tangible shape as a performance'.[50] The author, as a person distinct from the teller; that is to say, distinct from the possessor of that narrative voice which addresses us from the story, can only emerge with the arrival of written, as distinct from oral narrative. It is in written narrative that those subtle discriminations between author and teller can be made through which irony and self-conscious art are introduced into story-telling in order to add variety and richness to the possibilities of narrative technique. Where the author exists as a separate person, responsible for, but standing back from the story, it is possible for the teller to become a distinct 'character': one who is separate both from the persons involved in the events and from the real personage who has decided to invent or transmit a record of the events to his contemporaries. In making this distinction, of course, I am not suggesting that every narrative which, as a matter

[50] Scholes and Kellogg, p. 53. I am indebted to this work for much of the argument in this paragraph.

of contingent fact, has come to be written down involves the distinction of author and teller, or that every story which is told by word of mouth renders the distinction inconceivable. There are many 'traditional' narratives which in the course of time have taken on written form, just as there are many examples of narratives of the written type being told or read aloud to a group of listeners. The distinction I have in mind concerns the genre of the narrative, not the contingent circumstance of its presentation to us. Bearing this in mind, I think we can say that the traditional Old Testament stories in which Yahweh figures as a quasi-human character are narratives of the epic, or traditional kind, whereas the stories of the New Testament, and in particular of the gospels, are characterised by their specifically written form. The New Testament writings are notable for their association with particular named persons: 'Matthew', 'Mark', 'Luke', 'John', 'Paul' etc. The point is so obvious that it is easy to forget it, especially when the Biblical critics begin to throw doubt upon the traditional ascriptions of authorship, and to reveal the many layers of narrative tradition that underlie the New Testament stories as we have them in the canonical texts. But the point remains valid despite the critics. We read the story of Jesus Christ in a different way from the mighty acts of Yahweh precisely because it reads like the record of experiences authenticated by the very persons who underwent them, or at least by persons in direct contact with the original witnesses. This is particularly true of the earliest strands of the narrative material, such as these parts of St Paul's letters which contain the most primitive tradition (e.g. 1 Cor. 15:3–8). Now the idea of a story told about an individual's experiences by that individual himself is a comparatively late development in the history of human story-telling. It is something that emerges very slowly and rather late out of the primordial idea of the story that is designed to perpetuate a body of tradition in which fact and fiction are more or less indistinguishable. In the case of the New Testament 'story' this evolutionary process is reversed. The earliest strands in that story are those which take the form of personal experiences recorded for the benefit of others (such as 1 Cor. 3ff): and the material which overlays these earliest personal accounts is that which fills out the personal witness by adding legendary, reflective or didactic elements of a not-directly-personal kind. To put it another way, there is a clear distinction in the New Testament, especially in the gospels as we now have them, however complex their textual history, between author and teller. By author, here, I mean the person *supposedly* responsible for the book: 'Matthew', 'Mark' etc. Such a person may, in fact, have had little or nothing to do with the text as we now have it. Nevertheless, the point remains, and we cannot and should not escape it, that the gospels are presented to us as the work of particular 'authors' and this is a significant, inescapable fact about the kind of books the gospels are, however complex the process by which they came to be formed. The identification of the story of Jesus with a certain kind of story-telling, that is the kind which allows for, and indeed entails, a distinction between teller and author, is itself a very significant fact about the kind of story that the story of Jesus is supposed to be. In Christianity the various possibilities that this genre of story telling opens up are exploited. There is now a crucial difference from the story-telling of the Old Testament, where we may say that the teller of the stories is simply the 'instrument through which the tradition takes on a tangible shape', and there is no distance between the teller and the author, no possibility of ironic or self-conscious narration. In fact it is just because of the anonymity of the Old Testament teller that he can assume the omniscience and the authoritativeness required to be able to tell stories in which Yahweh can figure as a character. Only a tradition which transcends the teller and imposes a kind of impersonality upon him, through its characteristic narrative form, can authorise the presumption which is implied in 'placing' Yahweh in the limited circumstances of place and time, and involving him even in embarassingly human situations. For a particular person like ourselves, say 'Luke' or 'Mark' to *place* God in such a manner would be blasphemously presumptuous. This is why in the New Testament, God does not figure as a character in the stories. He is implicit, hidden, present in the wings but never on stage. He is not named. He is simply 'the Father' etc. He is present only as related to human characters, not as a character in his own right. He intervenes only indirectly, through Jesus or through those ordinary men to whom he entrusts special powers, as recorded in the Acts of the Apostles. His spirit is at work, but he is not present in person. He is available only indirectly in Jesus the man whose personality reveals, in a glass darkly, something of his 'character'.

In the light of modern scholarship on the New Testament what I have just said may sound absurdly naive. Yet I think it is basic to the difference between the Old and New Testaments. It is perfectly obvious when we reflect upon the experience of reading the gospels. This experience is not radically altered by the discovery that, say, the organising principle of the gospels is that of the early church's liturgical requirements, not that of straightforward historical sequence.[51] Whatever we may discover about the way in which, say, the resurrection narratives were put together,[52] or about the degrees of historical reliability we should ascribe to their various parts, or the amount of literary or religious symbolism that has been built into them, the fact remains that they are what they are, narratives personally vouched for. As such, they are of a more modern genre than the tales of Yahweh's mighty acts narrated in the Pentateuch. Precisely because God has become man, he has ceased to be a character having dealings with other, human characters. He has in one sense been made more familiar and humble, present *within* a particular human person, Jesus; but in another sense he has become more remote and ineffable, a Holy Spirit to be discerned only from experience, to be invoked in prayer or mobilised in miracle but never to be 'placed' by a human narrator.

Of course the distance between author and teller which is implicit in the gospels, and which is crucial to the *Christian* conception of God, has been overlaid by the long centuries during which the gospels were regarded as literally true accounts of the biography of Jesus. Such a literal reading of the gospels, with their multifariously legendary or mythic elements, led many people inevitably to docetism. A man who could literally be the subject of such wonders could hardly be a real man. But presumably the gospels, and the source material from which the gospels as we know them now were written, were originally recognised by those who read or heard them for what they were. There was little temptation to interpret them throughout in a uniformly literal mode, as history or biography. But under the pressures of a culture in which narratives were separated out into either the empirical or the fictional[53] it may have been inevitable that they should be misread. On the one hand, they had to be established as literally true, as history, for without this basis of fact, it was felt, the faith could collapse.[54] On the other hand they could be read didactically, whether

---

[51] See M. D. Goulder, *Midrash and Lection.*

[52] R. H. Fuller's is the most recent study of this subject.

[53] According to Scholes and Kellogg these are the two main streams into which narrative divides when written narrative supervenes upon oral transmission.

[54] Aquinas's interpretation seems to imply this. *Summa Theologiae*, I, Q. 1, Art. 10c.

as sources of moral, or mystical teaching. Hence the elaboration of the medieval theory of the four levels of meaning in scripture.[55]* But this separation of the narratives into watertight historical or didactic levels of meaning was fatal to the true understanding of them as written narratives. The connection here between an inadequate theory of metaphorical language and an inadequate theory of narrative structure seems, in retrospect, plain enough. An essential element in their comprehension was the recognition of the difference that separated teller from author. Perhaps it is only now, as a result of our long experience of reading *novels*, that is, narratives that once again combine the empirical and the fictional in a mode of narration more complex than either of these can be by itself,[56] are we able to recover the true nature of narratives that were written before that split occurred. The distance between author and teller in the gospels is discernible as soon as we begin to realise, as those who first heard or read them must have realised, the kind and degree of *art*, that is of deliberate organisation of material for eliciting a complex kind of assent,[57] which has been involved in them from the outset. When we understand, for example, that St Matthew's gospel is written to illustrate and fill out the liturgical readings of the religious year and to reinterpret them in the light of the life, death and resurrection of Jesus we have to recognise at once the presence of an author, and an authorial 'point of view' which is quite distinct from that of the implicit teller whose voice simply narrates the story as we have it. (I am not of course suggesting that there is no such art in the Old Testament books. But I am saying that we are not aware of it in the same way, and it makes no difference to the essential objectivity of the story, because the Old Testament stories are not, and do not claim to be told by individuals vouching for them personally, whether as actual witnesses of the events or as persons directly connected to those who were witnesses.) 'Matthew' is a self-conscious narrative artist as are 'Mark', 'Luke' and 'John'. Their presence in their books is of a different order from that of the merely implicit teller whose voice exists in any piece of narrative (as distinct from dramatic or lyric) discourse. And the self-conscious art of each is the source of the

[55] *Summa Theologiae*, loc. cit.

[56] Scholes and Kellogg argue that the novel is the product of an attempt to reunite the separated streams of 'empirical' and 'fictional' in narrative.

[57] I have borrowed the phrase, though not in quite the original sense, from Newman's *Grammar of Assent*, Part 2, Chap. vi.

theological insights which make each gospel a Christian document, and which make the God they imply into the Christian God. This art is one which interprets the story of Jesus *as* one about the activity of God in Jesus. In this sense the Christian vision is radically dependent not only upon narrative as such, but also upon the distance which written narrative sets up between the author and teller of the tale.* In other words, there is a close connection to be observed between what may be called the 'rhetoric' of Christian belief and the 'rhetoric' of fiction. In Part Two of this book I have tried to show what some of these connections are by a study of a number of modern fiction-writers and their work.

Notes to Part One

p. 16. See James F. Ross, *Analogy as a Rule of Meaning for Religious Language*, in *Aquinas: A Collection of Critical Essays*, ed. Kenny, p. 114: 'Aquinas's rule for analogy of attribution contains a provision that the secondary uses of the term will signify a causal relation of their subject to the normal subject of the property'; and Burrell, p. 132: 'The justification for analogous usage and the line of argument distinguishing it from the "merely symbolic" theories (of a Maimonides or a Tillich) itself depends on an analogous use of "cause" '. This argument is clearly circular; but not viciously so. For Burrell argues that in the end we have simply to recognise that we *do* invoke notions which resist analysis—such as the notion of cause which underlies Aquinas's theory of analogical language—and there is no getting away from that fact. I do not want to deny this: but to supplement it with an argument to show that this is not just a fact about the way our minds are constituted (and so vulnerable to the criticism that reality is not necessarily tailored to fit our minds): it is also a fact about the very structure of language as a medium for saying *anything*—including, of course, saying that perhaps the way our minds work does not fit the way things are! Thus the hostile critic of 'analogy' is hoist by his own petard as soon as he opens his mouth.

p. 23. Even in Gardner's paraphrase the metaphor remains irreducibly itself. It cannot be put into purely non-figurative terms. On the metaphors in Hopkins see Robert Boyle, *Metaphor in Hopkins*. Boyle's discussion of the poem, which I did not come across until I had written this section, differs in certain respects from my own but my general drift is, I think, confirmed by Boyle's approach.

p. 24. Indeed it may be that this kind of growth of metaphor is what theological development consists of. According to Newman, the first note of a genuine doctrinal development is 'preservation of type' on the analogy of physical growth, while other notes are a capacity for anticipating the future and conserving the past. See *The Development of Christian Doctrine*, II, 5.

p. 25. The distinction between metaphor and simile, though less significant for my argument than the distinction between metaphor and analogy, is nevertheless important. Aristotle could see little or no difference between the two (*Rhetoric* III, 1406b), nor apparently could Cicero (*De Oratore*, III, 39). Among the ancients, only Hermogenes of Tarsus (c. A.D. 170) saw that metaphor had a creative role to play in the joining of two meanings and was not merely a matter of 'diction' (see W. B. Stanford, *Greek Metaphor*, p. 14). Christine Brooke-Rose, criticising Aristotle, insists on the difference, but even goes so far as to say that we can tell the difference by a merely syntactic test: simile 'merely states that A is like B, never that A is B' (*A Grammar of Metaphor*, p. 14). This is making the distinction between simile and metaphor too rigid, though Miss Brooke-Rose is certainly right that when Aristotle says there is no difference between 'he rushed on like a lion' and 'a lion, he rushed on' he is failing to distinguish simile from metaphor. But then the important point, as she says, is that in the first case it is the man's *action* that is compared to a lion, whereas in the second it is the man himself, 'possessing himself of all the lion's attributes'. Philip Wheelwright is nearer to the heart of the matter when he insists that metaphor has an inbuilt *tension* which is lacking in a simile. Simile is merely the joining of two expressions, each conveying one idea (e.g. 'he ran like a scared rabbit'). On the other hand there is another kind of joining in which a single expression carries two or more meanings at once. (e.g. Marvell's 'fine and private place', referring to the grave; in which 'fine' suggests both approval and narrowness and finality). Metaphor is the merging of these two opposed kinds of linking and embodies a tension within itself for that reason. We need a kind of 'stereoscopic' vision to keep both aspects of the tension in mind. (See Wheelwright, *The Burning Fountain*, Chap. 6 and, Stanford, p. 105). But this sort of account of metaphor can be taken further. Sometimes it may be preferable to say that a metaphor 'creates' the similarity rather than to say that it formulates some similarity antecedently existing. (See Max Black, *Models and Metaphors*, p. 28). On the other hand, to say this might lead us back to simile, in which the deliberate linking of things together is the essential point. Perhaps we need to formulate the idea in terms of 'technique as discovery', to adopt Mark Schorer's phrase. Thus, to take an example from Donne's comparison of a pair of lovers to a pair of compasses (in *A Valediction: Forbidding Mourning*) we may say that by the poetic technique of metaphor Donne has 'discovered the potential transference' between lovers and compasses, not devised it (see Hawkes, p. 21). S. L. Goldberg gives a couple of examples from Joyce's *Ulysses* which usefully sum up the difference between simile and metaphor. At the end of *The Cyclops*, Bloom is compared to Elijah and this is a 'live' metaphor, whose effect, 'like that of all metaphor, is to cast its component elements into a new, unexpected but significant relationship. Its critical, or ironical effect is as inevitable as its universalising effect, just because it cannot be simply reduced either to "Bloom is Elijah" or to "Bloom is not Elijah" '. On the other hand the extended comparison of Bloom to Sinbad the Sailor at the end of *Ithaca* is not so effective, Goldberg says, because it 'no more arises naturally from the action than does, say, a parallel with Alice back from the Looking-Glass. The Sinbad conceit is funny in its way, and Joyce elaborates it as far as it will go: nevertheless it remains fanciful, extrinsic in origin and effect. At best it illustrates, not illuminates' (*The Classical Temper*, pp. 147–8). The use of the word 'fanciful' here reminds us that simile is to Coleridge's 'fancy' as metaphor is to his 'imagination'. Finally, it is worth noting that the distinction between simile and metaphor may be extended when we see whole stories as either expanded similes (i.e. allegories) or as extended metaphors (i.e. myths). Thus, D. H. Lawrence maintained that the Apocalypse of St John had originally been a myth, but that Christian authors reduced it to a mere allegory. Allegory, for Lawrence, is an artificial and delimited form, for 'an allegorical image has a *meaning*' and allegory is 'narrative description using . . . images to express certain definite qualities'. But 'you can't give a symbol a "meaning" . . .

symbols are organic units of consciousness with a life of their own, and you can never explain them away.' And since, according to Lawrence, symbols are the 'images' of myth, you can't explain a myth as you can explain an allegory. See D. H. Lawrence, Introduction to Frederick Carter's *The Dragon of the Apocalypse*.

p. 31. In the first preface to *Lyrical Ballads*, Wordsworth describes the purpose of his poetic ventures in terms that echo Hartley: 'to make the incidents of common life interesting by tracing in them . . . the primary laws of our nature: chiefly as regards the manner in which we associate ideas in a state of excitement'. How far Wordsworth in 1800 was still intellectually under the influence of the Hartleian psychology seems uncertain: but what does seem clear is that even if he did not fully accept the implications of the Hartleian doctrine, he was not troubled by the us of Hartleian terminology.

p. 44. Even so anti-metaphysical a thinker as Jacques Monod seems to admit that no egg suggests a chicken and that science has no way of forming the connection. Thus he admitted in a radio discussion with Peter Medawar on 20 August 1972 that the scientific way of describing a chicken is 'one egg's way of making another egg'. That is, science cannot describe the chicken at all! Similarly the whole biological world is simply 'DNA's way of making more DNA!' On the inadequacy of our understanding of the logic of causal propositions see Geach, *God and the Soul*, Chap. 6.

p. 53. Norman Mailer gives a neat illustration of what Mill means, in his description of the lift-off of a Saturn rocket: 'For the moment the spaceship does not move. Four giant hold-down arms large as flying buttresses hold to a ring at the base of Saturn V while the thrust of the motors builds up in the nine seconds, reaches a power in thrust equal to the weight of the rocket. Does the rocket weigh six million, four hundred and eighty-four thousand, two hundred and eighty pounds? Now the thrust goes up, the flames pour out, now the thrust is four million, five million, six million pounds, an extra million pounds of thrust each instant as those thousands of gallons of fuel rush every second to the motors, now it balances at six million, four hundred and eighty four thousand, two hundred and eighty pounds. The bulk of Apollo-Saturn is in balance on the pad. Come, you could levitate it with a finger . . .' (*A Fire on the Moon*, pp. 169–70).

p. 54. This seems to be Monod's view of the origin of what he calls the 'animist projection' though of course he regards it as incompatible with the true objectivity of science. See *Chance and Necessity*.

p. 55. Monod seems to fall into the Cartesian confusion when he says: 'The cornerstone of the scientific method is the postulate that Nature is objective. In other words, the *systematic* denial that "true" knowledge can be reached by interpreting phenomena in terms of final causes—that is to say, of "purpose". An exact date may be given for the discovery of this canon. The formulation by Galileo and Descartes of the principle of inertia laid the groundwork not only for mechanics but for the epistemology of modern science, by abolishing Aristotelean physics and cosmology'. *Chance and Necessity*, p. 30.

p. 56. Of course, for Thales, this 'something' was a kind of 'stuff' since change only occurred by the redisposition of the four elements (the hot, the wet, the cold, the dry) out of which reality was constituted. This meant that only a portion of 'the hot' could make something else hot. Such views have often also been ascribed to later, Aristotelean thinkers. Thus Anthony Kenny thinks it a fatal objection to Aquinas's first proof of God's existence, from motion, that the premiss 'a thing cannot be brought from potentiality to actuality except by something which is itself in actuality' (or, in Kenny's somewhat inaccurate paraphrase, 'only what is actually F will make something else become F') is often falsified; for example by the conduction of heat, whereby something can be made hot by the friction of two sticks against each other that are not themselves hot. But, as Geach has pointed out (*Philosophical Quarterly*, 20 (July 1970), pp. 311–12), Aquinas *cannot* have meant such a thing, since although he knew e.g. that the sun made things hot, he thought it was an equivocation to say that the sun itself was hot (*Summa Theologiae* 1, Q. 13, Art. 5). The sun, being an incorruptible heavenly body, was not itself hot or fiery, for it was not made of earthy elements at all. Hence it could not bring about heat in a terrestrial body by the transfer of its own heat. Whatever 'actuality' meant when ascribed to the sun's capacity for making things hot, it did not mean that the sun was actually hot itself. It rather meant having the power or tendency to make things hot. This is not tautologous for Aquinas, since it implies that the sun does indeed have a certain natural tendency to behave in a determinate way. It *would* be tautologous to say 'only something which has the power to make something else hot can make something else hot' if 'having the power' were merely a long-winded way of saying 'can'. But for Aquinas, having the power to bring about F in B implies more than this: namely an actual tendency to do so which *will* bring it about unless thwarted by the exercise of some other intervening tendency on the part of some other agency.

p. 62. On this, see *Blueprint for Survival, The Ecologist*, 2 (January 1972), reprinted by Penguin Books, 1972: 'The greater the number of different plant and animal species that make up an eco-system, the more likely it is to be stable. This is because . . . in such a system every ecological niche is filled. That is to say, every possible differentiated function for which there is a demand within the system is in fact fulfilled by a species that is specialised in fulfilling it. In this way it is very difficult for an ecological invasion to occur, i.e. for a species foreign to the system entering and establishing itself, or worse still, proliferating and destroying the system's basic structure'. But, as the authors go on to point out, 'as industrial man destroys the last wildernesses, as herds of domesticated animals replace inter-related animal species, the vast expanses of crop monoculture supplant complex plant eco-systems, so complexity and hence stability are correspondingly reduced'. Hence the very activities of man in trying to increase production, and thus to provide for the needs of developing peoples, are adding to the possibilities of ecological disaster.

p. 63. The second law of thermodynamics states that in any closed system all differences of temperature must tend to even out spontaneously. That is to say, a dissipation of energy tends to proceed throughout the system, thus increasing the randomness, or lack of order, within the system. Now the irony at the heart of this idea, which has caught the imagination of creative artists, is that whereas the presence of *life* within a system is always the presence of a certain order, or organisation of matter and energy, which is counter-entropic, i.e. is a centre of 'negentropy'; the communication of *information* always hastens the dissipation of that organisation, since the transmission of any message dissipates the information it contains. Hence human civilisation, which depends on communication between people, is itself bound to undermine the resistance of mere biological life to the increasing randomness in the system. (This may be seen as the basis for Lawrence's emphasis on the 'greater morality of life itself' over the merely 'social' morality of civilised man). See Norbert Wiener, *The Human Use of Human Beings*, Chap. 2; Jacques Monod, *Chance and Necessity*, Appendix 4; Tanner, *City of Words*, Chap. 6; Lévi-Strauss, *A World on the Wane*, conclusion.

p. 64. Caird notes that Philo of Alexandria (b. around 25 B.C., d. A.D. 40) mingles Greek (Platonic) and Jewish (scriptural) thought on the angels in a remarkable way. 'Philo uses the word "powers" . . . to denote one of three things: sometimes they are attributes of God, sometimes they are created beings identical with the Platonic ideas, and sometimes, again, as in Stoicism, they are immanent causes in the material world, though Philo censures the Stoics for imagining that such powers could be corporeal and independent of any higher cause. In their third capacity, the powers are occasionally to be identified with angels'. See also Newman, sermon on 'The Powers of Nature', in *Parochial and Plain Sermons*, ii.

p. 64. The traditional notion of the fall of Satan, in Jewish apocalyptic, represented it as having occurred at the beginning of the world: the God of suffering and service could no longer be identified with the great accuser, who had therefore to be cast out. But in the New Testament this tradition is modified: the fall of Satan is there represented as happening at the moment of Christ's triumph (Rev. 12:10; Luke, 10: 17–20). But I do not think the traditions are really contradictory: we are dealing with a description of a state of chaos (disorganisation, entropy) in the world, brought about by a 'fall', not with a temporal event. It is also worth noting that, according to Caird, the consorting of unclean animals with demons testifies 'to the existence of a strong popular feeling that not only in human life but in the world of nature there is a residue which cannot be brought into congruity with the holiness of God,—and which is under the control of the demonic powers (Caird, p. 59). Caird refers to Deuteronomy, 32:17; Psalm 106: 38; Leviticus, 16: 7ff; Isaiah, 34: 13–15.

p. 67. Of course, according to Newman (and Christian tradition generally), the angels are not *just* the powers of Nature. That is to say, the term 'angel' is not just equivalent to the term 'natural tendency' *tout court*. But I am not concerned here with the theological question whether, or how, angels are said to be more than the powers of Nature. That they are this is enough for my argument.

p. 76. See, for example, Monod, pp. 64–5: 'We should keep in mind the essential idea developed in this chapter: it is by virtue of their capacity to form, with other molecules, *stereo-specific* and *non-covalent complexes* that proteins exercise their "demoniacal" functions . . . by virtue of its extreme specificity an "ordinary" enzyme. . . constitutes a completely independent functional unit. The "cognitive" functions of the "demons" is restricted to the recognition of their specific substrate to the exclusion . . . of all other compounds'. It is the 'cognitive' here which is particularly problematic when put in quotes.

p. 77. Of course, process theory goes back much further than this: in a recognisably modern form at least as far back as Hegel. A full discussion of this topic is not possible here. On Hegel's place in the process-theology tradition, see Patrick Masterson, *Atheism and Alienation*, Chap. 3 ('Hegel and the Immanent

Absolute'). For a critique of Whitehead and his disciples see E. L. Mascall, *The Openness of Being*, Chap. 10.

p. 85. Kaufman, pp. 105–6, would seem, in passing, to concede this, for in arguing for the view that believing in God simply means 'to order all of life and experience in personalistic, purposive moral terms and to construe the world and man accordingly', he notes in a mere parenthesis that 'a doctrine of God (or of the gods in a polytheistic system) means that meaningful or purposive forms of order are not confined to human history and society'—as though it makes no intrinsic difference whether the 'referent' is singular or plural.

p. 90. As Von Rad points out, the oldest version of the story pictures the construction of the tower as a threat to the gods. The 'come let us' of Yahweh 'presupposes the idea at one time of a pantheon, a council of the gods', which in Israel became the heavenly King's council. But the Yahwist has removed the *explicit* motive of anger, or jealousy on Yahweh's part, so that Yahweh's response is seen as both punishment and prevention. He is angry, but also in the long-run caring in that he will not have to punish men later by more severe measures as they degenerate further. On the sources, Von Rad shows how the Yahwist 'marks that decisive line of demarcation in the history of culture which we can observe for so many peoples: he was the collector of the countless old traditions which until then had circulated freely among the people. With him began the writing down of those poetic or cultic narratives which previously had circulated orally and without context among the people. . . What a profound change occurred when materials from the most dissimilar cult-centres became unified and even substantially altered by a superimposed plan, when, in a word, they became available as literature . . . in this process those traditions were gradually liberated from their imprisonment in the hereditary sphere of the sacred cult . . . becoming literature meant in a sense an end for this material, which until then had a long history behind it.' G. Von Rad, pp. 145 and 16–18.

p. 92. An illustration of the illicit use of metaphorical language for divinity is given in Wisdom, 13. Those who think of God in terms of the natural elements are wrong, but relatively blameless, for at least they are looking in the right direction, namely among the things God has himself made. But those who think of God in terms of human artifacts are 'wretched' for they suppose mere images to have divine power. This distinction is only intelligible as part of a tradition which sanctions one sort of metaphor but outlaws another.

p. 95. The ultimate source of Aquinas's inadequacy on metaphor is no doubt Aristotle, and the classical tradition of Rhetoric, although the principal influence on medieval rhetorical theory did little to change the basic classical view of metaphor as merely compressed simile, an ornament of discourse rather than a cognitive use of language. (On this see Hawkes, pp. 16ff and Stanford, pp. 28–30.) Certainly Aquinas under-estimates the value of metaphor in theology, and gives poetry the lowest place of all the kinds of 'doctrine' or modes of instruction (*Summa Theologiae* I, Q. 1, Art. 9). Metaphor is systematically treated only in the first question of the *Summa Theologiae*: thereafter it is mentioned only in passing. Aquinas even goes so far as to suggest that the things in Scripture which are treated metaphorically in one place are always dealt with more plainly elsewhere (*Summa Theologiae* I, Q. 1, Art. 9 ad 2), thus giving evidence of his view that metaphor is no more than a device which can be translated without cognitive loss into other, non-figurative terms. Indeed, the whole issue of metaphor is raised in the context of the loaded question whether poetry is a sufficiently elevated form of discourse to be appropriate in speaking of God: and although Aquinas's answer is in the affirmative, he seems to be somewhat grudging even here. On the other hand, when he is not dealing with metaphor specifically, he elaborates a theory of the meaningfulness of *things* which is eminently capable of generating a rich and cognitive view of metaphor.

p. 97. Aquinas's remarks on the Tetragrammaton are worth noting in this connection. He admits that the Tetragrammaton (i.e. the name Yahweh written in Hebrew, which has four consonants) is perhaps used as the name of an individual, as distinct from the word God (Deus) which is not the name of an individual (*pace* Kaufman—see above, pp. 84ff) but a term for the divine nature. But unfortunately he does not pursue the significance for theology of the fact that the name Yahweh is used in this way. (*Summa Theologiae*, 1, Q. 13, Art. 9).

p. 105. Dante, in his *Letter to Con Grande della Scala*, prefacing the *Paradiso*, elaborates the four levels of meaning that are to be read into the whole *Commedia*. See P. Toynbee (ed.), *the Letters of Dante*, pp. 162–211, and also the Introduction to Vol. 3 of *The Divine Comedy* by Dorothy L. Sayers and Barbara Reynolds, p. 39 and pp. 44–45. I am not suggesting that the literal level of fact is irrelevant to a Christian understanding of Scripture.

p. 106. Of course, it is still a question whether it is the authorial mode which constitutes the novelty of Jesus or whether it is Jesus who constitutes the novelty of the authorial mode, as has been pointed out to me by Fr. Cornelius Ernst OP. In other words, if Christianity rules out tragedy, as many people have thought, may we also say that it created the novel? As Fr. Ernst puts it to me in a letter: 'Wouldn't the efforts to say just what Jesus means for man and God inevitably make "eye-witnesses" important? Is this not the implication of Acts 1: 21–2?'

Part Two: Critical

Introductory

In this second part I try to show the relevance of what has already been said in a theoretical way, to the work of certain writers of modern fiction. My choice of authors has been governed by a number of factors: their intrinsic importance, their influence upon fiction generally, the variety of approaches which they represent. But in each case I have also chosen to concentrate attention upon some particular aspect of their work which exemplifies my general theme in a distinctive way. Thus I have chosen to contrast Lawrence's and Joyce's responses to what may be called the domestication of the metaphysical dimension; that is of the vertical dimension in fiction which relates man to some superior reality. In Lawrence's case this dimension had already been domesticated, not only by the forms of secularised and 'privatised' Protestantism by which he felt himself to be surrounded, but also in the fiction with which he was most familiar. Hence his work may be understood as a persistent and life-long attempt to reclaim by means of a systematic use of metaphorical language a lost metaphysical dimension, to make contact once more thereby with 'unseen presences' and even to re-create in imagination—and indeed in historical fact—the social forms necessary for such a reclamation. Joyce's experience was somewhat different. His problem was that of living in a milieu in which the 'unseen presences' had become all too familiar, the vertical dimension domesticated in quite another sense; not abolished or forgotten, but made part of a routine that had ceased to be creative or relevant. Joyce therefore tried to transpose the given forms of religious awareness into a new key: the key of art. The sacramental system which was the embodiment in Catholicism of the metaphysical dimension had ceased to nourish: so Joyce said, let us then replace it, using such parts of its framework as seem appropriate or useful, by a new kind of sacramentalism: that of an artistic vocation which would satisfy the deepest aspirations of the individual and of an art which would itself be a celebration of the spiritual meanings to be found in material things, the 'solid bodies' of this world. But both Lawrence and Joyce are hampered in their efforts by their own inescapable immersion in the very culture they try to transcend. Lawrence cannot finally rid his religious visions of the posivistic presuppositions inherited from his social past and from the voices of his 'accursed human education'[1]: Joyce's work suffers from an equivalent dissociation between celebrating the world of 'solid bodies' for its own sake and celebrating it for its capacity to embody immaterial and timeless values.

In the case of Waugh and Beckett, I have chosen to concentrate on a different area, or perhaps it might be better to say, a different expression of the same theme. As I have said, one of the most important ways in which the 'vertical' dimension expresses itself in fiction is by means of the structural relation that holds between the teller and his tale. The changing nature of this relation is a clue to the changing nature of a society's way of viewing itself in relation to whatever 'gods' or unseen presences it acknowledges. In the cases of Waugh and Beckett we have two particularly clear and eloquent instances of a relationship between teller and tale that is on the point of total disintegration. The perilous and uncertain relationship that we see between Waugh, as narrator, and the world he contemplates is one of the most striking testimonies we have to a common feeling of social and spiritual chaos within a world of extreme modernity. Here the narrator is an omniscient God who has deliberately and irresponsibly abandoned his creation to its own fatal devices. The disintegration of the narrator, and the subsequent collapse of fiction into monologue, which is a persistent trend in the work of Beckett, is an equally expressive testimony to a somewhat similar, but even more desperate sense of loss.

Finally, I have used the contrasting work of Robbe-Grillet and Norman Mailer to illustrate two radically different, but equally intelligible and relevant, sorts of solution to the problems posed by the fiction of the recent past. That of Robbe-Grillet consists, essentially, in rejecting the implicit diagnosis underlying that fiction. The problem is not how to resurrect a lost dimension, but how to bury it. The job of the novelist is not to reclaim a forgotten truth, but to do without an illusion; not to bolster up a false ideology but to abolish it. One way of accomplishing this work of demolition is to abandon the

[1] D. H. Lawrence, 'Snake' originally published in *Birds, Beasts and Flowers*.

metaphorical means by which it is perpetuated. Mailer's solution seems to be just the opposite: even if the ideology is false and the metaphysic obsolete, the kinds of attitude expressed by it and the metaphorical language needed to express it are still necessary to our own psychological health. Perhaps, therefore, if we persist—and indeed rejoice—in adopting those attitudes and employing all the resources of that language, we shall, by a kind of lucky accident, hit upon what we need to put in the place of the worn-out mental and spiritual furniture that, for the moment, we are stuck with.

5

Lawrence and the Unseen Presences

A great deal of narrative art in the modern period is concerned with redefining the relation between the horizontal and the vertical dimensions of narrative. The greatest masters of realistic fiction in the nineteenth century had, for a precious moment, transcended the older division of literature into tragedy (in which the primary emphasis was upon the 'vertical' relationship of men to the gods) and comedy (in which the primary emphasis was upon the 'horizontal' relation of men to each other). But modern experience has shattered the foundations of that temporary synthesis. The technological urbanised 'corporation-land' of today is intrinsically hostile to the all-inclusive novel which bridges the gap between town and country, between culture and nature, novelty and tradition. On the other hand it is also hostile to the conceptions upon which tragedy and comedy in their classical meanings depended.

I suppose it is not surprising, therefore, to find that many of the greatest writers of the modern period have looked for a way back beyond both tragedy and comedy. Thus when Lawrence diagnosed the modern age as tragic precisely because it refused to take itself tragically,[1] he was able to do so only because he had tried consistently, from the time of his exile from Europe, to go back to a social world where men could live in an integrated relationship to the material environment and the 'unseen presences' that were to be found there. From that position the tragedy of the modern world seemed plain to see—as did its refusal to take itself tragically. The fundamental reason for this refusal lay in the progressive reduction of metaphysical conceptions of man's relationship to the material world to merely illustrative ones. Similarly, Joyce's backward glance throughout

---

[1] *Lady Chatterley's Lover*, opening sentence. Except where otherwise noted, page numbers in Lawrence's works refer to the Penguin editions. See Bibliography for further details.

Ulysses to the Homeric antecedents, though not especially helpful in understanding the novel, is highly significant in registering a search for an 'epic' unity[2] which would include every modulation of experience in a 'sane and joyful spirit'* which, as with Homer, refused to be compartmentalised.

For Lawrence, the fundamental reason why the modern world failed to take the measure of its own tragic predicament was that it had replaced the metaphysical conception of man's place in Nature, characteristic of the religious societies of the past, by merely illustrative images of Nature. Nature was no longer an order of real causes and effects: it had become, for the scientist, nothing but a series of inexplicable associations of phenomena and, for the poet, nothing but a series of free-wheeling metaphors. In order to restore the validity of these metaphors it was necessary, therefore, to take seriously once more (to use Mailer's phrase) the necessary 'measures'.

In Lawrence's own work, the question of man's place in Nature and of the 'unseen presences' to be found there, became explicit in his *Study of Thomas Hardy*. One of the things that rightly or wrongly troubles Lawrence about Hardy's tragedies is that they contain 'nothing more metaphysical than the division of man against himself'.[3] This lack of metaphysical perspective enables Hardy to separate the foreground theme of man divided against himself from the merely background theme of the 'deep black source' of tragedy—namely some offence against 'the greater morality of life itself'. Whereas in the great tragedies of the past, for example of Sophocles or Shakespeare, the tragedy arises because the hero transgresses against, and is actively punished by, this greater morality of life itself, in modern tragedies it is only the social code which is transgressed and the offence against 'life itself' is kept to the background, in the 'scenery' (p. 177). Although the typical Hardy hero is a profoundly social being, the community is a prison to him. The imperative he feels towards self-fulfilment forces him to break out of the social bonds that nurtured him. But always such a course leads to self-destruction and tragedy. Meanwhile, because life itself, or Nature, is not directly involved in the tragedy, but at the

[2] On Joyce's theory about the relation of 'lyrical', 'epical' and 'dramatic' forms of art (perhaps one should say, Stephen Daedalus's theory) see *A Portrait of the Artist as a Young Man* (henceforth, *A Portrait*), Chap. 5.

[3] *Study of Thomas Hardy*, in A. Beal (ed.), *D. H. Lawrence: Selected Literary Criticism*, p. 168.

same time supplies the 'deep black source' from which the tragic lives are drawn, it is possible for Hardy to regard his characters as merely accidental victims of an ongoing reality far greater than themselves. 'What matters if some are dead or drowned, and others preaching or married? ... The Heath persists. Its body is strong and fecund, it will bear many more crops beside this.' (p. 172)

The attitude to tragic waste here attributed to Hardy is developed further in Birkin's moment of cosmic optimism as he is confronted by Gerald's death in *Women in Love*. In the presence of that death, Birkin reflects on how

> the eternal creative mystery could dispose of man, and replace him with a finer created being. Just as the horse has taken the place of the mastodon. It was very consoling to Birkin to think this. If humanity ran into a cul de sac, and expended itself, the timeless creative mystery would bring forth some other, finer, more wonderful, some new, more lovely race, to carry on the embodiment of creation. (p. 538)

But we must note that this optimism about the 'creative mystery' and its limitless possibilities, does not console Birkin for very long. He is soon overborne by an opposite feeling, of the tragic finality and irreparability of Gerald's death.

> But now he was dead, like clay, like bluish, corruptible ice. Birkin looked at the pale fingers, the inert mass. He remembered a dead stallion he had seen: a dead mass of maleness, repugnant. He remembered also the beautiful face of one whom he had loved, and who had died still having the faith to yield to the mystery. That dead face was beautiful, no one could call it cold, mute, material. No one could remember it without gaining faith in the mystery, without the soul's warming with new deep life trust.
>
> And Gerald! The denier! He left the heart cold, frozen, hardly able to beat. Gerald's father had looked wistful, to break the heart: but not this last terrible look of cold, mute Matter.

A few moments later Ursula comes to console Birkin.

> 'But need you despair over Gerald?' she said.
> 'Yes' he answered. (pp. 540–1)

Now at the end of *Women in Love*, even if nature does not supply a fatal avalanche to order, as in Ibsen, the logic of Lawrence's tragedy is nevertheless clear. If, like Gerald, you offend against your own 'real, potent life', the deep black source of your own being, than that source will in the end bring you to destruction, if not by active punishment then by the immanent logic of the offence itself. The snow and ice of the Alps is much more than mere 'background': nature is not reducible to scenery there. What begins in the novel as a mere figure of speech— Gerald's tendency to 'snow-abstract annihilation' (pp. 286–7)[4]— turns at the end into literal, physical reality. The imagery of snow and ice is unmistakably metaphysical in its implications for the tragedy. As Gerald approaches the summit of the snow ridge he comes across a half buried alpine crucifix:

> He sheered away. Somebody was going to murder him. He had a great dread of being murdered. But it was a dread that stood outside him like his own ghost.
>
> Yet, why be afraid? It was bound to happen. To be murdered! He looked round in terror at the snow, the rocking, pale, shadowy slopes of the upper world. He was bound to be murdered, he could see it. This was the moment when the death was uplifted, and there was no escape.
>
> Lord Jesus, was it then bound to be—Lord Jesus! He could feel the blow descending, he knew he was murdered . . . (p. 533)

Immediately afterwards, Gerald falls forward in death, unmistakably murdered by the 'greater morality' of which the pattern is the crucifix and of which the executioner is the snow and ice. He is murdered as a punishment for that whole movement towards 'snow-abstract annihilation' which has been his life, and which has come to its consummation in the attempt to kill Gudrun, the one whom he loved.

Nature then, in *Women in Love* is very far from being just 'a wood you retreat to, as a solace from human experience'.[5] Lawrence is trying to restore a concept of Nature as 'the vast incomprehensible pattern of some primal morality greater than ever the human mind

---

[4] Birkin is here recalling the African statuette seen earlier in the novel: 'The white races, having the Arctic north behind them, the vast abstraction of ice and snow, would fulfil a mystery of ice-destructive knowledge, snow-abstract annihilation . . . Birkin thought of Gerald. He was one of those strange white wonderful demons from the north, fulfilled in the destructive frost-mystery.'

[5] Raymond Williams, *Modern Tragedy*, p. 136.

can grasp',[6] and out of the defiance of which the greatest tragic deaths inevitably come. Of course he does not succeed. It was not a task that could be expected of one man, writing for the most part against the grain of his own age and generation. The long slow process of narrowing and secularising Nature, and of eliminating the metaphorical language needed to describe it, had much further to go yet: through Kafka and Hemingway, through Camus and Sartre, to Beckett and Robbe-Grillet and John Cage and computer poetry and the ruptured monosyllables of the astronauts—to where? We do not know.

However, even if we do not know how far the process has to go we can at least consider how far Lawrence himself took the theme in his later works. Of these, perhaps the most explicit is *St Mawr*. In this *nouvelle* Lawrence makes his most conscious and systematic attempt yet to reclaim the metaphysical dimension of tragedy, and the metaphors he needs to express it. But the work also shows clearly the difficulties in his way and the reasons for his ultimate failure: why, in the end, he had no other advice to give but 'retreat to the desert, and fight' (p. 79).*

In the first half of the story, the theme of a living and meaningful Nature is embodied in the image of St Mawr himself, a living stallion to balance Birkin's dead one. St Mawr, though certainly a 'mass of living maleness', is far from repugnant to Lou Witt, even though it is true that at the beginning of the story the horse seems to be—to use Graham Hough's terms—only a somewhat 'obvious and unmodulated symbol of primitive energy'.[7] This is certainly how St Mawr strikes Lou: 'She was startled to find the vivid heat of his life come through to her, through the lacquer of red-gold gloss. So slippery with vivid, hot life.' (p. 21) But soon St Mawr begins to work his power over her, compelling her to see *herself* as threatened:

> Almost like a god looking at her terribly out of the everlasting dark, she had felt the eyes of that horse; great, glowing, fearsome eyes, arched with a question, and containing a white blade of heat like a threat. What was his non-human question, and his uncanny threat? She didn't know. He was some splendid demon, and she must worship him. (p. 22)

[6] *Study*, p. 176.
[7] Hough, *The Dark Sun*, p. 213. The horse symbol had been in evidence in *The Rainbow*, in *Women in Love*, and in such stories as *The Horse Dealer's Daughter*. But in *St Mawr* the horse itself takes the centre of the stage.

Finally, the answer to Lou's question comes out: St Mawr is a symbol of the 'greater morality of life itself', that 'deep black source' from which tragedy springs. In this story, the 'heath' of Hardy and *King Lear* is now transposed into a Mexican desert. St Mawr, the life-breathing horse is but the means by which Lou first understands the need to retreat to this desert to fight: he seems to her

> like some living background, into which she wanted to retreat. When he reared his head and neighed from his deep chest, like deep wind-bells resounding, she seemed to hear the echoes of another darker, more spacious, more dangerous, more splendid world than ours, that was beyond her. And there she wanted to go. (p. 34)

The Mexican landscape in which Lou finds herself at the end is her 'heath', then, 'the real stuff of tragedy . . . the primitive, primal earth where the instinctive life heaves up'.[8] Naturally, there is now no more need for the horse. His symbolic role has been played out: he has brought her to this place, this 'living background' of which he was but the foreshadowing. He is therefore put out to grass and forgotten. For what was at first merely symbolic has now—as in *Women in Love*—become reality. Yet the place, like the horse, is ambiguous in its meaning for Lou. Just as the horse was part domestic animal and part dragon* so the landscape is part holy retreat and part terrifying waste land. In its presence Lou feels 'like one of the Virgins of the holy fire in the old temples', for, like the priestess in *The Man Who Died*, she is weary of incompetent men, and turns 'to the unseen gods, the unseen spirits, the hidden fire . . . receiving thence her pacification and her fulfilment'[9] (p. 146). She finds the hidden fire 'alive and burning in the sky, over the desert in the mountains' and she feels a kind of holiness in its presence: 'For me this place is sacred' (p. 147). But as she confronts this sacred world, she finds herself struggling against an active, eternal and invincible enemy, even at times a kind of plague:

> At one time no water. At another a poison-weed. Then a sickness. Always, some mysterious malevolence fighting, fighting against the will of man. A strange invisible influence coming out of the livid

[8] *Study*, p. 172.

[9] There are other premonitions of *The Man Who Died* in *St Mawr*. For example, in Lou's letter to her mother in which she writes 'I feel all bruises, like one who has been assassinated. I do so understand why Jesus said: *Noli me tangere*' (*St Mawr*, p. 124).

rock-fastness in the bowels of those uncreated Rocky Mountains, preying upon the will of man, and slowly wearing down his resistance, his onward-pushing spirit. (p. 151)

The beauty of the place is awe-inspiring, but it is an inhuman landscape. Yet man has to live in it. Whenever he tries to make the 'nearness' (in which he has to live) as perfect as the distance in which the beauty of the landscape manifests itself, the 'grey rat-like spirit of the inner mountains' attacks, or 'rivers of fluid fire' suddenly fall from the sky. At such times the conclusion seems plain: there is no merciful God in the heavens (p. 156). But Lou is not allowed to draw that conclusion: and it is at this point that we see Lawrence refusing to take his story to the tragic limits. There is always, for Lawrence, a way out of tragedy into the world of what Frank Kermode has called the 'archetypes'. That is to say, the inexorable drive of time and history towards the tragedy of the irreparable moment, the moment of Birkin's necessary despair, is replaced by the 'myth of the eternal return',[10] a seeing of things in a pattern within which the individual tragedy is only incidental, just 'one year's accidental crop' to be followed always by the next year's flowering. This was Birkin's immediate answer to the tragedy of Gerald: and it is Lawrence's answer to the tragedy of Lou. Instead of making Lou discover in her retreat both life and death, the pacifying unseen spirits *and* the absence of any merciful God, he gives that conclusion to her predecessor in the ranch; the New England women who had fought the enemy to the utmost and had then been driven to accept defeat. The significance of the story of the New England woman's efforts to bring life out of the desert is that it shows the struggle to be unending, forcing her to retreat from the terrible tragic despair she finds within herself. Whenever there is a storm she sees the 'fretful elements' as signs of the malignancy of the universe. But after any storm the voice within her would say 'What nonsense about Jesus and a God of Love, in a place like this! This is more awful and more splendid. I like it better' (p. 156). So what was at first an authentic expression of the nihilism which is always embedded in tragedy—the nihilism that prompts men to defy the universe or be destroyed by it—is immediately taken back,

---

[10] The phrase is Mircea Eliade's, from his book of that title. Kermode refers to this work in connection with Lawrence in *Shakespeare, Spenser and Donne*, pp. 20–3.

and replaced by a kind of religious aestheticism, a thrill of enjoyment in the presence of the Holy. The reaction is understandable, as a response to 'what the chapel folks believe in' (p. 112), i.e. to Jesus and a God of Love humanised and made 'humble and domesticated like dogs' (p. 57). But it is a sign of defeat all the same, a refusal to take the full implications of the tragic facts. And the logic of the story surely must be that Lou will go the same way as her predecessor, though Lawrence conveniently ends the tale before having to make up his mind about this.

There is a good deal in *St Mawr* which comes out of the 'shabbiest aspect of Lawrence's mind': the side which tended to refuse tragedy by escaping into the cyclic mysteries and the underworld of occultism and exotic scholarship. But there is also a great deal which represents 'his true vein [in which] he celebrates life and quickness'.[11] The description of the Mexican landscape may at times recall *The Waste Land* (itself not far from a similar kind of shabbiness),[12] but it is also full of precisely etched observations that give it concreteness and a location in place and time. The question whether, in *St Mawr*, the shabby side or the true vein prevails seems to me to be very open: Lawrence does not choose to reveal the answer. His answer, if he had chosen to give one, would surely lie in the fate of Lou: would she give up, as the New England woman did, and go back to the life of the comfortable, hospitable valley (where, no doubt, Lawrence's 'pillars of society' would still be living, just as Ibsen's were at the end of *When We Dead Wake*)? Or would she carry on to the bitter end, carrying the logic of the landscape's metaphysical meanings, its housing of unseen presences, to the only possible conclusion? Perhaps we can gain some idea of the answer by looking at two other short stories of Lawrence's later career: *The Woman Who Rode Away* and *The Man Who Died*.

In tragedy of the Shakespearean or the Sophoclean kind there is always a solution, at least to this extent: people are destroyed, but life still goes on. Of course this sense of an ongoing life stretching beyond the immediate confines of the book is one of Lawrence's greatest strengths: it makes him, in Barbara Hardy's sense of the term, one of fiction's great realists. It is a sense of life itself, as a continuing force

[11] Kermode, *Shakespeare, Spenser and Donne*, p. 25.
[12] The similarity between *St Mawr* and *The Waste Land*, in terms of theme, was remarked by F. R. Leavis, in his *D. H. Lawrence: Novelist*, Chap. 6.

greater than anything that a single book can contain, which is transferred in Lawrence's art from the real world to the world of the novel: and it is transferred without being totally 'transubstantiated'. The substance of ordinary experience remains, even after the artistic transference, as an unmistakable and tangible residue in the fiction. One element in this sense of life must, of course, be a recognition of the tragedy of unnecessary death: of Birkin's 'necessary' despair. But as I have said, tragedy—as Lawrence himself insists—takes various forms. Yet one of its characteristic features is the fact that even when individuals are destroyed, life still goes on. Sometimes there may be hints of a redemptive renewal coming mysteriously from these deaths; sometimes it may simply be that the power of life to reassert itself, of wounds to heal and be forgotten, is recalled at the end; but in either case we are shown the effects of the destructive elements upon those who survive and thus are somehow, as survivors, brought into the action and made to learn from it. But without the destruction there can be no such 'solution'—unless it be, as in *The Tempest* or *The Winter's Tale*, that the deaths themselves are not absolute. Now *St Mawr* perhaps suffers from the absence of just such a resolution, because it lacks the deaths. But in *The Woman Who Rode Away* Lawrence seems to be feeling towards such a resolution through the death of another kind of Lou. Here we have the story of another essentially virginal figure, at thirty-three 'still the girl from Berkeley' whose marriage has made no difference to her conscious development (p. 46). The world around her, transformed by her husband's mining enterprises into a totally humanised landscape, is altogether dead to her and she to it. She has to get out of it or die. So she rides away to the mountains in search of the Chilchui Indians, who live in another Las Chivas, a retreat in the mountains where it is possible to be free, amid the unseen presences and the hidden fires. But whereas the Mexican landscape in *St Mawr* remains empty and ambiguous, its presences unseen and its fires unpredictable, the valley of the Chilchui is peopled by a society that has come to terms with those presences and actually lives by the light of the fires. Their society is the model of a human life lived in relation to the 'living background', the 'greater morality of life itself': they are the opposites of the society of Lou and Rico, 'pillars of society' in Europe or America. The logic of confronting such a world and such a society is here pursued to its bitter conclusion: the Western woman who is brought into contact with it is inevitably destroyed by its terrible, unlivable power. The gay pleasantry of the New England woman's 'I like it here' (echoed near the end of *St Mawr*, surely, by Lou herself: 'Don't you think it's lovely?' (p. 161) is revealed, in this later story, to be the superficiality that it really is. It is not the place for aesthetic poses: life is lived here in earnest, to the bitter end.

Yet even in this story, Lawrence refuses to explore the situation in fully tragic terms. By simply cutting the action short at the very moment when the knife is to fall and the woman's heart is torn from her body in ritual sacrifice, all 'solution' is prevented. This is not because of any shrinking from the thought that 'there is no merciful God in the heavens': on the contrary the story takes that despair at its starting point. The woman was a nihilist from the beginning, in the lifeless isolation of the house which cowered under the shadow of the refuse-plant. And long before she arrives at the Chilchui settlement she has heard something in the night which she interprets as a 'great crash at the centre of herself', which was either the crash of her own death, or else it was 'the crash at the centre of the earth' (p. 52). No, what prevents this re-working of Lou Witt's predicament from fully taking up the implications left unaccepted in *St Mawr* is the fact that the final destruction which 'the very forces of life itself' wreak upon the woman is not lived through. There is no sign of life continuing, surviving and healing itself; we are shown nothing of how the death works through the body of the living. This is not sacrifice, it is sheer extinction. Yet the story is clearly supposed to be about sacrificial action: a return on the part of the white civilisation to the sacred sources which Lou sought for, and could not find, in the horse, and did find but could not quite come to grips with, in the ranch. In *The Woman Who Rode Away* a more single-minded and disillusioned Lou understands, quite clearly, that the end of her retreat to the desert is to be her own sacrificial death; the end of her exile from life is to be the knife in her breast. The dance of the villagers makes this plain to her, even before the young Indian guard tells her the myth which explains it all; a sexual myth which implies the renewal of life through a sacrificial death: 'when the man gets the woman, the sun goes into the cave of the moon, and that is how every thing in the world starts' (p. 72). But it is also a cosmic creation myth. White civilisation, having stolen the secret of creativity from the Indians, has debased and distorted it. The cosmic order and the human order alike can be restored only by the sacrifice of white civilisation itself on the altar of the Indian. Only by such means can the Indian, who represents the future as much as the past, 'accomplish the sacrifice and achieve the power' (p. 83). The myth is thus explicitly causal, attributing creativity to the heavenly bodies in language that goes back to the pre-enlightenment mode. Yet the total effect of the story, with its brutally truncated ending, is to deny the meaning of this kind of language, to shed doubt upon its implications for the renewal of life. In the end Lawrence hesitates to turn mythical hypothesis into metaphysical assertion, to move from the subjunctive to the indicative mood.* It is clear enough why: he cannot put himself beyond the consciousness of the woman herself. He cannot, as narrator, put himself above the white civilisation he himself belongs to. The woman must remain, for him, the 'central intelligence' from whose viewpoint everything is told. Once that intelligence is extinguished, everything goes black: there is no more to be said. The infinite possibilities of human renewal that the myth suggests are cut short: the story freezes into an eternal gesture.

If we want to find what Lawrence makes of a death that is not final, and out of which some kind of human renewal comes, we must look to *The Man Who Died*. In this reworking of the Christian resurrection story, the retreat to the desert to fight, and indeed the sacrificial death which should end it, are both over. Now the harvest is to be reaped from the sowing. The cosmic myth of the renovation of man by the sun, restated in terms of Isis and Osiris, is now made actual in the return to life of the man by the sun's radiance; literally in Part 1, as he lies in the peasant's backyard in the sunshine, but more profoundly still in the sexual encounter of Part 2.[13] Yet despite the imaginative effectiveness of the actual awakening in the tomb and the man's slow reluctance to face the world again after having left it, the result is curiously uncertain. Not only are there times when the pressure of fiction-writing leads Lawrence into stylistic absurdities (e.g. some of the pseudo-hieratic dialogue) and, worse still, catastrophic vulgarities (such as the man's worry, when he makes his assignation with the priestess, about possible mother-in-law troubles): the very basis of the

[13] *Short Novels of D. H. Lawrence*, ii, pp. 42–3: 'Slowly, slowly in the perfect darkness of his inner man, he felt the stir of something coming. A dawn, a new sun. A new sun was coming up in him, in the perfect inner darkness of himself.' The new dawn is both a carnal and a spiritual resurrection: 'He crouched to her, and he felt the blaze of his manhood and his power rise up in his loins, magnificent. "I am risen" '.

story is an evasion. Despite the constant authorial insistence that the man actually died, Lawrence is too aware of the biblical critics and rationalist sceptics who are looking over his shoulder not to hedge his bets. He is too much of a secular man himself not to put into Jesus's own mouth the suggestion that they took him down too soon and that this explains his return to life (pp. 7, 12). Of course, this is quite consistent with Lawrence's thorough-going humanisation of the whole story. Yet, it is unnerving, and I think stultifying, to find him surrendering the 'creative mystery' to rationalistic pressures so completely, without acknowledging the fact. For what is the deliberately religious ambience and atmosphere of the story for, if it is to be so casually and yet so completely frustrated by worries about finding a naturalistic explanation?

I think that it was because he himself recognised this difficulty that Lawrence added a second part to his original story of *The Escaped Cock*. Presumably he felt that a reworking of the gospel accounts within a humanistic framework, such as we find in Part 1 of *The Man Who Died*, was inadequate. So he added the second part, which suggests that the real awakening of the man comes not from the conquest of death but from the discovery of sex. But the two parts are not really compatible. The renewal to be found in Part 1 consists in the man's discovery that his preaching of a moral code of self-giving and renunciation was a mistake, an illegitimate interference in other people's affairs. But the renewal in Part 2 is purely sexual, and secret. (True, the woman is the priestess of a public cult: but this seems to make very little difference to the story.) Thus, although there is a connection between the two awakenings, the emphasis changes, and the upshot is a feeling that the first resurrection was not enough. This can only mean that the resurrection itself was not a conquest of death through a sacrificial renewal but merely a temporal process of self-realisation. In fact, the death hardly matters in this perspective. This is why the ambiguity about whether the man really died at all can be pushed into the background. Yet in that case the story ceases to have the kind of significance that its Christian ambience suggests and which underpins Lawrence's attempt to go beyond the limits set in previous works.

Of course the giving of the self in sex and the giving of the self in a sacrificial death are closely linked in the Christian tradition. Yet this is something that Lawrence does not want to emphasise, for he regrets the giving of self as a kind of greed, a mode of exercising power over others, from which the man who has died is now free. He is 'risen' into 'proud singleness', a state symbolised by the cock itself. But the cock is proudly single because it has a life that goes beyond the little personal life of the individual, trapped in his own little body. The contrast between the cock, tethered though it is, and its owner make this plain:

> The man who had died was sad, because the peasant stood there in the little, personal body, and his eyes were cunning and sparkling with the hope of greater rewards in money later on. True, the peasant had taken him in free, and had risked getting no reward. But the hope was cunning in him . . .

On the other hand the cock, in which 'the flame of life burned up to a sharp point . . . so that it eyed askance and haughtily the man who had died' suggests at once the 'greater life of the body, beyond the little, narrow personal life' (p. 17). A little earlier, it had been the sight of the cock which led the man to recognise

> a vast resoluteness everywhere flinging itself up in stormy or subtle wave-crests, foam-tips emerging out of the blue invisible, a black and orange cock or the green flame-tongues out of the extremes of the fig tree. They came forth, these things and creatures of spring, glowing with desire and with assertion . . . (p. 10)

The connection here with *St Mawr* seems clear enough. The cock, like the horse/dragon, symbolises the 'greater morality of life itself' which the truly tragic heroes offend directly, and die at the touch of. In taking over the Christian resurrection story, it might have been expected that Lawrence would discover at last how to present, in his own way, just such a hero and just such a tragic, redemptive death.* And this is indeed the implication of his view of what the resurrection is about; the man's sin has been to offer a merely human code where he should have been preaching the 'greater morality of life itself'. His renewal after death comes from the recognition of his mistake. Yet precisely by refusing to admit consistently that the consequence of this mistake was truly a death, Lawrence in effect refuses to see his own story in those terms. By surrendering to the critics and evading the problem of his hero's death, Lawrence has turned down the chance of writing a tragedy based upon a conflict to the death between man and the powers of Nature, and has reduced his story to the level of a merely human tragedy, of a human code defied. In this he defines himself, to use his own term, as characteristically 'modern': perhaps even, by the ultimate failure to supply the lost metaphysical or vertical dimension in fiction, as a 'one-dimensional' man.

6

Joyce and the Sense of an Ending

In the work of D. H. Lawrence we have seen the attempt to reclaim, for the twentieth century, the meaningfulness of a long lost sense of 'unseen presences' within the world's 'fretful elements'. Lawrence, we feel, takes the loss of this sense, which is also the loss of the vertical 'warp' of fiction's fabric, the tragic dimension in life, as a major, indeed calamitous enfeebling of the whole culture and ultimately of the society which produced it. One could put the same point another way by saying that Lawrence was a man in whom the horizontal (metaphorical) dimension, always powerfully present, was forever in search of its vertical (metonymic) counterpart. That the language of metaphor, which bridged the 'heart-breaking schism'[1] between men and things, was both necessary and valid, Lawrence never doubted. But in the modern world of life-denying commercialism, secularism and tragic despair where was to be found the 'tender care that nothing be lost' that underlies—if Whitehead is right—the creative mystery of sustaining causality in Nature? The end of *Women in Love* is surely Lawrence's most eloquent testimony to the problematic nature of that question. Faced with Gerald's death in the snow, as we have seen, Birkin's first response is to celebrate the optimistic faith that it is best to leave things to 'the vast, creative, non-human mystery' which has 'brought forth both man and the universe'. This mystery has its own great ends of which man's petty circumscribed life is not the measure. 'God can do without man,' Birkin affirms in hope: the death of Gerald is not the end of the mystery even though it is the end of Gerald: 'the eternal mystery could dispose of man' but it could still replace him with 'a finer created being'. Yet the tragic finality of Gerald's death, brought home to Birkin by the frozen, brittle corpse, forces from him a different, more absolute and tragic cry, at the very end of the novel:

[1] Robbe-Grillet, *Snapshots*, p. 92.

'But need you despair over Gerald?' she said.

'Yes,' he answered...

'Aren't I enough for you?' she asked.

'No,' he said.

However the argument between Birkin and Ursula which concludes the novel is clearly unfinished. She insists, as if to clinch everything, that he cannot have two kinds of love: love for her *and* love for Gerald. But Birkin will not accept this. 'I don't believe that', he answers, and from that point, the whole argument clearly starts again. And not only the argument between Birkin and Ursula, but also the argument of the novel itself; the argument about whether the death of Gerald is simply a tragic waste or whether, beyond it, lies a new and finer kind of being still to come; the argument about whether or not there *is* an eternal creative causal mystery underpinning the Lawrentian metaphors.[2]*

The absence of a strong sense of ending is both a strength and a weakness in *Women in Love*. It is a strength in that it shows Lawrence's realism (in Barbara Hardy's sense of the term) in refusing to pretend that life can be packaged and polished into a tidy aesthetic whole. Lawrence's best fiction springs unmistakably out of 'a primary act of mind transferred to art from life',[3] and the rambling loose-endedness of reality itself remains as a substantial residue even when the transference has been made. The temptation to provide *Women in Love* with an aesthetically harmonious ending, a perfect final cadence, must have been strong. The Ibsen-like scenario invites such an ending: it seems so 'final'—to use a favourite Lawrentian word. Yet the temptation was resisted, and we recognise the moral force of Lawrence's resistance. The 'greater morality of life itself' has the last word. Yet there is also a kind of weakness about this open-endedness. A strong ending, however unlike life, does at least help to remind us that what we have been through is only a story. The fictiveness of the story's middle is retrospectively enforced by the obvious fictiveness of the end: and, as Frank Kermode has reminded us, it is the consciousness of a story's fictiveness that is the best protection against its degeneration into myth.[4] Of course there is a paradox here: it is precisely the strong sense of an end that is already present in the beginning that most obviously characterises myth, and turns a 'marked respect for

---

[2] *Women in Love*, pp. 539–41.   [3] *Novel*, 2 (Fall 1968), p. 5.

[4] *The Sense of an Ending*, p. 39.

things as they are' into a tidy pattern of coherence that is dangerously delusive.[5] So in the end—if I may put it so—what matters is the *kind* of strength or weakness of the ending; whether it comes 'naturally' or is forced upon us. There is a place for the open ends of Lawrence's novels, which take us back from the fiction into the stream of life: but there is also a place for the strong, harmonious ending which emphasises the fact that we have been engaging only in make believe; that— as an harmonious ending would obviously suggest—we have been involved with the kind of art that aspires to the condition of music; or which, like the Grecian urn, sculptures every movement of thought and feeling, every ray of illumination and every slightest contact with things, into an eternal gesture, creating a perfectly finished work of art; perhaps an object itself bereft of feeling, but redolent with the distant memory of it.

To speak in this way of the virtues of the closed, harmonious ending takes us immediately into a different world from that which Lawrence inhabited or wished to inhabit: indeed into the world of his greatest contemporary James Joyce.

We might put the difference between them in the following way. Whereas Lawrence tried to restore a concept of sacral, if unseen presences within nature, a vertical dimension to a world that had become, in his view, denatured and one-dimensional, Joyce tried to secularise an over-religious, indeed neurotically religious culture, in order to allow the ordinary things of 'the now, the here' to come into their own, to be given their rights. The man with the grocer's assistant's mind, as Joyce once described himself, wanted to show that the world was a supermarket of things, feelings, impressions and actions all of which had their place in a general scheme. But the scheme was not that of a sacral 'nature'. Joyce, with good reason, was suspicious of too much talk of 'nature'. The old analogical ties with which a textbook scholasticism neatly parcelled the world into a 'great chain of being' were not only obsolete: they were rotten with the 'true scholastic stink' which only Dublin life could give off.[6] Thus, to give coherence and order to his patterns, Joyce substituted for Nature, artifice: the artifice of an Homeric or Renaissance synthesis, drawn from a bookish mythology. Within the splendid supermarket of things that he parades

[5] Ibid., p. 17.

[6] The phrase is Lynch's, *A Portrait*, Chap. 5. All page numbers in *A Portrait* and in *The Dead* refer to the Penguin edition of *The Essential James Joyce*.

before us, Joyce is able to be indiscriminately bountiful towards the things of the here and now, without imposing upon them the cold touch of an authorial personality. Joyce is the greatest of novelistic levellers for this reason; the most democratic of major novelists—far more so than Tolstoy, for all the latter's peasant aspirations.[7] But a price had to be paid for the achievement. That price is a certain pedantry and coldness, even perhaps a touch of what Lawrence diagnosed in discussing Thomas Mann as the Flaubertian disease: the tendency to stand aloof from life—a tendency which lies at the root of any craving for perfect form in art.*

In order to make the contrast with Lawrence more explicit, it may be illuminating to consider the ending of Joyce's first great master-piece, *The Dead*. Like *Women in Love* this last story of the *Dubliners* sequence ends in a kind of snow-abstract annihilation, but of a very different sort. Gabriel and Gretta Conroy are attending his aunt's Christmas party, with a large number of other friends and relatives. Gabriel, as a college man and as favourite nephew, is asked to make the speech of welcome and propose the toasts. Before he can do so, a Miss Ivors proposes to him a summer trip, with his wife, to Connacht. When he refuses, she runs away from the party. After the speeches, and just as the party is breaking up, he overhears one of the guests singing a song—a song which his wife seems strangely taken with. When the pair of them arrive back at their hotel, but before the excited Gabriel has any chance to make love to Gretta, she tells him why she loved that song: it reminded her of her former lover in the West of Ireland, the sickly Michael Furey who died for love of her. *He* used to sing the same song. Gabriel is at first appalled to discover that he does not after all occupy the first place in his wife's heart; that she is still haunted by the aching memory of the boy who, visiting her in the rain, died soon afterwards for love of her. In the hotel bedroom, Gretta falls asleep; but Gabriel lies awake, thinking:

> Generous tears filled Gabriel's eyes. He had never felt that himself towards any woman, but he knew that such a feeling must be love. The tears gathered more thickly in his eyes and in the partial darkness he imagined he saw the form of a young woman standing under a dripping tree. Other forms were near. His soul had ap-proached that region where dwell the vast hosts of the dead. He was

[7] Ellmann, *James Joyce*, pp. 2ff., for a comparison between Tolstoy and Joyce.

conscious of, but could not apprehend, their wayward and flickering existence. His own identity was fading out into a grey impalpable world: the solid world itself, which these dead had one time reared and lived in, was dissolving and dwindling.

But this cosmic 'dissolution' is not merely subjective; it has an 'ob-objective correlative' in the snowstorm that is blotting out Ireland, in a kind of 'snow-abstract annihilation':

A few light taps upon the pane made him turn to the window. It had begun to snow again. He watched sleepily the flakes, silver and dark, falling obliquely against the lamplight. The time had come for him to set out on his journey westwards. Yes, the newspapers were right: snow was general all over Ireland. It was falling on every part of the dark central plain, on the treeless hills, falling softly upon the Bog of Allen and, further westwards, falling softly into the dark mutinous Shannon waves. It was falling, too, on every part of the lonely churchyard on the hill where Michael Furey lay buried. It lay thickly drifted on the crooked crosses and headstones, on the spears of the little gate, on the barren thorns. His soul swooned slowly as he heard the snow falling faintly through the universe and faintly falling, like the descent of their last end, upon all the living and the dead. (p. 514)

Now the problem about this ending, it seems to me, is that it fails fully to reconcile the contradictory impulses that went into the making of *The Dead*: the impulse towards what Joyce called 'epiphany' and the impulse towards the telling of a story, the revealing of a secret. Epiphany one might say implies the evocation of a specific world, and as such it emphasises the vertical dimension of narrative. But the unfolding of a secret is, equally clearly a matter primarily of horizontal 'plot'. So Joyce's uncertainty in *The Dead* is an uncertainty about the right relation of the two dimensions.

The first part of the story is clearly on the side of epiphany. Joyce is here concerned to render with scrupulous and revealing precision an aspect of Dublin life that he felt he had hitherto neglected: namely Irish hospitality. Most of the other stories in *Dubliners* were epiphanies of the dreariness of Dublin, its spiritual paralysis. *The Dead* would make amends.[8] So the first impression we get from the opening pages

---

[8] Ellmann, p. 254.

is one of the extraordinary authenticity of Joyce's memories. The description of the dinner table, for example, is Dickensian in its relish, but in its objectivity, its lack of humanising metaphor, it verges on the *chosisme* of Robbe-Grillet:

> A fat brown goose lay at one end of the table and at the other end, on a bed of creased paper strewn with sprigs of parsley, lay a great ham, stripped of its outer skin and peppered over with crust crumbs, a neat paper frill round its shin, and beside this was a round of spiced beef. Between these rival ends ran parallel lines of side-dishes: two little minsters of jelly, red and yellow; a shallow dish full of blocks of blancmange and red jam, a large green leaf-shaped dish with a stalk-shaped handle, on which lay bunches of purple raisins and peeled almonds, a companion dish on which lay a solid rectangle of Smyrna figs, a dish of custard topped with grated nut-meg, a small bowl full of chocolates and sweets wrapped in gold and silver papers and a glass vase in which stood some tall celery stalks. (p. 493)

There is a loving delight too in the eccentricities and idiosyncrasies of character, the sheer variety and spice of Dublin life. The sense of place, the evocation of the old days when Italian opera-companies came to Dublin and the tenor Parkinson was at his peak, the memories of the old-fashioned pictures on the Morkans' drawing-room walls— all of these impress upon us that the principal object of the story is to make us *see*, in Conrad's sense;[9] to make us feel that we are at the table with the guests.

But now Joyce introduces what might be called in musical terms a 'second subject' which gives further solidity to his evocation of Dublin hospitality by casting a certain shadow across it. Gabriel's own in-security and aloofness acts as a counterpoint to the gaiety of the party. This insecurity comes out first in his patronising banter with Lily, the servant-girl, over her 'young man'.

> 'I suppose we'll be going to your wedding one of these fine days with your young man, eh?'
> The girl glanced back at him over her shoulder and said with great bitterness:

[9] *Nigger of the Narcissus*, Preface.

'The men that is now is only all palaver and what they can get out
of you'.
Gabriel coloured, as if he felt he had made a mistake and, without
looking at her, kicked off his goloshes and flicked actively with his
muffler at his patent-leather shoes. (p. 479)

From that moment onwards we are continually reminded of Gabriel's
insecurity; for example by Gretta's sarcasm over the wearing of
goloshes, by Gabriel's unease in company compared to the jollity of
the 'screwed' but well-liked Freddy Malins, by the 'superior' taste in
music which inhibits him from enjoying Mary Jane's piano piece, by
the curtness of his reply to the Gaelic Leaguer, by Miss Ivors' irritating
questions about his disloyalty to Ireland. Gabriel's insecurity persists
despite the fact that he is the favourite nephew of the hostesses and
their principal guest. Joyce shows us Gabriel continually trying to
retreat into a private, protective fantasy-world where he can remain in
control of things: a world in which a quotation from Browning would
not go over the heads of his hearers, where a sentence of his own from
one of his articles in the *Daily Express* would be duly appreciated,
where Aunt Julia would be able to understand his reference to her as
one of the 'Three Graces of the Dublin musical world', and above all
where he would be able to keep his own wife to himself in a kind of
private portrait-gallery of his own creating, and contemplate her as a
work of his own art:

He asked himself what is a woman standing on the stairs in the
shadow, listening to distant music, a symbol of. If he were a painter
he would paint her in that attitude. Her blue felt hat would show off
the bronze of her hair against the darkness and the dark panels of
her skirt would show off the light ones. *Distant Music* he would call
the picture if he were a painter. (pp. 503–4)

Thus far, *The Dead* could easily be fitted into the general framework
of the rest of *Dubliners*, as another naturalistic evocation of an aspect
of Dublin life, an 'epiphany' of its hospitality and its 'ingenuous
insularity'.[10] But Joyce has another end in view, a personal theme to
explore: the theme of the dead lover from the past who still haunts the
present. Now, whatever may have been Joyce's private motives for
treating this theme, its function in the story is to *explain*, by way of

[10] Ellmann, p. 254.

a sudden revelation, the secret cause of Gabriel's insecurity, especially his awkwardness with Gretta herself. Their relationship has been shown, from the very beginning, as uncomfortable. Gabriel's very first words about Gretta are cutting: a would-be stroke of joviality that misfires. As they arrive he makes a remark at Gretta's expense to the little servant girl. Confided to his own relations, perhaps, the sarcasm might be tolerable: to a servant, it is merely bad taste:

> 'O, Mr Conroy,' said Lily to Gabriel when she opened the door for him, 'Miss Kate and Miss Julia thought you were never coming. . .
> 'I'll engage they did', said Gabriel, 'but they forget that my wife here takes three mortal hours to dress herself.' (p. 478)

As the story proceeds, more hints are dropped that all is not well between Gabriel and his wife: Gabriel fussily insists on Gretta wearing goloshes and she resents this; they differ over the invitation from Miss Ivors to go to Connacht; and finally a mysterious rift opens up between them as a result of the singing of the song. But none of this would by itself *entail* the final episode of the story, in which the secret source of their unhappiness is revealed. Yet as the narrative moves away from the genial warmth of the house to the streets where the guests depart, and finally to the hotel bedroom where Gretta confesses her past to Gabriel, we begin to feel that a different kind of story is emerging; a a story in which explanation takes over from naturalistic description as the driving force of the narrative. We are now seeing things exclusively through Gabriel's eyes. His personal problem has come to the surface, obliterating the residual omniscience of the former narrative mode. The scene in the hotel bedroom, in which Gretta comes out with her love for Michael Furey, is of course a masterpiece of tact and delicacy of feeling in its own way. Indeed it reveals a humanity and compassion which Joyce seldom rose to in any of his later works. The pathos of Gretta's memories and the artless simplicity of her speaking are immediately striking: so too is the pathos felt for Gabriel's side of the case. He has to suffer the humiliation of knowing not only that he has always taken second place in Gretta's heart to a dead rival, but also—and this is a masterly touch—that the rival was simply a consumptive lad from the local gasworks. But fortunately, Gabriel is capable (as, I think, Stephen Daedalus would not have been) of rising to the challenge of this humiliation. Although he sees himself as 'a ludicrous figure, acting as a pennybody for his aunts, a nervous, well-meaning sentimentalist, orating to vulgarians and idealising his own clownish lusts', and even as the victim of 'some impalpable and vindictive being [who] was coming against him, gathering forces against him in its vague world' (pp. 511–12) Gabriel succeeds in fighting off this intruder by an 'effort of reason'. He continues to comfort Gretta despite his own inner shame, and in this he reveals his own maturity (p. 512). For this he is duly rewarded in the end by a final peace of mind, a consoling loss of all feeling:

> Gabriel, leaning on his elbow, looked for a few moments un-resentfully on her tangled hair and half-open mouth, listening to her deep-drawn breath. So she had had that romance in her life: a man had died for her sake. It hardly pained him now to think how poor a part he, her husband, had played in her life. (p. 513)

Nevertheless there is a difficulty about the ending of *The Dead*. For whereas the story as we might have predicted it from the early scenes would have remained open to the Dublin life beyond itself, simply by being a disinterested epiphany of Dublin hospitality and insularity, the theme of an explanatory secret seems to draw it into a different, less expansive narrative dimension. A story which is simply an epiphany has the kind of openness which comes from seeing the rest of life as surrounding it on all sides. The 'greater morality of life itself' is implicitly present in the chosen instance, precisely because the latter is only an instance. But a story which seeks to *explain* a situation by a device of plot can be open only in a different way; by showing the ongoing consequences, in the greater life outside the confines of the plot itself, of the revelation given within it. As we have seen it is the virtue of *Women in Love*, and indeed of most of Lawrence's best fiction, that we are allowed to see past the fictional events that determine the ending of the narrative itself—for example, the death of Gerald Crich—and to glimpse their flowing back into the stream of life. Lawrence's openness to 'the greater morality of life itself' is largely a result of his allowing us to do just this. But in *The Dead* Joyce does not permit the reader to see anything of the life that continues after the discovery of Gretta's long-treasured secret. We do not behold their ongoing life together, are not even given a hint of it. On the contrary, the story ends with a 'coda' which dreamily describes Gabriel's vision of a welcome death, and his hopeless yearning for a passion which he knows he can now never attain. The symbolic snowstorm that finally envelops everything and everybody in a shroud of elegiac sadness certainly provides a perfect cadence, in a minor key, to round the story off. But in so doing it blocks off any further reference to ongoing life: and it does so not because this blocking-off is part of the logic of the plot, but because Joyce prefers to substitute for that logic an aesthetic literary device. The snow is a symbol only: it has no roots in the process of causality.

In saying this, I should not like to be thought of as trying to detract from the true value of the ending of *The Dead*. That value remains, a monument to Joyce's mastery not only of symbolism and the music of a poetic prose, but of the 'epiphany' as a form of narrative art. But what I am suggesting is that the ending marks a return to the mode of the beginning—the mode of epiphany—which has been interrupted, for a good many pages, by another kind of narrative: the narrative centering upon the unravelling of a secret, on the dimension of plot. And despite the triumph of art which the ending undoubtedly represents, it cannot quite hide the seam between the two, for there is a certain incompatibility between them. In order fully to be part of the 'plot' the snow would have to have some causative influence upon, as well as symbolic function in, the events. In *Women in Love* (as too in Ibsen's avalanches) it does have this function, as we have seen: for however important the snow in that novel may be as a symbol of Gerald's coldness and abstractness, it is also the cause of his physical death. Similarly the logic of the plot in *The Dead* seems to require that the snow should have some effect on what actually happens in the story. But to give it such a function would involve making it the agent of some purposeful 'unseen presence' as Lawrence did when he talked of Gerald's death as a 'murder' by the snow. The recognition of such unseen presences, however, is just what Joyce wants to avoid: perhaps, as I have suggested, because he has had a surfeit of religious persuasions concerning them. So he tries to turn his 'plot' back towards the mode of 'epiphany' and uses the snow to do just that—with masterly eloquence.

In *A Portrait of the Artist* we find a somewhat different answer to the same basic problem. Joyce saw very clearly the need for a corrective to the tendency of his catholic milieu to see everything in supernatural terms. Stephen's struggle to free himself from that milieu is partly a search for the significance of things *as* things rather than as manifestations of 'unseen presences'. Yet in order to justify that struggle he had to interpret it in the terms he knew. The artist seeking to prove the validity of the classical temper, with its emphasis on the value of 'solid bodies' nevertheless found it impossible not to express his ideal in terms of a priestly vocation to art, 'transmuting the daily bread of experience into the radiant body of everliving life' (p. 226). Such an ideal comes perilously close to what Stephen thought of as the very opposite of his own view: namely the 'romantic temper' which can find no earthly place for its ideals and 'chooses therefore to behold them under insensible figures'.[11] In the very act of trying to concentrate the artistic vocation on the here and now of the horizontal dimension, Stephen finds himself forced to suggest just the opposite: that this vocation is one in which the vertical dimension, the sacramental dimension in which outward forms hide invisible religious meanings, is very prominent. Thus Joyce substitutes art for religion, but of course the substitution will not do. The tension between the two dimensions of narrative, between secular art and religious sacrament, remains in *A Portrait of the Artist* because it was built into it from the beginning, in the very terms in which Stephen's struggle against his milieu was first formulated. Not until a later stage of development, in which Stephen's own formulation could be subjected to a more radical criticism, by being 'placed' critically within a larger and more all-embracing perspective, could the tension be resolved.

The unresolved tension in *A Portrait of the Artist* comes out in the fact that even at the moments when Stephen is condemning 'kinetic' art in favour of 'stasis', *A Portrait of the Artist* remains itself obstinately kinetic.[12] According to Stephen, the kinetic feelings—*desire*, which 'urges us to possess, or to go to something', and *loathing*, which 'urges us to abandon, to go from something'—are improper feelings to arouse in art. 'The arts which excite them, pornographical or didactic, are therefore improper arts. The aesthetic emotion is therefore static. The mind is arrested and raised above desire and loathing' (*Portrait*, p. 213). This is all very well: but in Stephen's case, at the stage of personal development which he has reached in *A Portrait of the Artist*, this aesthetic is combined with an abstract and loftily rigid distinction between the physical and the intellectual, between facts and values, between morality and aesthetics, which it is the business of Joyce, the narrative voice mediating Stephen to us, to show as crippling. Stephen's actual practice, both as artist and as an ordinary human being, betrays

---

[11] *Stephen Hero*, Chap. XIX, p. 78.
[12] Goldberg, *The Classical Temper*, pp. 64–5.

the inadequacy of his way of thinking, and shows it as arising from evasions of responsibility. It is part of Stephen's problem that he has yet to sort out the difference between seeing his artistic vocation as something impelling him from within, like a natural instinct, part of the life-force that is within him, and seeing it as a conscious moral choice between alternative possibilities that are open to him.[13] Although he grows, in moral understanding, during the course of *A Portrait of the Artist*, he does not mature enough to recognise that his choice of vocation must be a free, and therefore moral responsibility: and this immaturity is reflected in the immaturity of the poetry he writes. It is true of course that Joyce does convey to the reader through narrative style, tone and nuance that he is fully aware of Stephen's immaturity: and to this extent, *A Portrait of the Artist* is a 'dramatic' rather than a 'lyrical', a classically rather than a romatically-tempered book. But it is noticeable, all the same, that by comparison both with the earlier *Stephen Hero* and the later *Ulysses*, *A Portrait of the Artist* embodies a residual Shelleyan platonism, a romanticism—to quote Stephen Hero himself—that 'sees no fit abode here for its ideals and chooses therefore to behold them under insensible figures'—or, to use A. E.'s (Russell's) term from *Ulysses* (p. 236) 'formless spiritual essences'.[14]

In *Ulysses* we find the fully-worked-out corrective to the over-religious milieu, which Stephen sought but could not find by himself in *A Portrait of the Artist*. Here Joyce succeeds in keeping to the ground-level of the horizontal dimension in narrative. There is no uncriticised wandering into romanticism, no indulgent embracing of ideals seen under insensible figures. Stephen himself has now put behind him Russell's platonism, replacing it by his own maxim, 'hold to the now, the here, through which all future plunges to the past' (p. 238). But holding to the here and now also entails holding to the fact that the romantic and the kinetic cannot be finally expunged from a work of art in favour of the purely classical temper without eliminating all its human meaning, and reducing its moral values to mere aestheticism. Goldberg gives an illustration of this which sums up the matter neatly.[15] The trashy art of *The Sweets of Sin* is unable to arouse in Bloom any feelings other than kinetic ones:

[13] Goldberg, p. 55.
[14] See also *Stephen Hero*, p. 78.
[15] p. 49.

Warmth showered gently over him, cowing his flesh. Flesh yielded amid crumpled clothes. Whites of eyes swooning up. His nostrils arched themselves for prey. Melting breast ointments (*for him! For Raoul!*). Armpits' oniony sweat. Fishgluey slime (*her heaving embonpoint!*) Feel! Press! Crushed! Sulphur dung of lions! (p. 303)

But later on, the fine rendering by Simon Daedalus of a splendid song from *Martha* gives Bloom an experience which can only be the authentically Joycean 'luminous silent stasis of aesthetic pleasure':

It soared, a bird, it held its flight, a swift pure cry, soar silver orb it leaped serene, speeding, sustained, to come, don't spin it out too long long breath he breath long life, soaring high, high resplendent, aflame, crowned, high in the effulgence symbolistic, high, of the ethereal bosom, high, of the high vast irradiation everywhere all soaring all around about the all, the endlessnessnessness . . . (p. 355)*

But the deepest stasis lies in the fact that Joyce, as narrative voice, has here reconciled Bloom's properly aesthetic response (a response very different from Gabriel Conroy's under similar circumstances) and the multifarious surrounding elements of 'the now, the here' which alone make such a response possible and which contribute—whether Bloom recognises it or not—to the total effect of the song upon him. Bloom's response is an advance on the response (if not on the theory) of Stephen in *A Portrait of the Artist*. But Joyce's narrative 'placing' of Bloom's response in a larger context still, shows a further stage in his own maturing. In this comprehensive, dramatic poise of the narrative voice in *Ulysses*—a voice that is so far 'refined out of existence' as to give the *impression* of a sheer, unmediated transparency to the given facts[16]—the tragedy of Gabriel's and Stephen's inability to go beyond themselves is transcended and becomes the subject of a comprehensive comic vision.

A comprehensive poise of this kind is possible only through a classical detachment, a refusal to take sides. The artist in this mode can take no special responsibility for transactions that may take place between his art and life outside. The Stephen of *Ulysses* recognises, as the Stephen of *A Portrait of the Artist* did not, that within the work, life's kinetic, moral, political and other responses have their place,

---

[16] *A Portrait*, p. 221. The 'impression' is produced, of course, by the most elaborate use of rhetorical artifice.

beside the evocation of aesthetic 'stasis', helping to make up for what the other lacks. But even if art of this comprehensive, reconciling kind, which is inevitably comic rather than tragic, is necessarily self-enclosed and autotelic, it ought to come, we feel, from a visible struggle to achieve objectivity in life. Stephen in *A Portrait of the Artist* demanded a detached critical objectivity in art, but he did not demand the same critical objectivity about himself. This was his weakness: and the greatness of *A Portrait of the Artist* lies in the way Joyce makes us see it as a weakness, through the exercise of his narrative voice and its nuances, without alienating us from Stephen or his predicament. For it is the predicament of all representatively 'modern' heroes; the search for an identity in a world which does not seem to provide the conditions for achieving one. And in *Ulysses* Joyce goes further, seeing even the strength of *A Portrait of the Artist* as only relative; the strength of a still immature work. *Ulysses* places and judges *A Portrait of the Artist*.

Yet the maturity of *Ulysses*, and of the Joycean voice that hovers about it, is still only a poise: something perilous and uncertain, like the slippery footholds of the lookout in *Moby Dick* who sees beneath his feet the 'Descartian vortices' that threaten to swallow up anyone who loses his balance (*Moby Dick*, Chap. 35). The vortices that threaten Joyce, however, are either older or more modern than Descartes's. They make themselves felt for example in the primitive superstitions that Joyce entertained about thunderstorms. As a man brought up in Catholic Ireland he could not skake off the *feeling*, even if he had shaken off the thought, that the 'fretful elements' manifested some 'unseen presence' of a terrifying and possibly lethal kind.[17] But they also made themselves felt in more modern insecurities, for example in the *Circe* episode, which is an expression of the nightmarish Freudian horrors to be found in the unconscious, once the tenuous hold of reason on human affairs is allowed to loosen. But the perilousness of Joyce's comic poise comes out even more clearly when we consider the kind of freedom and maturity that *Ulysses* itself embodies: a freedom and maturity which, despite the splendour of the achievement, are surely still too limited and too easily won. In *Stephen Hero* there is an awkward contradiction between the claims of the 'classical temper', with its emphasis on art as rooted in the now and the here, the earthy

[17] Ellmann, p. 25 and note.

and the morally problematic, and Stephen's romantic, Shelley-like claims for art as a way of mediating 'between the world of [the artist's] experience and the world of his dreams'.[18] In *A Portrait of the Artist* this problem is not so much solved as systematically evaded, by Stephen's insistence (on theoretical, allegedly Thomist grounds) that the kinetic—which the world of the here and now, the earthy and the morally problematic inevitably is—has no place in art at all. By forcing this distinction on art, the contradiction is temporarily avoided. But in the anti-platonic *Ulysses* it had to be faced and (if possible) resolved. And it *is* solved: by rejecting both the Thomist metaphysic of *A Portrait of the Artist* and the Shelleyan platonising of *Stephen Hero*. But a price has to be paid in this solution. As Goldberg puts it, Stephen in *Ulysses* does not see

> how much more acute [his] difficulties are made by his adopting casual ideas from St Thomas without adopting the metaphysics which gave them their coherence... The problem of the poetic meaning and truth of art is capable of *some* kind of solution if we hold a philosophy that gives 'intelligibility' a metaphysical range: if we believe, that is, that the intelligibility of art ought to reveal and reflect the intelligibility inherent in all things in the world... The fact is, however, that neither Joyce nor Stephen accepts any such metaphysical philosophy.[19]

As for the Shelleyan platonism of *Stephen Hero*, which would see the role of art as mediating between this world and some other transcendent world, this is given very short shrift by the Stephen of *Ulysses*, in his silent retorts to Russell's platonic and symbolistic musings (pp. 236–8). In its place, the opposing classically-tempered notion of art as rooted in the now and the here is given full expression in Stephen's new theory about Shakespeare's earthy private life and the relation of this to *Hamlet*. But is this emphasis on the need for a comprehensive objectivity about oneself, coupled with a steadfast rejection of any systematic metaphysic to back it up, a sufficient basis for the kind of freedom to which Joyce in *Ulysses* seems to aspire? Ultimately what emerges as the ground of this newly-won freedom and maturity is only an unblinkered individualistic liberalism of a very familiar kind. No doubt this liberalism is unusually 'democratic' for a modernist

---

[18] *Stephen Hero*, p. 77. See also Goldberg, pp. 68–9.
[19] Goldberg, pp. 61–2.

writer[20] and helps to exonerate Joyce from the charges brought by Snow against most of his contemporaries in the literary world. And in any case, Joyce did not claim to have any original *ideas*. He remained a lower-middle-class Irishman with, as he accurately put it, a 'grocer's assistant's mind'.

But an unblinkered liberalism, however admirable in itself, was hardly an adequate response to the 'flood' which, as Lawrence accurately saw in the twenties was about to engulf the world. But of course, Joyce's response was much more than a mere liberalism. In a situation where not only European civilisation, but even the continuance of civilisation itself was in question, the artist could, it seems, take one of two paths. He could fight against the trend of the times by attempting to recreate in his fiction a world that he no longer found about him in reality, hoping thereby to preserve at least the image of civilisation. Or he could register his protest by creating wholly autonomous worlds of words which would stand up for themselves like beacons lighting the dark, revealing the impending tide of evil for what it was by their own scandalous self-sufficiency. If the former was the 'kinetic' way, the latter was the way of 'stasis'. And given the historical fact, or apparent fact, that very few artists have ever been able to change the course of history even a little by their art, who is to say that the way of stasis that Joyce took was not as responsible and as effective as the other?

Joyce's art, then, was his most potent weapon. But the autonomy of the work of art, which *was* his contribution to the battle against the flood, was possible only as long as the artist's own personal ends were kept out of it. The achievement of a self-sufficient style and the extinction of the egocentric narrative personality had to go together. But inevitably this meant an absence of what had hitherto been expected from a novelist: the implicit imposition of some kinds of moral 'standards', if not in the behaviour of the characters then at least in the moral vision implied by them. This Joyce refused, in any direct way, to provide. In his own case, such absence itself becomes a kind of standard, of honesty, artistic integrity, sheer perseverance. But in another kind of artist, with another kind of vision, this absence truly becomes a scandal. With benefit of hindsight it is not difficult to see where Joyce's view of the story-teller's art has led. The montage of

[20] See Gross, *Joyce*, p. 53 and Ellmann, pp. 1-5.

bits of reality that we find, for instance, in the work of William Burroughs, is only one extreme case of a more widespread breakdown. In the process of this breakdown, the distinctive personality of the teller tends, inevitably, to disappear altogether. If he is supervising anything, it is not a connected sequence of events, but a chaos in which causality and sequence have ceased to operate, and in which he has no place. Just as any theory of blind cosmic evolution makes the notion of 'nature' impossible,[21] so the novel of sheer chance, or total subjectivity makes the creative teller's voice inaudible. Of course, in eliminating the teller such fiction renders impossible any protest against the 'flood' through comic stasis and the achievement of a self-sufficient style. But it also rules out another kind of comic response as well: the sort of comedy in which a moral protest against the flood is registered by a calculatedly scandalous refusal of moral discriminations among its effects. Such comedy depends for its life on a sharp distinction between the irresponsibility of the world that is created in the fiction and the latent but easily discernible sense of responsibility manifested, but not stated, by the teller. If the poised static comedy of Joyce is a protest against the flood, so too, in a different way, but in the same general tradition, is the dandyish amoral comedy of Evelyn Waugh.

[21] On this see Monod, pp. 159ff.

7
Waugh and the Narrator as Dandy

In Chapter 1 I drew attention to two different ways in which we can speak of a 'vertical' dimension in the fabric of fiction. The first was the sense of depths and heights, of unseen presences above and below ground level within the fictional world itself: a sense which the one-dimensional novels of one-dimensional men in the contemporary era seem to have lost, partly through that process of levelling which Lawrence thought of as the reduction of 'nature' to mere scenery. Much of the space I have so far given to Lawrence and Joyce has been concerned with examining the problems attaching to the recovery of this lost vertical dimension. However, when we come to the next generation of novelists, and in particular the two I have singled out for special mention—Evelyn Waugh and Samuel Beckett—it is the other kind of thread which seems to have been disturbed or broken: I mean the vertical relation between the world of the fiction and the supervisory narrative direction given to it by the author himself, through the narrative voice implicit in the story. How this relation changes and develops or even disintegrates in response to the pressures of the age we live in, is the main focus of interest of these two sections, and what I have to say about the role of metaphorical language in these authors flows from that primary concern. In the further cases of Robbe-Grillet and Mailer, my emphasis is more or less the opposite. There I have concentrated upon the horizontal dimension, as it comes to be embodied in questions about the possibility of a valid metaphorical language in today's world, and the metaphysical commitments that such a language must inevitably entail. If the work of Waugh and Beckett seems to show, each in its own way, that the old coherent relation between teller and tale, and more fundamentally the analogies upon which it rested, no longer hold, in the case of Robbe-Grillet and Mailer the reverse side of this collapse comes into view in the contradictions each seems to be presented with as he either affirms or denies the validity of metaphors which, in any case, if my argument is valid, cannot be sustained once the corresponding vertical axis has itself collapsed.

Evelyn Waugh has often been thought of as a reactionary, a man with a message. True, his private religious commitments suggest a man whose sense of moral purpose is strong, even over-powering. But Waugh's novels, especially those of the thirties are anti-moralistic: or so it seems until we dig very deep indeed into them. What is most striking about them is the scandalous absence of moral discriminations. Virtue and vice, instead of being inverted as in much satire, simply cancel each other out, in a world where chaos seems to have come again. Metaphors are no longer able to bridge the metaphysical chasms. No amount of tender care can prevent everything from being lost.

This being so, I think it is best to think of Waugh as a comedian in the tradition of which the purest representative is Sterne. In this kind of comedy—a comedy born of insecurity, not of security—we find an imaginative habit of mind which is rooted in an old harmony that has been disrupted but not forgotten.[1] In other words, like tragedy, such comedy comes from a disintegration which has not yet become a total loss. Waugh's pugnacious, backward-looking vision, of which his Catholicism is only one expression, is the key to his art because it enables him to maintain contact with a kind of 'harmony' which, to more modern and liberal minds, seems long since dead. When, as in Waugh's novels, contact is lost with those pedestrian realities which are the stuff of ordinary experience, order itself becomes chaos by the logic of its own self-infatuation, the 'unbridling of reason' to use Whitehead's phrase.[2] But the loss of contact with the ordinary universe that we experience in the novels rests upon the feeling that contact is being maintained by the author himself: his own stance of self-assurance about ultimate realities gives us a security behind which to enjoy the comic horrors. For the chaos in Waugh's world is not a romantic loss of control, but a controlled and calculated loss. His comedy is of limitations, implying the need for a sense of due proportion, a balance

[1] See Jefferson, 'Tristram Shandy and its Tradition' in B. Ford (ed.), *From Dryden to Johnson* and his longer article, 'Tristram Shandy and the Tradition of Learned Wit' in *Essays in Criticism*, 1 (1951), pp. 225–48.

[2] Quoted in *From Dryden to Johnson*, pp. 334–5.

between the claims of the mind and of the emotions, over against the unbridled rationality of a scientific age. But the balance it pleads for is only implied—by the scandal of its absence in the fictional world. What we have in the comedy itself is a delight in destructiveness which comes through as a self-sufficiency, a concern for style, in which morality, piety, even compassion seem to be mere irrelevancies. The rules of decent behaviour, feeling and thought, which apply in the real world, are here suspended, producing an art which is self-enclosed within its own comic frame of reference. The autotelic character of this sort of comedy, which gives it a non-kinetic stasis of the kind Stephen Hero pleaded for, is foreign to (say) comedy of situation (Fielding) or comedy of manners (Jane Austen). It takes no responsibility for the outside world. It is morally neutral, even irresponsible to the point of outrage, telling with poker-face and dead pan accents of moral and emotional enormities which, in another context would be tasteless and grotesque. The maiming of Tristram Shandy by a falling window is only one notorious example of this kind.[3] In the same tradition W. S. Gilbert can revel in the punishments meted out by the Mikado to pathetically vain ladies:

> The lady who dies a chemical yellow
> Or stains her grey hair puce
>> Or pinches her figger
>> Is blacked like a nigger
> With permanent walnut juice etc![4]

and P. G. Wodehouse can note, in his non-committal way, how one of his characters 'groaned slightly and winced, like Prometheus watching his vulture dropping in for lunch';[5] while Waugh himself can flatly inform us, of the missionaries and ambassadors who came to Ishmaelia,

> None returned. They were eaten, every one of them; some raw, others stewed and seasoned—according to local usage and the calendar (for the better sort of Ishmaelites have been Christian for many centuries, and will not publicly eat human flesh, uncooked, in Lent, without special and costly dispensation from their bishop).[6]

[3] *Tristram Shandy*, vol. v, chap. 17.

[4] The Mikado's Song in Act II.

[5] Quoted by Usborne, *Wodehouse at Work*, p. 194.

[6] *Scoop*, Bk. 2, Chap. 1. All page numbers in Waugh's works refer to the Penguin editions.

It has been objected to passages in Waugh such as this that their satire fails because they do not offer any alternative moral position to which appeal might be made.[7] But surely Waugh's own point is correct: such writing is not satire at all. His reason for saying this is that 'Satire is a matter of period. It flourishes in a stable society, and presupposes homogeneous moral standards . . . It has no place in the century of the Common Man where vice no longer pays lip-service to virtue'.[8] Whether Waugh is historically right about satire is unimportant. What matters is that his reasoning is a clue to his own art. Waugh yearns for homogeneous moral standards, but is completely frank in admitting that they no longer exist. Perhaps it is because he faces the prospect of disintegration with such honesty that his fiction does not embody a disgusted reaction against modern life. (In this respect Waugh is quite different from Huxley. Huxley's work is all either in the satiric mode (*Crome Yellow*, *Antic Hay*) or in the didactic (*Eyeless in Gaza*, *Time Must Have a Stop*). Huxley lacks the dandyish ability to be irresponsible, for all the indiscriminate learning which, given another temperament, might have made him a great learned-wit comedian.) It is not disgust with human civilisation that motivates Waugh's comedy, but a sense of its precariousness. When we look closely at his books, especially the early ones, we begin to understand how thin is the ice over which Waugh, the comic narrator, skates so deftly, and with such apparent ease and perfect timing. His artistic poise, or pose, is self-assured, but it is a self-assurance born, as with Oscar Wilde's dandies, of a sense of desperation.[9] The self-assurance is largely self-assurance. For the dandy, like the revolutionary, is alienated from his society. Bourgeois moral sanctions seem to him irrelevant. The proper response to civilisation's disintegration therefore is not action for the sake of a better future, but the achievement of a personal style by which to repudiate the values which have led to the brink of disaster. For the dandy, style is everything: but the style is that of the tight-rope walker, both superior and precarious. Any hint of personal involvement in the goings on that the dandy observes beneath him, in the world of

---

[7] Graham Martin, 'Novelists of Three Decades' in B. Ford (ed.), *The Modern Age*, p. 396.

[8] Quoted by Stopp, *Evelyn Waugh*, pp. 194–5.

[9] On Waugh as dandy, see Bradbury, *Evelyn Waugh*, p. 2. On the dandy in Wilde see I. Gregor, 'Comedy and Oscar Wilde' in *Sewanee Review*, 74 (1966), pp. 501–21.

'Descartian vortices' beneath his feet, would be fatal to his poise. Nothing must trammel his free intelligence; no conventional sense of 'decency', no respect for hurt feelings, no interest in the solid world of the ordinary man in the street. The precariousness of the dandy's style is expressed in the risky, precarious nature of his speech—that is to say, his command of preposterous paradoxes. But he also has a sense of the precariousness of the world he inhabits. The dandy can only be safe in a world of dandies; that is, a world of pure play, an arbitrary world. Only a preposterous plot can match his sense of the preposterousness of life itself. Yet the dandy provides at the same time a standard of truth, insight, intelligence, even of other worldliness, by which others are judged and found wanting. The dandy is more, not less aware than those around him, of the vortices that lurk beneath the feet of those ordinary mortals who fondly imagine they have solid earth to walk upon. His ability to move through 'the incertitude of the void'[10] comes, not from an earthy commonsense like Leopold Bloom's, but from a brilliant and audacious defiance of common sense. The dandy is the embodiment of reason unbridled in a world of seeming dull reasonableness.

Because of his devotion to style, the bourgeois world judges the dandy to be morally, politically and emotionally irresponsible. But the bourgeois world is wrong. The dandy exists to prove it is wrong. His assertion of the value of a personal style is, in fact, a kind of moral responsibility. By the outrageousness of the figure he cuts, he makes himself into a mirror by which an irresponsible age can see itself truly. In a roundabout way, the dandy is moralist after all. His inability to live in the real world shows up the real world for what it is: an intolerable place for real people to have to live in. Only those who are lucky enough to be free of the world's trammels can survive in it unscathed.

Waugh's contribution to the literature of dandyism consists in his development, not of the dandyish character, but of the dandyish narrator. It comes out in the special tone of the early novels, and particularly in the narrator's studied neutrality towards actions and attitudes which, by ordinary decent standards, cry out to be judged. This refusal to judge, coming as it does from a recognition that the only standards available from the bourgeois world, by which to make

[10] *Ulysses*, p. 818.

a judgement, are themselves irrredeemably corrupt, gives the early novels their scandalous and outrageous, but also their valuably invigorating character.

Waugh's first novel, *Decline and Fall*, shows the dandyish narrator in his scandalous garb from the very outset. The very first incident it records is the stoning to death of a fox with champagne-bottles by a gang of drunken aristocratic Oxford thugs: and the first moral response the narrator asks us to make is to go along with his own gleeful enjoyment of the fun; 'What an evening that had been!' (p. 9) he exclaims, with characteristic relish. The novel proceeds from there, taking its prevailing tone from that first salvo of dandyish irresponsibility. The novel depicts two kinds of apparently irresistible barbarism, between which the flitting shadow of civilisation, in the shape of Paul Pennyfeather, is tossed and tormented mercilessly. There is the primitive barbarism of Grimes (a grim comment on Lawrence's 'greater morality of life itself') who is the life-force incarnate,[11] and is 'singularly in harmony with the primitive promptings of humanity' (p. 35), and there is the over-sophisticated, mechanised barbarism of Otto Silenus, whose philosophy is Swiftian in its loathing of humanity.* From the narrator's point of view, there is nothing to choose between these two forms of barbarism; their atrociousness is equally repugnant. But the thing that strikes us most as we read the novel is Waugh's exuberance in describing the antics of both sides. He personally feels, strongly, the attractions of moral anarchy, the life of 'fun'. When Silenus describes life as a huge mechanical wheel, which you can leap on to if you wish, in order to enjoy the thrills it offers, or which you can simply watch amusedly as a detached observer (pp. 208–9), we feel that he is expressing a philosophy that fascinates Waugh himself. The narrator's scandalous neutrality between the crimes and atrocities of the competing barbarisms, even in their most outrageous manifestations, seems to be simultaneously a gleeful contemplation of gratuitous brutality and a defence against its implications for himself. Beneath the glee there is the horror. This combination of glee and horror is typical of Waugh's early work, and it expresses his feeling that the world is moving in-

---

[11] 'Grimes . . . was of the immortals. He was a life-force. Sentenced to death in Flanders, he popped up in Wales; drowned in Wales, he emerged in South America; engulfed in the dark mystery of Egdon Mire, he would rise again somewhere at some time, shaking from his limbs the musty integuments of the tomb . . .' (p. 199).

exorably away from order and civilisation—the civilisation of Kings Thursday, where visitors might reflect 'how they seemed to have been privileged to step for an hour and a half out of their own century, into the leisurely prosaic life of the English Renaissance' (p. 116), towards the mechanised barbarism of Silenus's new creation, where the perfect buildings will be factories, because they are built to house machines, not men. As the title suggests, Waugh's is a 'world on the wane', a world gripped by the irresistible tide of increasing entropy.*

In the face of an imminent descent into barbarism, the only sane attitude to adopt is that of the dandy: a man who is not interested in trying to communicate a message of salvation or hope (it is already too late for any such messages) but in using language to strike an attitude of defiance, and to find a style that will satisfy himself; a style well-made and lasting, as 'hard, bright and antiquated as a cuirass' (*Ordeal of Gilbert Pinfold*, p. 15). By rejecting all attempts to communicate last-minute calls for action, in favour of creating something that is aesthetically self-sufficient and self-justifying, the dandy defies the process of disintegration itself. For this disintegration is proceeding by a remorseless levelling, the obliteration not only of that hierarchy of values which is civilisation, but also of any variety at all, the very spice of life. Under such conditions, communication itself only contributes to the accelerating of entropic decay. Art for art's sake then takes on an historical, even metaphysical, significance as the last line of defence against irresistible collapse.

The structure of Waugh's fiction mirrors the content. As I have already said, the value of narrative as a mode of explanation depends upon its two-dimensional structure, its embodiment both of a syntagmatic order, or plot, and of a paradigmatic, vertical order which relates the fictional world to the real world, and the teller to the tale. We have seen the consequences, in Lawrence's fiction, of trying to restore to an essentially tragic age a valid vertical dimension through the re-creation of the concept of unseen presences within Nature. And we have seen the opposite, but complementary process in Joyce's attempt to secularise and control an obsolete, but hypertrophied concept of sacral Nature, an over-developed vertical dimension, by enclosing Nature within the confines of art. But Waugh, in a later generation, and perhaps confronted by a more immediate threat of disintegration, is unable to offer achievement on that scale. Yet the structure of his fiction is an eloquent testimony to his understanding of the crisis he confronted. On the vertical plane, the relation of teller to tale in Waugh's early fiction, as we have seen, is largely negative. The teller is conspicuous by his scandalous policy of non-intervention. It is not that he is impersonal, merely 'paring his fingernails'. On the contrary, he is very much alive as a personal presence. But whatever view of the world he, as author, holds is almost entirely unrelated to the real world that, as narrator, he finds himself forced to contemplate. At the end of *Decline and Fall*, when Paul Pennyfeather is back at Oxford studying theology, he attends a lecture in which he hears about the heresies of second-century Christianity.

> There was a bishop in Bythinia, Paul learned, who had denied the Divinity of Christ, the immortality of the soul, the existence of good, the legality of marriage, and the validity of the Sacrament of Extreme Unction. How right they had been to condemn him! (p. 212)

The elegance of this altogether characteristic touch of Waugh's art lies in its timing, at the end of the hero's 'education' in a school of suffering and in the studied ambiguity of that 'learned'; in its combination of pugnacious logical consistency and the appearance of calculated irrelevance. Has Paul learned nothing? we are inclined to ask ourselves. We are lured into wondering whether the remote academic subtleties of second-century theological debate are not more important to Paul, even now, than the crimes of the twentieth century in which he has been personally involved. His academic fiddling while civilisation burns seems to be on a par with the rest of his 'shadowy' nature—his ability to order a dinner in creditable French, and see to luggage at foreign railway stations (p. 122): both are expressions of the shadowiness of his 'civilisation', his incapacity to cope with the reality of modern barbarism. And yet, Waugh makes us feel, a world in which such things as the theology of Extreme Unction are matters of overwhelming importance, is somehow much more civilised, more truly human, than the world we have been witnessing in the novel itself. In this sense Paul is right to see that more is to be gained from studying the past than from involving oneself in the idiocies of the modern world. The irrelevance of the author's implicit private attitudes to the world he has revealed publicly to us is here so artfully placed that it becomes more of a judgement on that world than on the author himself. Waugh's art has made us feel that the author's stance of pugnacious and anachronistic concern with the past is somehow more important than anything the modern world has to offer. Its outrageous irrelevance to the novel's world *is* its relevance, its responsibility to the real world.

The studied irrelevance of the author's opinions to the world he is describing is part of that dandyish sense of superiority that the tight-rope-walking narrator in Waugh's fiction constantly maintains in the early novels. Poised above the chaotic world, he sees below him, perilously spread out, like the *Waste Land* typist's combinations, to catch the last rays of civilisation's sun, the lengthening shadows of European history. This sense of superiority, together with the scanda-lous absence of authorial intervention in the action, helps to emphasise the arbitrary and pointless character of the actions that are going on down below. In place of an unfolding of cause and effect in an intel-ligible sequence, we find in Waugh's fiction only aimless disconnec-tions, arbitrary turns of event, the staccato inconsequential chatter of idle layabouts. Paul's condemnation of the Bishop in Bythinia for his views on marriage becomes relevant, precisely by its startling ir-relevance to modern reality, when we overhear a conversation such as the following from *Vile Bodies*:

> 'Darling, I've been so happy about your telegram. Is it really true?'
> 'No, I'm afraid not.'
> 'The Major *is* bogus?'
> 'Yes.'
> 'You haven't got any money?'
> 'No.'
> 'We aren't going to be married today?'
> 'No.'
> 'I see.'
> 'Well?'
> 'I said, I see.'
> 'Is that all?'
> 'Yes, that's all, Adam.'
> 'I'm sorry.'
> 'I'm sorry too. Goodbye.'
> 'Goodbye.' (p. 183)

However it is not only in the idle conversations that the arbitrary pointlessness of the world is manifested. We find the same purposeless disconnected inconquentialities in the world of things, especially of man-made things. (Natural objects are in rather a different case as we shall see.) Just as he refuses to allow his attitudes or opinions to impinge in any direct way upon the action, objects too, in Waugh's world are left to their own devices. But, as Gulliver found in his voyage to Laputa, things without words attached to them are meaningless. So too in the world of Waugh objects left to their own devices are meaningless. In the past, of course, or in memory a person's treasured things have meant something:

> Morgan le Fay had been his room since he left the night nursery. . .
> He had taken nothing from the room since he had slept there, but
> every year added to its contents, so that it now formed a gallery rep-
> resentative of every phase of his adolescence—the framed picture
> of a dreadnought (a coloured supplement from *Chums*), all its guns
> spouting flame and smoke; a photographic group of his private
> school; a cabinet called 'the Museum' filled with the fruits of a
> dozen desultory hobbies, eggs, butterflies, fossils, coins . . . (*A
> Handful of Dust*, pp. 15–16)

But to the person who is completely modern, and therefore free of all ties of 'language, history, habit or belief' (*Scoop*, p. 75) things are quite simply broken images, with—to use Robbe-Grillet's phrase,— 'no cultural fringes':

> There was only the colour of the paint to choose and some few
> articles of furniture. Mrs Beaver had them ready for her inspection, a
> bed, a carpet, a dressing table and chair—there was not room for
> more. Mrs Beaver tried to sell her a set of needlework pictures for
> the walls, but these she refused, also an electric bed-warmer, a
> miniature weighing machine for the bathroom, a Frigidaire, an
> antique grandfather clock, a backgammon set of looking glass and
> synthetic ivory, a set of prettily bound French eighteenth-century
> poets, a massage apparatus, and a wireless set fitted in a case of
> Regency lacquer, all of which had been grouped in the shop for her
> as a 'suggestion'. (*A Handful of Dust*, p. 56)

Or if they have cultural fringes, these have been so detached from their origins that they are no longer intelligible:

> . . . mats made for prayer were strewn on the divan; the carpet on
> the floor had been made in Bokhara as a wall-covering; while over

the dressing table was draped a shawl made in Yokohama for sale to cruise passengers; an octagonal table from Port Said held a Tibetan Buddha of pale soapstone; six ivory elephants from Bombay stood along the top of the radiator ... (Ibid., p. 114).

As one might expect from a narrator of such scrupulous detachment, there are very few metaphors in Waugh's descriptions of the modern world's artifacts; no verbal bridges are thrown over metaphysical abysses. Yet the abysses themselves are there: traps for the helpless victims to fall into. The absence of metaphors gives us the sense of disjointedness, the absence of any sense of ordered Nature, that is the hall-mark of Waugh's vision of modernity. And it is because modern man has interfered with everything that the world is unintelligible, lacking in depth and resonance; essentially superficial, like the hotel room William Boot finds himself in when he goes to London:

The room was large and faultless. A psychologist, hired from Cambridge, had planned the decorations—magenta and gamboge; colours which—it had been demonstrated by experiments on poultry and mice—conduce to a mood of dignified gaiety. Every day carpets, curtains, and upholstery were inspected for signs of disrepair. A gentle whining note filled the apartment emanating from a plant which was thought to 'condition' the atmosphere. (*Scoop*, pp. 36–7)

But if human interference has made everything unintelligible, this is because man has upset the balance of Nature. That is to say, while the *things* that modern man has made are essentially unintelligible, incapable of being metaphorically humanised, the creatures of the natural world, if left to themselves, have all too obvious a meaning. The animal world, for example, is irremediably metaphorical because, whether man likes it or not, animals mean something to him. If he misuses them, then they fight back at him—as in the case of little John Last, in *A Handful of Dust*, who is kicked to death by a horse. Men and animals are connected, whether they like it or not, by natural bonds of a radical kind. They cannot get away from each other. If man cannot establish a superiority to the animals, then he will find himself reduced below them. For example, the only characters in *A Handful of Dust* who retain any kind of dignity are those who remain superior to the animals, like Mrs Rattery (who redirects the savagery of the murderous horse into a game of animal snap) and the impoverished but conventionally decent relations who take over Tony Last's estate at the end of the novel and tame the animals by putting them in cages (pp. 111–13 and 221). Everyone else is reduced to living in a jungle: either the literal jungle of Mr Todd's Brazilian hideout, or the metaphorical jungle of London 'society'. Thus, the ordinary run of modern people, according to Waugh's vision of things, are patently inferior to animals, and they have to suffer, if not death, then at least indignity at the hands of the animals they cannnot control. If the animals cannot be humanised, men will be animalised: and the metaphorical language of this transformation reveals itself at once when this occurs. In striking contrast to the studied absence of metaphor in the descriptions of modern artifacts, we find a plethora of metaphors in the descriptions of the animals modern men have reduced themselves to:

> The milch-goat looked up from her supper of waste-paper; her perennial optimism quickened within her, and swelled to a great and mature confidence; all day she had shared the exhilaration of the season, her pelt had glowed under the newborn sun; deep in her heart she too had made holiday, had cast off the doubts of winter and exulted among the crimson flowers; all day she had dreamed gloriously; now in the limpid evening she gathered her strength, stood for a moment rigid, quivering from horn to tail; then charged, splendidly, irresistibly, triumphantly; the rope snapped and the welter-weight champion of the Adventist University of Alabama sprawled on his face amid the kitchen garbage. (*Scoop*, p. 153)

In Waugh's early novels, the metaphors, particularly those concerned with the world of living nature, are predominantly ironic, as in the case just quoted. By deliberately humanising Nature, Waugh is equally deliberately showing the modern dehumanisation of man. The things man has made, when simply catalogued and left to speak for themselves, automatically come to symbolise the disconnectedness and meaninglessness of the modern world they belong to: Waugh's unerring eye for the modern sees to that. Nature, on the other hand, is much more than a meaningless heap of broken images (to use Eliot's *Waste Land* phrase). Indeed, in *A Handful of Dust* the animal world is so important as a commentary on the human world that the novel almost becomes a totemic myth: we understand the meaning of what is happening to the human beings by watching the behaviour of the animals. By adopting so deliberately archaic a narrative technique, Waugh seems to be implying something about the regressiveness of the modern world itself, its natural tendency to revert from over-sophistication to sheer primitivism, from fiction to myth.

However, during the second world war, things changed for Evelyn Waugh. Like Guy Crouchback, he now had a cause to fight for. The change is registered most emphatically in *Brideshead Revisited*, written as a reaction to the period of 'soya beans and basic English' (p. 7). In this novel Waugh's critical, invigorating poise of neutrality above the abyss is lost: and the loss of detachment is evident first of all in his language. In particular, this novel shows Waugh using metaphorical language in a wholly new, uncritical and unironic way. The deliberately inflated absurdity of the humanised animal in *Scoop*, now becomes an ersatz poetry, a rhetoric cut off from critical dandyish intelligence, in *Brideshead Revisited*, where the world of Nature, instead of being either subject to or superior to man, simply becomes the receptacle of 'pathetically fallacious' feelings about the past:

> My theme is memory, that winged host that soared about me one grey morning of war-time.
>
> These memories, which are my life—for we possess nothing certainly except the past—were always with me. Like the pigeons of St Mark's, they were everywhere, under my feet, singly, in pairs, in little honey-voiced congregations, nodding, strutting, winking, rolling the tender feathers of their necks, perching sometimes, if I stood still, on my shoulder; until, suddenly, the noon gun boomed and in a moment with a flutter and sweep of wings, the pavement was bare and the whole sky above dark with a tumult of fowl. Thus it was that morning. (p. 215)

In passages such as this, Waugh's disturbingly metaphorical language tends to suggest a humanisation of Nature that is also a capitulation to it. The hard, bright, antiquated refusal to be browbeaten by the modern world has given way to a sense of its tragedy: and what Robbe-Grillet says of tragedy seems peculiarly apt for *Brideshead Revisited*, and its hero: 'Since the harmony between man and things has finally been denounced the humanist saves his empire by immediately setting up a new form of solidarity, the divorce in itself becoming a major road to redemption.' Thus Ryder's tragedy 'becomes an ordeal where victory consists in being vanquished'.[12]

Even more disturbing to the balance of the dandyish narrator's poise than *Brideshead Revisited* was the revealing inner agony described in *The Ordeal of Gilbert Pinfold*, written almost as if the tensions involved in trying to be neutral in a world that cried out for commitment on everyside had grown too burdensome, and the moral pressures had burst the fictional vessel. From that moment on, it seems that the ethical vacuum which it was Waugh's greatest triumph to have anatomised by an art of scandalous non-intervention (an art which unerringly lighted upon the most telling images of a decadent modernity with all the enthusiasm of a dedicated symbolist) had sprung a small, but irreparable leak of personal commitment. The closed universe of the 'bright young things' had been fatally exposed to the winds of common decency. The brilliant evocation of the twentieth century's idiocies through the sharp, selective observation of relevant details:

> ... The first to come were the Hon. Miles Malpractice and David Lennox, the photographer. They emerged with little shrieks from an Edwardian electric brougham and made straight for the nearest looking glass. (*Decline and Fall*, p. 128)

> The younger generation for the most part allowed their cases to be settled out of court and later gave a very delightful party on the proceeds in a captive dirigible ... (*Vile Bodies*, p. 109)

> Later that afternoon, as she lay luxuriously on the osteopath's table, and her vertebrae, under his strong fingers, snapped like patent fasteners, Brenda wondered whether Beaver would be at home that evening ... (*A Handful of Dust*, pp. 41–2)

subsided into a predictable list of Mr Pinfold's grumpy opinions:

> His strongest tastes were negative. He abhorred plastics, Picasso, sunbathing, and jazz—everything in fact that had happened in his own lifetime. (p. 14)

Of course, springing a minor leak did not spell the end of Waugh's fictional voyage: it simply marked a change of course. Nevertheless, even in such a major work of fiction as the *Trilogy* the unlooked-for

---

[12] *Snapshots*, p. 83.

influx of reality into the comic world took its inevitable toll. Superb though it is as an evocation of the farcicality of modern war, the *Trilogy* is not farcical in the old, scandalously neutral and therefore morally invigorating way. The trouble begins at the very outset in *Men at Arms*, with Guy Crouchback's disillusionment, not only with the modern world, but with himself. The war provides him with something to live for, a cause, a way of ending eight years of shame and loneliness by offering up the loyalties which should have sustained him, loyalties above all to God, to country and to family: 'Whatever the outcome there was a place for him in that battle.' (p. 13)

This opening suggests a commitment to seriousness of a kind very familiar to the readers of *Brideshead Revisited*. Guy's social position and antecedents—upper-class Catholic recusant—are very similar to those of the main characters in that book. Nevertheless the *Trilogy* is far less self-indulgent than the earlier war-novel and one of the things that redeems it is the fact that, ironically, Guy finds that at the end of it all his place in the battle has been quite unheroic. As a moral challenge the war was a failure to him. As a source of sustaining loyalties, it was worse. Guy's closest comrades are mostly incompetent fools and proven cowards. The actions in which he takes part all exemplify the incompetence and bungling which Waugh sees as the bread and butter of modern war. So Guy's commitment to seriousness is revealed as misplaced. His pretensions to be a successor of the crusading Christian knights, to whose prayers he entrusts 'our endangered kingdom' as he sets out on his military career, are cut down cruelly to size by the ignominious events which make up 'his' war. To this extent, then, the *Trilogy* is a far more poised and self-critical book than *Brideshead Revisited*. On the other hand, it has little of the audacity and verve of Waugh's earlier dandyism. Instead the *Trilogy* presents us with something new in Waugh's fiction: an eloquent and loving portrait of a wholly good man and a wholly sympathetic character: namely Guy's father. In the earlier books, including *Brideshead Revisited* and *The Ordeal of Gilbert Pinfold*, the Christian gentleman had been subjected to a good deal of fairly savage mockery. Waugh's emotional commitment to the myth of a high aristocratic civilisation embodied in the ancient Catholic families of England was usually held in check by his delight in the myth's absurdity, its inconsistency, its sheer irrelevance, as revealed by the actual characters who had to carry the burden of embodying it. In the *Trilogy*, however, the myth has been shorn of its ancient glory: Waugh no longer seems to believe in it. Instead we are confronted by a character who embodies what is left of it with neither the old glamour nor the old absurdity. Guy's father is an unpretentious, thoroughly likeable human being with more than a touch of genuine sanctity about him. Waugh has succeeded in making a saint who is both credible and sympathetic: but only because the old proud myth has been superseded by a new, and genuine humility.

Not surprisingly, the new humanism of the *Trilogy* has its effects upon the language. The style is no longer 'hard, bright and antiquated' like the language of the earlier novels, and the eye for the telling detail is not so keen. If some of Waugh's outrageous nostalgia for the past has gone, so has our sense of its invigorating non-conformity. It is interesting to compare the country houses of Hetton and Kings Thursday in the earlier novels, with that of the Campbells of Mugg, in *Officers and Gentlemen*. Tony Last's love of Hetton, with its absurdly inefficient and fake medievalism, infinitely preferable though it be to the modernity of the Beavers' London apartments, is revealed for the semi-idiocy that it is by the narrator's self-conscious hyperbole: 'there was not a glazed brick or encaustic tile that was not dear to Tony's heart' (*Handful of Dust*, p. 14). But there is no such consciousness, and hence no such covert irony, about the description of the great hall of Mugg. In the later novel, the description is both fairer and more undistinguished, less inhumane and less interesting, more like a good average novelist's work, less like Waugh's:

> A candelabrum, consisting of concentric and diminishing circles of tarnished brass, hung from the rafters. A dozen or so of the number-less cluster of electric bulbs were alight, disclosing the dim presence of a large circular dinner table. Round the chimney piece, whose armorial decorations were obscured by smoke, the baronial severity of the rest of the furniture was mitigated by a group of chairs clothed in stained and faded chintz. Everywhere else were granite, pitch-pine, tartan and objects of furniture constructed of antlers . . .
> (p. 60)

Throughout the *Trilogy* there is a tendency for this humanisation of the environment—that is, for the reinstatement of Nature—to make the whole fictional world more reassuring, more compliant to the vanity of human wishes, more open to redemption than in the earlier work. In the *Trilogy*, *things* are no longer symbols of an irredeemable meaninglessness: they become vehicles of meaning. (Even the war is more meaningful, more purposeful, despite its farcical aspects, than the pointless antics of the 'bright young things' of the early novels.) Thus, when in *Unconditional Surrender* old Mr Crouchback's personal effects are being collected together to be sold after his death, they appear to Guy not as a heap of broken images, nor as fallacious and pathetic vehicles of nostalgic sentiment, but simply as the living record of a good man's life:

> The brass bedstead, the triangular wash-hand stand, the prie-dieu, the leather sofa, the object known to the trade as a 'club fender' of heavy brass upholstered on the top with turkey carpet, the mahogany desk, the book case full of old favourites, a few chairs, the tobacco jar bearing the arms of New College, bought by Mr Crouchback when he was a freshman, the fine ivory crucifix, the framed photographs . . . these were what Mr Crouchback had chosen from his dressing-room and from the smoking room at Broome to furnish the narrow quarters of his retreat. (p. 71)

We have here a new tone in Waugh's attitude to things. In the early novels, objects existed either to mirror human idiocy in the present or to recall an irredeemably lost past. But here we see how things can be humanised even in the modern world, even in war-time. Old Mr Crouchback's dignity has dignified his things, by the touch of his own humanity. The world of objects is not, then, irredeemable after all. Even human artifacts can be given meaning.

As I have said before, in the early novels we have a narrator whose voice betrays, in roughly equal proportions, as he surveys the doomed world below him, both glee and horror. But in the *Trilogy*, the glee and the horror have both vanished: for they depended upon the narrator's dandyish, lofty poise above the abysses of modernity, his refusal to take part in the world's madness, or to judge its actions in its own corrupt terms. But now, the narrator is involved; he has a cause; he has intervened. The war is neither a spectacle for gleeful exuberance and outrageous neutrality, nor for horrified and appalled detachment. It demands participation. It is certainly a farce and certainly a tragedy; but above it is the epitome of human nature at its best and at its worst. Flesh and blood are of its key essence, civilisation—'our endangered kingdom'—is at stake in it. It has toppled the dandy from his superior position above the fray: there is no alternative left but to join in.

But the dandy has not just been toppled; he has been made super-flous. Old Mr Crouchback makes redundant the dandy's precarious poise over metaphysical abysses. For him the 'Descartian vortices' are no threat: he has, in a real sense, 'overcome the world' of Waugh. But in doing so he has also undermined what was most valuable in it; namely the sense of a universal insecurity that attended the business of being alive, and of the impossibility of attaining any dignity in the Modern Age. These features of Waugh's earlier vision could only be presented in a fiction that stood wholly apart from commonplace reality, in an autonomous world of fantasy and farce, dominated by a dandyish contempt for conventional morality, order and reason. In creating old Mr Crouchback (not to mention other elements in the *Trilogy* which I have no space to discuss here) Waugh sacrifices the autonomy of the dandy for a moral universe that has direct relevance to the real world. The comic decline and fall of the Christian gentleman, in the shape of Paul Pennyfeather, has here been 'tragified' by the appearance of a character who bridges the gulf between life and art and thus turns fantasy into something like fact, with all the heartbreak that such a transformation entails. The *Trilogy* is a comedy that is profoundly shot through with tragic meanings. From the stasis of the earlier, brittle and brilliant works of perfect poise and almost inhuman precision, Waugh has moved in the *Trilogy* towards a kinetic art of moral compassion and understanding, a 'comedie humaine'. In doing so, he has in a sense re-established one of the 'vertical' threads of narrative: that which links an intelligible fictional world with the moral personality of the narrator. Yet it was just the absence of such a link, indeed the scandalous fracture of all such links, which made the early novels such evocative expressions of contemporary moral chaos. If it is one implication of my general argument that we need to reestablish the vertical dimension in narrative, it is another that we need to recognise that the enterprise must begin by acknowledging the depth of the contemporary un-yielding despair which is the starting point of any modern and free man's search for something to worship.

8

Beckett and the Death of the God-Narrator

We have seen how, in Joyce and in Evelyn Waugh, the poise of the comic narrator, perilously perched as he is over the terrors of the void, the 'Descartian vortices', has served the twentieth century as a kind of last-ditch defence against metaphysical monsters. In the work of Samuel Beckett we are privileged to watch what happens when this poise is lost. As we move from the world of Belacqua and Murphy to the world of Malone and The Unnamable, and beyond him to the world of *The Lost Ones*, we see rational man falling over the abyss and into the incertitude of the unfathomable void, shouting stories to 'calm' himself during his eternal fall.[1]

A study of Beckett's work seems to me to lead to the following conclusion: that the progressive disappearance of the reassuringly sane and rational narrative voice inevitably involves an equally progressive deterioration of the world into chaos. When the warp of the fabric is loosened from the frame of the loom, the texture of the material universe, the patterns which we had hitherto been able to discern in it, are lost to view. The separate colours merge into a uniform greyness, outlines dissolve. It is true that in the plays of his 'middle period'— if we can thus speak of a writer still actively at work—there is a certain recovery of intelligible order and pattern, resulting from the very nature of the theatrical experience. But in the latest short pieces, the disintegration seems to have progressed even beyond that which was envisaged at the end of *The Unnamable*.

In Beckett's first major work, *Murphy*, a 'rational' comedy of very learned wit,[2] the rationalism that is mocked is that of Cartesianism

---

[1] See *The Calmative*, in *No's Knife*, pp. 25–42. A calmative is of course a sedative, or pain-killer. All page numbers refer to the appropriate English editions of Beckett's works.

[2] See above, p. 152, note 1.

taken to its 'logical' conclusion in the arbitrary occasionalism of Geulincx. Geulincx is obviously the kind of thinker whose rationalism leads to absurdity. He is a natural butt for learned wit. But for Beckett there is more to the Cartesian heritage than Geulincx. There is also Pascal. And for Pascal, the Cartesian philosophy is not only the apotheosis of reason, it is also the apotheosis of a tragic humanism. Pascal exposes, as no one else can, the depth and the terror of the vortices that lurk beneath the feet of any profound Cartesian thinker. Reason, for Pascal, leads to insoluble problems because, in its Cartesian form, it establishes radical discontinuities and metaphysical gulfs that cannot be bridged: between mind and body, man and the external world, cause and effect. In each case, rational analysis leads to intolerable deadlock. For Pascal the impasse is tragic because (he insists) we know in our hearts that the deadlock must be overcome. If the God of the Philosophers leads us to the brink of the abyss, the God of Religion offers us the faith to leap over it to the other side. If Beckett owes the comic element in his early work to a learned wit which is applied to the Geulincxian absurdities, he owes the tragic element in it to Pascal's uncompromising insights.

In *Murphy* the paradoxes generated by the unbridled rationalism of the Cartesian tradition—such as Murphy's inability to overcome his body's desire for Celia despite the supposedly 'bodytight' nature of his mind, or his resort to astrology as the 'logical' extension of Geulincx's philosophy of cosmic co-incidences—are presented against the pull of a countervailing commonsense. The book does not contain sentiment, in Sterne's sense, or Joyce's feeling for the ordinary: but we do find the implicit critical authority of a narrator who is not identified with Murphy himself and who remains above and apart from the action. This narrator is constantly interposing himself between the reader and the characters, by giving us information to which the characters do not have access. For example in Chapter Six, he tells us, objectively and authoritatively, facts about the nature and content of Murphy's mind which could not be given in any other way. He also provides us with details of Murphy's earliest moments to which Murphy himself has no access (p. 52). In this way the implicit omniscient narrator sets up a standard by which we can judge the 'unbridled rationalism' of the characters for what it is. He represents a reassuring standard of sanity against which we can evaluate the absurd thoughts and behaviour of the characters. The fact that their irrational rationalism *can* be controlled, and put to aesthetically effective ends, is itself an insurance against apparent anarchy. The narrator's very stance of reticent intervention, standing back and letting the lunacy of the action proceed for the most part unimpeded according to its own remorseless logic, is itself a sign of his (and hence of our) confidence that things will not be allowed to get completely out of hand.

Although *Watt* too is organised for us by an implicit omniscient narrator who has authoritative information for the reader, what he tells us is a good deal less reliable and reassuring than in *Murphy*. If Murphy is still recognisably a citizen of the world, Watt is certainly an outcast.[3] Thus the things that Murphy loathed about life were limited and, in a sense, manageable: such as his own body, or the need to work. Watt's predicament is much bleaker and more total: 'If there were two things that Watt loathed, one was the earth, the other was the sky' (p. 34). Murphy has dealings with a large number of real, if crazy people; but Watt's dealings are with unrealities, with mere negations like Mr Knott and his shadowy servants. Murphy keeps his balance on the tight-rope of life—just. Watt, it might be said, is a man in the act of falling from the comic poise into the metaphysical abyss. If his chronicle is a comedy, it is comedy of a desperate kind. The rationalism it mocks is purer, but less substantial than that of *Murphy*. The mathematics of irrational numbers has replaced the mind-body problem as the submerged rock upon which the hero's quest for his own identity founders. Although the omniscient narrator begins his book with an engaging show of knowledge about the world we are to be led into and the characters we are invited to meet, the whole introduction leads us only into a cul-de-sac:

> Mr Hackett turned the corner and saw, in the failing light, at some little distance, his seat. It seemed to be occupied. This seat, the property very likely of the municipality, or of the public, was of course not his, but he thought of it as his. This was Mr Hackett's attitude towards things that pleased him . . . (p. 5)

—and this promising start to a story about Mr Hackett peters out. Mr Hackett and his acquaintances disappear after a few pages, never to return. Meanwhile the book proceeds, without regrets, in quite a different direction. The narrator attempts no explanation for this

[3] See Fletcher, *Novels of Samuel Beckett*, p. 35.

arbitrary change of course; not even the 'absurd' kind of explanation
that a comedian in the learned wit tradition might have been expected
to give. Thus he establishes himself as a much less reassuring personality
than the narrator of *Murphy*. In *Watt* the narrator cannot stop
Arsene's 'short statement' from turning into a tedious and erratic
monologue of twenty-five uninterrupted pages (pp. 37–62). He cannot
supply the information that is necessary to complete some of his own
anecdotes (p. 99). He occasionally says Knott when he means Watt and
has to correct himself (p. 113); and he contradicts himself in his own
footnotes on matters of simple fact (pp. 100–1). Despite being *Watt*'s
'mouthpiece' (p. 66) he is obviously not in control of his own narrative,
and cannot supply that implicit standard of commonsense which, in
Murphy, reassured the reader that the comic poise would, if only
precariously, be maintained.

It is not surprising to find that after *Watt* Beckett's fiction manages
without the, by now dubious, benefit of an authoritative narrative voice
altogether. From the three *nouvelles*, *The Expelled*, *The Calmative*
and *The End*,[4] through the 'Trilogy' (*Molloy*, *Malone Dies*, *The
Unnamable*) to the *Texts for Nothing*[5] there is a steady development of
the monologue form. The origins of the form are, perhaps, to be found
in Arsene's 'short statement' in *Watt*, but in the three *nouvelles* the
Beckettian hero as 'I' takes over completely. It is not until the appearance of *Waiting for Godot* that any kind of 'dialogue', whether between
characters or between character and narrator, reappears in Beckett's
work. The significance of the monologue is that in it we are confronted
by a one-dimensional narrative form. The elimination of the narrative
voice means the apparent elimination of artistic organisation. The
speaking voice who addresses the reader from wherever he finds himself—perhaps from some place he has just been thrown out of, as in
The Expelled, or from the prison of his bedroom as in *Malone Dies*—
is simply recollecting his own past. In doing this, of course, he is
putting it into narrative form: making up that primitive story which is
the retracing of the past in memory.[6] But, to use E. M. Forster's
distinction, his story can hardly be called a plot; it is no more than 'the
chopped-off length of the tape-worm of time'.[7] And plot, after all, is
the novelist's business. The difference between story and plot is the

[4] English versions in *No's Knife*.   [5] English versions in *No's Knife*.
[6] See Crites, pp. 301 ff. (This work is cited above in Chap. 2, n. 17.)
[7] *Aspects of the Novel*, p. 93.

difference between 'the king died and then the queen died', and 'the king died and then the queen died of grief'.[8] And this difference can be brought about only because the narrator has 'access to self-communings and from that level he can descend even deeper and peer into the sub-conscious'.[9]

Beckett's monologues eliminate the possibility of this descent into the private life of a character—that life of which he is himself unaware, but to which the narrator has the privileged access of a creator. (Forster says that a novel in which story replaces plot 'ought to have been a play':[10] and it is no accident that Beckett's monologues, even in the prose narratives of the *Texts for Nothing* and the 'Trilogy', read very much like the monologues to be found in the plays. They are best heard, rather than read.)[11] The elimination of the vertical dimension of narrative—the dimension of depth which makes possible the descent into the character's subconsious—means also, as Forster sees, the elimination of that causal connectedness which is the essence of plot, the horizontal dimension of narrative art. The Beckett speaker cannot keep his mind on one thing for long. The logic of his 'story' is not that of causality, but of mere association. Sometimes even the speaker's own name changes, inexplicably, from episode to episode.[12] But to say 'inexplicably' is itself to misunderstand Beckett, for there is nothing to explain. Everything is on the surface, open to inspection in the words on the page: there is no sub-conscious because there is no dimension of depth. Beckett, like Robbe-Grillet, refuses to be a vulgar fictional speleologist, giving his readers the cheap thrill of exploring his characters in order to bring to light some dark disturbing secrets.[13]

One important consequence of displacing the narrator's voice is that the novels cease to be comedies in any recognisable sense of the term, though local patches of bitter and sardonic wit still remain. It is an important fact about the kind of comedy that the earlier Beckett novels represented, that there should be some implicit standard of rational

---

[8] Ibid.　　　　　[9] Ibid., p. 92.　　　　　[10] Ibid., p. 93.

[11] The recordings by the late Frank McGowran make this very clear.

[12] In *Malone Dies*, Malone is first called Saposcat (*Trilogy*, p. 187) even before he is called Malone (p. 223). By p. 230 he has become McCann. Page numbers in *Malone Dies*, *Molloy* and *The Unnamable* refer to the single volume edition; henceforth 'Trilogy'.

[13] *Snapshots*, pp. 56–7.

control against which to assess the absurdity of the comic action. Beckett's early comedy involves a detached narrator who coolly manipulates things in favour of himself and his jokes, whose authority is assumed at the expense of any sympathy we might otherwise feel for his characters,[14] and whose total control of the material is in complete contrast with the lack of control of their destinies evident among the characters themselves. The apparently unbridled rationalism that we see within the action is, in fact, checked by the narrator's rein and whip. So naturally, when the narrator falls, the rationalist horse bolts. In the *nouvelles* and the 'Trilogy', the Cartesian/Pascalian deadlock takes over completely, so that these works cease to be self-contained comedies of learned wit and turn into philosophical explorations of man's tragic predicament. All the metaphysical abysses that rationalism opened up yawn wide to swallow the 'hero', and there is no comic poise to save him from being engulfed. The relation of body to mind, of consciousness to its objects, of cause to effect, of time to eternity are still pressingly problematic, still central to the hero's quest for identity, security, peace, heaven. But they are now not only insoluble: they are not even funny, except by accident. Instead of receiving a narrator's invitation to view the spectacle of a clown like Murphy 'seeking the best of himself' (p. 52) the reader is now drawn into the hero's own situation, identified with an archetypal 'I' whose predicament is essentially that of Pascal's everyman, lodged in 'this little dungeon . . . I mean the universe':

> We are floating in a medium of vast extent, always drifting uncertainly, blown to and fro; whenever we think we have a fixed point to which we can cling and make fast, it shifts and leaves us behind; if we follow it, it eludes our grasp, slips away and flees eternally before us. Nothing stands still for us. This is our natural state and yet the state most contrary to out inclinations. We burn with a desire to find a firm footing, an ultimate lasting base on which to build a tower rising up to infinity, but our whole foundation cracks and the earth opens up into the depth of the abyss. (*Pensées*, p. 92)

---

[14] See for example, the description of Murphy after the upset of his rocking chair: 'Murphy was as last heard of, with this difference however, that the rocking chair was now on top. Thus inverted his only direct contact with the floor was that made by his face, which was ground against it. . . Only the most local movements were possible, a licking of the lips, a turning of the other cheek to the dust, and so on. Blood gushed from his nose.' (p. 23)

Pascal's vision is also that of Beckett. The Pascalian predicament is also the predicament of Molloy and Moran, Malone and the Unnamable, the 'I' of the *nouvelles* and the *Texts for Nothing*. The only difference between Pascal's man and Beckett's is that, for the one, there is just one source of hope—God: the God of Abraham, Isaac and Jacob—whereas for the other there is none. Very likely Beckett would agree with Mother Angelique de Sainte-Madeleine in drawing comfort from St Augustine's saying: 'He who is not satisfied with God alone as a witness of his actions is too ambitious'.[15] Certainly his heroes are not too ambitious. Molloy's 'ambition' is to suck all of his sixteen stones equally often in due order ('Trilogy', pp. 69ff), MacCann's to be a good road-sweeper (ibid., p. 245), Mahood's regularly to receive the 'spiritual nourishment' of clear and simple things, like the invariable gravy supplied by the restaurant outside which he sits in his jar (ibid., p. 331). But even these petty ambitions are denied. God cannot deliver even these puny helps.

As I have said the progressive disappearance of the narrator in Beckett's fiction involves the progressive disappearance of the plot. In the end the Beckett hero is not a character in a story but a person, or rather a voice, whose existence is guaranteed only through the stories he tells himself.[16] In *Molloy*, admittedly, there are still the bare elements of a recognisable landscape with figures. Molloy and Moran exist in a certain kind of fictional time; they have different names, they are distinct 'characters'. But in *Malone Dies* the various names (Saposcat, Macmann etc.) are patently the speaker's own inventions, mere persona for himself. Even 'Malone' is only 'what I am called now' ('Trilogy', p. 221) and has no absolute authority as a name giving permanent identity. Although 'Malone' lives in a certain place—he is in bed, in a room, with his little heap of possessions—neither time nor place are clearly or consistently established. The temporal dimension of the book exists less in the events which occur to Malone as in the stories he invents in order to create a temporal dimension for himself. The stories exist to break up an endless time, without beginning or terminus, in which Malone seems to be caught. The collapse of plot into mere story inevitably means the collapse of the fictional 'world' into a mere heap of broken images. With *The Unnamable* these twin losses are more

---

[15] Quoted in Goldmann, Epigraph to Part 1.

[16] The reduction of the character to the voice, or mere speaking mouth, is brilliantly dramatised in the recent play, *Not I*.

apparent than ever before in Beckett's work.* Even Malone's story-telling resource, with its function of creating a kind of time-sequence in which Malone can try to live, has now collapsed. Not only is the narrative voice now totally anonymous, indeed is nothing but a function of the words it utters, but these words make no pretence at being stories. Malone at least began with a plan:

> While waiting, I shall tell myself stories, if I can . . . I think I shall be able to tell myself four stories, each one on a different theme. One about a man, another about a woman, a third about a thing and finally one about an animal, a bird probably. (Ibid., 180–1)

But the Unnamable has lost all sense of a time in which such a plan might be conceived, all sense of a self about which to speak:

> The fact would seem to be, if in my situation one may speak of facts, not only that I shall have to speak of things of which I cannot speak, but also, which is even more interesting, but also that I, which is if possible even more interesting, that I shall have to, I forget, no matter. And at the same time I am obliged to speak. I shall never be silent. Never. (Ibid., p. 294)

For the Unnamable, to speak is to exist. Words, any words, are defence against annihilation, and annihilation, even though it would be welcome, is alas impossible. For the Unnamable is already dead, and death has made no difference. Therefore he is compelled to speak, how-ever nonsensically, for ever:

> you must say words, as long as there are any, until they find me, until they say me, strange pain, strange sin, you must go on, perhaps it's done already, perhaps they have said me already, perhaps they have carried me to the threshold of my story, before the door that opens on my story, that would surprise me, if it opens, it will be I, it will be the silence, where I am, I don't know, I'll never know, in the silence you don't know, you must go on, I can't go on, I'll go on. (Ibid., p. 418)

In more familiar kinds of novel, the story constitutes its own time, its own world, which we recognise as a metaphor for the real world and real time. The implicit authorial voice creates a fictional time and space and places characters within it. But in Beckett's trilogy there is no such fictional structure, no world brought into being by the narrative creator. On the contrary, there is only a voice speaking to us from 'this little dungeon . . . I mean the universe'. And since this infinite vastness has to be filled somehow, given some kind of intelligible structure in order to accommodate the hero's unquenchable thirst for meaning, there is only one thing to be done in it: to tell stories, to turn reality itself into a fiction. Instead of the fictional world being an illuminating metaphor for a potentially intelligible reality, a mirror held up to nature, reality is now literally nothing until it has been made into something, given a content and a structure, by the fictions that those who live in it tell because, like *The Calmative*, they are too frightened to listen to themselves rotting, 'waiting for the great red lapses of the heart, the tearing at the caecal walls, and for the slow killings to finish in [the] skull, the assaults on unshakeable pillars, the fornications with corpses' (*No's Knife*, p. 25). For Beckett reality in itself is nothing because it is, quite literally, a contradiction in terms. Just as a net may be described as a set of holes tied together with string, so the Beckett universe is a set of contradictions tied together by the concepts of post-Cartesian reason, a 'matrix of surds' (*Murphy*, p. 79). In such a world, there can be no comedy, let alone of learned wit; for there is no meaning except that which man can invent. Yet meaning is of its nature *maior entis quam ens*, more genitive than nominative: it depends on there being that of which it is the meaning. It entails a dialogue between mind and object, between man and the world he confronts. If there is no such world and no such dialogue, then even the invention of meaning through the telling of stories becomes impossible, itself a contradiction in terms. As Beckett put it in 1956, 'In the last book, *L'Innomable*, there's complete disintegration. No 'I', no 'have', no 'being'. No nominative, no accusative, no verb. There's no way to go on.'[17]

However, by the time *The Unnamable* was written, *Waiting for Godot* was also finished; and with it a way to go on was found. What the drama provided, unlike a story-teller's monologue, was a recognisable scenario, and above all an audience. The Trilogy's monologues hardly implied even a reader: they certainly make excessive demands upon any reader's attention. But the drama implies a dialogue of author and audience. The audience in effect constitutes just that element of commonsense which is necessary to the comedy of unbridled rationalism. If there is no longer a presiding narrator whose

[17] Quoted by Fletcher, *Novels of Samuel Beckett*, p. 194.

presence ensures a standard of rational control, there is now, in Beckett's plays, an equivalent standard set by the expectations of theatre-goers. Against them, the absurdities of comedy can once more be set up. Further more, the stage becomes a world apart, a place where 'characters' live and move and have their being, in a special temporal and spatial dimension. The hero is not imprisoned in 'this little dungeon . . . I mean the universe': he is imprisoned, first of all, in a particular place, a particular time, a particular self. Of course, 'A country road. A tree. Evening' is not exactly explicit as stage directions go (Act 1). But a country road is not the universe, and 'Next day. Same time. Same place', especially when we see four or five leaves on the tree, is not the same, but recognisably different (Act 2). Estragon is not Vladimir, Pozzo is not Lucky. The endless monotony of *Waiting for Godot*, or *Happy Days*, is achieved by playing upon the assumptions of the audience (solid, middle-class assumptions) that the stage is not the place where they, the audience, live (it is not the universe) but is a special, fictional world inhabited by fictional characters. That it can be so little differentiated, so little specified, apparently so universal is because, as a stage, it is already constituted as a place apart, the locus of a fictional time and space. And furthermore, the cycle of repeated performances counterpoints, and thus emphasises the linear time of the play itself; its inexorable thrusting towards an unattainable extinction.[18] Because the drama depends upon the very strong sense of beginning and end which is engendered by the audience's coming for an evening's entertainment (a sense of beginning and end much stronger than that engendered by the intermittent picking up and leaving aside which is the normal experience of reading a substantial novel), it is all the more effective as a medium for expressing the monotony of an endless temporal extension. Because the theatrical conventions tell so strongly in favour of a limited time and a limited place, the slightest gesture of affront to them will make a significant impact. Hence the four or five leaves on the tree in *Waiting for Godot*, the difference between burial up to the armpits and burial up to the neck in *Happy Days*. Thus by taking the bourgeois theatre audience into his confidence, Beckett once more made contact with a reality which was solid, not self-contradictory or tragic but simply there. In so doing he was able to create fictional times and spaces, a sense of 'the now, the here' to use Joyce's

[18] Coe, *Beckett*, p. 92.

words, and thus to erect a two-dimensional structure in which to place characters and create a primitive kind of world. His works for the theatre in the nineteen-fifties became once more illuminating metaphors. And this partial recovery of the two-dimensional structure of narrative then spilled back again into the novel, into *How It Is* in which there is at least a material environment for the characters (albeit only a sea of mud) and even the beginnings of dialogue between torturer and victim. There is certainly a temporal progression from beginning, through middle to end (Before Pim, With Pim, After Pim) and even a rudimentary plot. With these goes a desire on the reader's part to find out what happens in the end. (That the end is also the beginning is, however, no surprise, not even a disappointment.) However minimally, all the ingredients of a novel are there, and each paragraph 'has the density of . . . a chapter of *The Brothers Karamazov* quintessentially reduced to the dimensions of telegram'.[19] However, if the solipsist monologue has been replaced by a kind of dialogue in *How It Is*, this does not imply any retreat by Beckett towards traditional narrative forms. On the contrary it simply heralds a new stage in his development: one which is carried further in the spate of short prose pieces which have followed *How It Is*. In *The Lost Ones* there is still a residual narrative voice that hovers over the events and which is distinguishable by its own doubts about the 'notion' of the world it is describing (p. 63). But the events themselves, and setting in which they take place ('Inside a flattened cylinder fifteen metres round and eighteen high', the 'abode where lost bodies roam each searching for its lost one') clearly place this work in the same group as *Imagination Dead Imagine*, *Ping* and *Lessness*.[20] In all these recent writings we encounter a consistently monotone world, hermetically sealed from any outside interference, and doomed eternally either to a round of predictable rhythmic changes that amount to changelessness (*Imagination Dead Imagine*) or to the total absence of change (*Lessness*). These sealed worlds are clearly related to earlier elements in Beckett's work: for example, to the set for *Endgame*, which suggests the inside of a skull[21] and—to go back almost to the beginning—to the interior of Murphy's mind, which turns out to be a description of a 'large hollow sphere, hermetically sealed to the universe without' (p. 76). (In *Lessness*, it is

---

[19] Ibid., p. 82.
[20] *Ping* and *Imagination Dead Imagine* are both in *No's Knife*.
[21] See Barnard, *Samuel Beckett*, p. 102.

true, we seem to have just the opposite of a sealed world, but the result is just the same. A completely open space, Pascal's 'medium of vast extent' which contains all there can possibly be, is necessarily self-enclosed. This universe is perhaps a development of the earth and sky which were the two things that Watt hated more than anything else, as well as of the desert scenario of *Happy Days*).²² In these writings, the impossibility of overcoming the nothingness of the universe by telling stories seems to be finally accepted. Molloy/Malone/The Unnamable's whole strategy of telling stories to defeat the encroaching inertia of a world on the wane, a world that is passing through its endgame to an inevitable stalemate (or, what amounts to the same thing, a perpetual check that can never be consummated into checkmate) is here shown to be useless. Nothing, it seems, can hold up the movement of matter towards final uniformity and changelessness. Clausius's law of entropy, which predicts an ultimate undifferentiated sameness throughout space, without structural organisation of any kind, is here given imaginative embodiment. We are left, in these latest works, and in *Lessness* above all, with a kind of frozen verbal sculpture, patterns of sound and imagery in which words have become simply objects in a vacuum, the mere nuts and bolts of communication. The two-dimensional structure of language itself is all but obliterated in a kaleidoscope of word-fragments endlessly juggled together. There can be no beginning, no middle or end in such a pattern; no progress of meaning from one statement to the next, no story, no narrator, no fictional world. In short, to quote Clov, in *Endgame*, 'there's no more nature' (p. 16).²³

For many writers in the contemporary world, the announcement that there is no more Nature comes neither as a shock nor as a misfortune. It is rather an invigorating return to the objective truths of science: a science that has at long last freed itself from metaphysical overtones. But for Beckett the conclusion that there is no more Nature is far from

²² 'Expanse of scorched grass rising centre to low mound . . . Maximum of simplicity and symmetry. Blazing light. Very pompier trompe l'oeil backcloth to represent unbroken plain and sky receding to meet in far distance' (stage direction to Act i).

²³ It is worth noting that one of the few phrases in *Ping* which is *not* repeated, and which therefore stands out as somehow peculiarly significant, is the phrase 'perhaps a nature'. The tantalising glimpse of a lost past which seems to be granted to us in this phrase is significant for its contrast with the repetitive present that is encapsulated in the recurring fragments of language which make up the body of the text.

reassuring. On the contrary it is terrifying. We are not surprised to find Hamm trying to extricate himself from Clov's bitter logic by any means available. Hamm wants to reassure himself by claiming that Nature has merely forgotten them—forgetting after all is an act possible only to something which is alive. Hamm adduces in evidence for his opinion, the fact that he and Clov are still in the process of losing their hair, their bloom, their ideals. As long as such changes go on, especially changes of so patently directional a kind, Nature must be still at work. But in that case, Clov returns with perfect logic, Nature has not forgotten them. So Hamm's attempted self-reassurance fails. Either Nature no longer exists, or it exists and continues to torture them. Only crooked thinking can suppose otherwise.

This pathetic little argument about Nature has profound resonances if we remember the meanings of Nature elaborated in, for example, John Bayley's distinction between the literature of Nature and the literature of the Human Condition. Bayley's thesis is that modern literature, with its tendency to 'fabulation' (i.e. to reject life in its untidy diversity as the primary subject of literature in favour of the tidy self-enclosed autonomy of the work of art), destroys the traditional idea of man as intimately related to the environing world which sustains him. In its place the modern age produces a literature of 'the human condition', in which the individual is alienated and alone, cut off from Nature. In short, for the modern writer, 'there is no more nature', only a universe of 'things that are there and . . . are nothing but things, each one restricted to its own self'.[24] Bayley sees this change as dehumanising, and incipiently totalitarian because of its one-dimensionality, its superficiality in the literal sense, i.e. its refusal to attend to anything but the surfaces of things.[25] I think Beckett's latest writings are the most eloquent statement so far made of what would thus become of a world in which there was no more Nature, only the human condition. There are three principal features in Beckett's picture of this condition. First of all, everything that is of value lies in the past, as the endless reminiscing of Molloy, Malone, the Unnamable, and Krapp too, testify. In the present, old age, decay, immobility and disintegration prevail. But the 'natural' immobility of old age is compounded in Beckett's view, by an immobility of apathy and helplessness. We can distinguish the immobility of Murphy in his rocking

[24] Robbe-Grillet, *Snapshots*, p. 99.   [25] Ibid., p. 57.

chair from that of Winnie, Hamm or the figures in the hermetically-sealed worlds of the later short prose works, by the fact that whereas Murphy sat still in his body voluntarily in order to come alive in his mind (p. 6), the immobility of the later characters is involuntary. They are all crippled, imprisoned or even unconscious. Secondly, corresponding to the immobility of persons is the slowing down, almost to the point of stopping altogether, of time itself. The image of Zeno's little heap of millet dominates *Happy Days*, and the notion of a steady deterioration that will never come to an end because its processes can always get slower without actually stopping, not only dominates *Waiting for Godot* but *The Lost Ones* too. But finally *The Lost Ones* also exemplifies to an appalling degree the torture that ensues upon the loss of those human feelings which, under the conditions of Nature flourish in order to lubricate the perpetual motions of social life. True, *Murphy* registers the beginnings of this loss of feeling. (It may be a Tristram Shandyish book in many ways, but it lacks the comforting lubrication of Sterne's sentiment.) Admittedly Celia, the prostitute with a heart of gold, has a certain feminine attractiveness, and she looks after her uncle with some devotion. But her warmth, such as it is, is ineffectual and certainly cannot prevent the steady drift towards Murphy's ignominious demise, cremation and scattering (p. 187). And no Celia-like figure returns to grace Beckett's pages again, except as one of Krapp's fond lost memories. For the rest of Beckett's work, there is virtually no warmth of human feeling anywhere to be found. It has all vanished with the bloom and the ideals which, as Hamm saw, once upon a time signified a loving Nature that cared for and solaced man in his little dungeon, the universe. In the place of such a 'Nature', we find the raw agony of bodily contact, the sheer 'human condition' of *The Lost Ones*. The climate of the closed cylinder which is their world has an inestimably terrible effect upon the soul, leading as it does to anarchy, fury and violence (p. 52). But the soul certainly suffers less than the skin 'whose defensive system from sweat to goose-bumps is under constant stress'. This stress 'robs nudity of much of its charm as pink turns grey and transforms into a rustling of nettles the natural succulence of flesh against flesh' (p. 53). Here sheer 'things', sheer 'surfaces' grind against each other without—to use Robbe-Grillet's words, though hardly in his sense—'false glamour, without transparency'[26]—and with what a vengence! The denatured world of

[26] *Snapshots*, p. 53.

things here pictured dissipates itself in *Lessness*, until it becomes nothing but—'Lessness'; that state of ultimate negation which Beckett evokes in memorable verbal variations on a simple theme:

> all sides endlessness earth sky as one no sound no stir . . . ash grey all sides earth sky as one all sides endlessness . . . grey air timeless earth sky as one same grey as the ruins flatness endless . . . all sides endlessness earth sky as one no sound no stir . . .

Pace Snow, nobody can say of this humanist that he doesn't understand the second law of thermodynamics.[27]

[27] Snow, *The Two Cultures*, p. 14. Unfortunately *Not I* appeared too late for discussion in the foregoing pages. However, I do not think it compels me to change any of the views expressed there.

9
Robbe-Grillet and the
One-Dimensional Novel

I said that in Beckett's *The Lost Ones* the principal torture that hell inflicts upon its inhabitants is the constant stress laid upon the surfaces of the human skin by endless bodily contact. This emphasis on surfaces as sources of pain could well be regarded as an ironic comment upon the praise of surfaces, and superficial textures, which we find in Beckett's best known contemporary in French fiction, Alain Robbe-Grillet. Robbe-Grillet rejects what he calls the old humanistic and romantic conceptions of man and nature, preferring to talk about the human condition as one of individual isolation in a world of discrete things (*Snapshots*, p. 57). Connected with this view of the human condition is the further notion that, with the removal of the old metaphysics of Nature—a metaphysic of 'depth', profundity', 'unseen presences'— the surfaces of things can come into their own again, and be seen truly for what they are, 'without false glamour'. When we recognise the existence of the surfaces of things as existing in their own right we shall experience 'the shock of this obstinate reality whose resistance we had been claiming to have broken down' (ibid., p. 53). To the person who has undergone this shock-treatment

> the first impact of objects and gestures should be that of their *presence* . . . the objects will gradually lose their instability and their secrets, they will forego their false mystery, and that suspect inner life that an essayist has called 'the romantic heart of things'. (Ibid., pp. 54–5)

Robbe-Grillet's case seems at first sight very like Ruskin's: a necessary plea to look again, disinterestedly, at things as they really are, without the false glamour they acquire through being constantly viewed through the tinted spectacles of a distorting ideology. Over the centuries, Robbe-Grillet argues, bourgeois romantics have tried to tame the things around them by renaming them 'Nature': that is by giving them a reassuring human meaning through the use of 'animistic or domesticating adjectives' (ibid., p. 53).* Thus 'Nature' itself is an ideologically loaded 'bourgeois' term. But today, Robbe-Grillet suggests we are beginning to recognise this ideological loading for what it is, with the result that the old literary imperialism in which things became merely 'the vague reflection of the vague soul of the hero' is under radical challenge (ibid., p. 55). At last we are beginning to know how to respect things for what they really are, simply there, 'alien to man': and the 'new novel' is one of the weapons for pursuing this struggle for liberation from bourgeois ideology. But Robbe-Grillet himself seems to be unclear as to the explanation for this new-found sense of liberation. He refuses to admit any vulgar Marxist account in terms of substituting the 'true' socialist ideology for a false bourgeois one: for he seems to want to get behind all ideology, to rediscover an unambiguous reality in its 'concrete, solid, material presence' without what he calls 'cultural fringes'. Yet he also knows that objectivity, in the sense of a completely impersonal way of looking at things, is impossible (ibid., pp. 70–1, 52). What he means by objectivity, then, amounts in the end to something negative: the absence of any 'magic, religious or philosophical appeal to any sort of spiritual resource "beyond" our visible world' (ibid., p. 68). As a personal option, this is legitimate enough: but as a philosophical position it is naive, in the sense that Robbe-Grillet has not established how the distinction between the kind of objectivity he espouses and the kind of objectivity he rejects is to be drawn. As usual, diagnosis turns out to be simpler than cure. It is easier to reject bourgeois ideology that it is to define exactly, or even coherently, what is to be put in its place.

Thus, if Robbe-Grillet's words seem to echo Ruskin's, the source of his artistic energy is more like Joyce's: rejection of a whole bourgeois milieu with its religious connotations. But even if his denunciation of the ideology of romanticism is a necessary corrective, just as Joyce's was, its results are not simple. Or perhaps one should say they are all too simple. For one result of Robbe-Grillet's new reduction of Nature to mere scenery is that narrative, including his own, becomes one-dimensional. Not only does Robbe-Grillet refuse to allow the novel to become an occasion for what he calls emotional 'speleology', plumbing the depths of the human heart. He also refuses the narrator any control of the world created by the very act of narrating. So the resulting novels not only give all their attention to the superficial, they defy what we ordinarily think of as the logic of reality. They are not logical pictures of the world, for despite a 'realistic' technique of description they are not pictures *of* anything: they are as opaque to 'interpretation' as the patterns of a Jackson Pollock canvas.

The first novel, *The Erasers*, bears all the external marks of a Simenon detective story: but in the course of the book it appears that the detective who is brought in to solve the puzzle of the murder committed at the beginning, actually commits that very murder at the end. What are we to make of this? Is the story a nightmare? or a hoax? Or is the whole thing a matter of mistaken identities? Such logical explanations are all carefully ruled out by the book itself. Its structure defies every explanation that seeks to make it conform to the logic of reality. There is no rational answer, and its very realism of surface treatment only underlines the falsity of such conventional realism. According to Robbe-Grillet 'realism' in the sense of conforming to the known rules of temporal and causal order is simply a subjective convention: something we arbitrarily read into things, largely for our own reassurance. Reality itself knows no such logic, no such rules. This is Barbara Hardy's notion of realism taken to a conclusion she can hardly have expected.

Robbe-Grillet's next two novels move steadily further in the same direction. *The Voyeur*, ostensibly a squalid little story of a *crime passionel*, focusses on the way a pathological sadist, during a day-long visit to the island of his youth, carefully avoids saying anything directly about the murder he seems to have committed during his visit. Did he murder the girl or not? This is a question the book forces us to ask, but it is designed to prevent us from ever being able to answer it. Since in a world of mere objects, each existing for itself, there can be no causal nexus linking one thing with another, it is impossible, and pointless, to ask questions of the sort we usually associate with a crime-story.

In *Jealousy*, the next novel, the obsessed character, instead of being in the centre of the picture, is removed to the edge of it. He becomes simply the all-seeking eye through which events are seen. The novel consists of impressions (we presume the husband's though we are never told) of an affair going on between a wife and another man. The 'husband's' jealousy is so total that it throws a jealousy-coloured tint over everything: and it is on the detection of this colouring that the reader's interest is focussed. From the spectacle of a jealousy-coloured world, the reader has to infer, first of all that it *is* jealousy-coloured, and then whose jealousy it is that colours it. If it were a normal magazine-type story, we should naturally begin to ask the question, is the husband imagining it all? Is his wife really having an affair or not? Yet once again, the book is designed to make such a question unanswerable. Indeed, the question is totally irrelevant: for it suggests that we might legitimately look beyond the frame of the picture to the real world, in order to discern some likeness in virtue of which we can ask, what really happened? Such a comparison between the picture and the world it pictures is impossible in the case of a novel like *Jealousy*. 'The novelist's strength lies precisely in the fact that he invents, that he is absolutely free to invent, without a model' (ibid., p. 63).

If the novelist is free to invent without a model, then there is no reason why his inventions should not contradict the logic of ordinary experience from the outset. In the fourth novel, *In The Labyrinth*, we are thrust straight away into a self-contradictory world. The narrator is sealed into a Proustian bedroom with no view outside at all. Yet his first remarks are about the weather: and furthermore even these contradict each other. It is both wet and dry, sunny and snowy outside. As we read on we begin to realise that everything we are told about this 'outside' world is in fact being invented by the narrator, using bits of furniture in the room as his source of inspiration. The story he tells is a fantasy designed to keep himself occupied.

In *The House of Assignation* the obsessed fantasist, who tells us in his first sentence that 'Women's flesh has in all probability always played a large part in my dreams. Even when awake my mind is constantly assailed by images of it' (p. 9), is apparently incapable of distinguishing between his own fantasies and real life. The story—we cannot call it plot—swings perpetually between the two poles of illusion and reality, in such a way that it is impossible for the reader to know how much of it is supposed to be 'true' and how much is the narrator's dream. Dream and reality are described with exactly the same precision. A murder seems to have been committed at least four times over, by different people each time, but this does not bother the narrator. In his kind of world, there are no obstacles to prevent such things happening. The logical picture of the world has been replaced by an apparently arbitrary sequence of words and images joined together by a logic entirely private to the novel itself.

The basis for Robbe-Grillet's thinking is plainly Cartesian. His world view emphasises clear and distinct ideas: everything must be itself and not another thing. The reason for making the novel a wholly self-enclosed world of words, with no function of picturing reality, is that this frees reality itself from the imperialism of the human imagination. Similarly, by insisting on the separateness of things from each other, the human being is freed from the potential tyranny of things: a tyranny to which the bourgeois humanist prefers to submit, rather than have the uncomfortable task of being himself, without the support of a friendly 'Nature'. Since man's overwhelming desire is to live in a *meaningful* way, he will give meaning to things wherever he can, in order to support his own ego. Even if such meaning can only be given to things by allowing them to become his master, he will do it. That is to say, he would rather 'tragify' the world, see himself as the victim of some overarching fate meted out by the world, than stand upright as a free individual in a world bereft of any reassuring meanings.

The result of this outlook in fiction is plain enough: the novel becomes a purely one-dimensional structure. The syntagmatic, or horizontal sequence of words and images is prevented, by the various devices I have already mentioned, from bearing any relation to a world-generating vertical dimension. There is no world-creating in Robbe-Grillet's novels. What appears, at first sight, to be a recognisable scenario soon turns out to be simply a mass of internal self-contradictions: that is to say, a nothingness, an empty concatenation of words that cancel each other out. Robbe-Grillet's case against the traditional 'realistic' novel of, say, Balzac is precisely that it was two-dimensional. In addition to telling a story, it insisted upon giving a depth of meaning to the things that made up the fictional world:

> The role of the writer traditionally consisted in burrowing down into Nature, in excavating it, in order to reach its most intimate strata and finally bring to light some minute part of a disturbing secret. The writer descended into the chasm of human passions and sent up to the apparently tranquil world (that of the surface) victorious messages describing the mysteries he had touched with his fingers. And the sacred vertigo which then overwhelmed the reader, far from causing him any distress or nausea, on the contrary

reassured him about his powers of domination over the world. There were abysses, it was true, but thanks to these valiant speleologists their depths could be sounded. (*Snapshots*, pp. 56–7)

Robbe-Grillet is of course quite right to see that if his programme is to be carried out, he must first of all rob language itself of all those elements which tend to create a false sense of mystery. In the first place, the 'pack of animistic and domesticating adjectives' must be eliminated. For in the old novel

> the literary phenomenon *par excellence* consisted in the global and unique adjective, which attempted to unite within itself all the internal qualities and all the hidden soul of things. The word thus functioned as an ambush into which the writer lured the universe and then delivered it into the hands of society. (Ibid.)

But it is not only the adjective that is the enemy of freedom: it is any kind of metaphorical language. For metaphor is never innocent. The choice of such language

> goes beyond the mere description of purely physical data, and this further content cannot simply be credited to the art of literature. The height of the mountain, whether one likes it or not, takes on a moral value; the heat of the sun becomes the result of someone's intention ... In practically all our contemporary literature these anthropomorphic analogies are too insistently, too coherently, repeated, not to reveal a whole metaphysical system. (Ibid., p. 78)[1]

Not surprisingly, adjectives are very rare in Robbe-Grillet's own work, and frankly metaphorical language is practically non-existent. But the question arises, as we read his novels, whether the blow struck for freedom by the elimination of the old 'depths' succeeds in its objective. In a sense, Robbe-Grillet is one of the most optimistic writers alive. Since he refuses to ascribe any kind of meaning, or direction, to the events that occur in the external world, his work is totally free of that sense of doom, of coming darkness and catastrophe, which pervades most of contemporary literature. He may agree with Clov, in *Endgame*, that

---

[1] Robbe-Grillet goes on to make some acute criticisms both of Camus's *L'Etranger* and Sartre's *La Nausée* on the grounds that they covertly 'tragify' experience by the use of metaphorical language of which the implications are never clearly brought to the surface. On the (characteristic) misuse of 'analogies' for metaphors, see above, p. 3.

'there is no more nature', but this is not because the world is coming to its end, but because the notion of Nature was never valid in the first place. In losing Nature all we have lost is one of our cherished illusions. The world can never be on the wane: for it is eternally what it is, simply there, directionless and meaningless. Yet Robbe-Grillet's own novels are far from cheering. This is partly, of course, because they are not supposed to be. They are not supposed to have any moral or emotional effect: they merely liberate by being what they are. But it is true nevertheless that this liberation has to be from the world as we experience it: and to that extent, a certain picture of the world does present itself in the novels. Robbe-Grillet cannot help giving us his idea of the kind of world we need to be liberated from; that is to say, his idea of what the modern world is really like. And when we look at his novels from this point of view, his liberating optimism soon seems to evaporate. Curiously enough, his work is even less encouraging than Beckett's. In Beckett, at least until the most recent works, the comedy and the wit somehow redeem the despairing vision so that, in an unexpected way, we feel more rather than less inclined to go on living after having made his acquaintance. Just as at his best Zola's exuberance overcomes his fatalism and somehow betrays it, so Beckett's zest for making images of our degradation and absurdity betray, triumphantly, that degradation. But Robbe-Grillet is an artist who refuses such contradictory honours. He is a novelist of remorseless logic even at his most 'illogical'. His novels provide us with a touch-stone of what it is like to live in the modern world without what he calls illusions. They turn out to be hells of a squalid and unheroic kind, expressing effectively and depressingly what it is like to live alone, to be alone, to move about in a world which leaves you alone, confronting you with its own meaninglessness. It is an ironic kind of 'libera-tion'.

The source of the irony lies, I think, in the contradictoriness of Robbe-Grillet's most fundamental philosophical presuppositions. The contradiction comes to the surface in a number of ways, of which perhaps the most significant is that in liberating things from the tyranny of human meanings, he makes them into mere instruments for human exploitation. The claim is that the time has come to liberate the world from our own clutches, because 'we no longer consider the world as a possession, our private property, designed to suit our needs, and domesticable' (*Snapshots*, p. 57). But in fact, the upshot of this revolution is almost an apologia for one-dimensional industrial man's exploitation of the environment for his own sordid ends:

Man looks at the world, but the world doesn't look back at him ... But this doesn't mean that he refuses all contact with the world. On the contrary, he agrees to use it for material ends; a utensil, as such, never has depth, a utensil is merely matter and form—and destination. (Ibid., p. 82)

Thus a man uses a stone for a hammer, but when he has finished with it, it ceases to have any meaning for him, for it has no meaning apart from its use. And the man of today, or at least the man of tomorrow, 'feels no sense of deprivation or affliction at this absence of meaning. He no longer feels lost at the idea of such a vacuum. His heart no longer needs to take refuge in an abyss' (ibid.). Whether this is a true statement of what man today feels is a large question too complex to discuss here. What seems clear is that a strange kind of liberation is here in question. Paradoxically, Robbe-Grillet's description reads curiously like the relation set up between Robinson Crusoe and his island.* The world bereft of meaning all too easily becomes the world as mere utensil. On the other hand, the kind of romanticism represented by Wordsworth, who is obviously one of the founding fathers of the tradition Robbe-Grillet opposes, is based upon a reverence for things in themselves that at its best is truly liberating. True, Wordsworth's admission that the 'influence of natural objects' often compelled him to acknowledge a 'grandeur in the beatings of the heart' makes him an obvious target for Robbe-Grillet's attack on the inevitable tendency of romanticism to encourage all our worst and most grandiose aspirations (*Snapshots*, pp. 79–80).[2] But Wordsworth is not so easily disposed of. Awe, submission, even power-worship may be present in Wordsworth's boyish attitude to natural objects such as mountains: but they are transformed, in the mature-poet, by the recognition that nature includes *people*. Human beings such as the leech-gatherer continually surprise us by their mysterious ambivalent reality, and it is *this* mystery which truly 'chastens and subdues' us (*Tintern Abbey*, 93). Persons are both objects and subjects: they are 'out there' among the rocks and

[2] See *The Prelude* (1805), I, 428–89, which incorporate Wordsworth's poem 'Influence of Natural Objects in calling forth and strengthening the Imagination in Boyhood and Early Youth'.

stones, but they are also 'in here', among us (*Resolution and Independence*, sts. ix and x).[3] Wordsworth begins by contemplating the leech-gatherer as a piece of natural landscape, but it is the discovery of the firmness of the *mind* that inhabits this decrepit body that most profoundly stirs him. And it has the effect of forcing the poet to laugh *himself* to scorn (ibid., st. x). If the boyish attitude included 'grandiose aspirations' before natural objects, that of the mature poet is just the opposite; humility before other people.

The trouble with Robbe-Grillet's thesis is that, in dividing man from objects, he has failed to take account of the fact that, as Wordsworth saw clearly in the case of the leech-gatherer, man is both an object and a subject. 'Man looks at the world, but the world does not look back at him' (*Snapshots*, p. 82) is true only as long as man himself is rigidly excluded from the world of objects. But such an unreasonable exclusion can be maintained only if what is meant by man is simply abstract human consciousness. Only if the 'essence' of man lies purely in his awareness of the world, and not at all in the fact of his being-in-the-world, can such a proposition make sense. Here the Cartesian *cogito* manifests itself as the root of the whole tradition underlying the 'new novel' of Robbe-Grillet. For the main ingredients of 'realistic' fiction; character, coherent temporal sequence, the whole machinery of realism, depend upon the fact of human bodiliness. Merleau-Ponty has shown, in painstaking detail, how conceptions of time and space, of persons and material objects, all arise 'from my relation to things' even while, at the same time, there is 'an element of truth in the Cartesian return of things or ideas to the self'.[4] Merleau-Ponty agrees with Robbe-Grillet to the extent of admitting that 'when I say things are transcendent, this means that I do not possess them, that I do not circumambulate them; they are transcendent to the extent that I am ignorant of what they are, and blindly assert their existence.[5] Yet even to be able to assert their bare existence and the impossibility of circumambulating them, I have to be one of them, among them, arranging them in spatial and temporal sequence. Robbe-Grillet often gives point to his 'chosisme' by emphasising the purely geometrical attributes of the things he describes, in contrast to the 'vaguer' attributes of colour

[3] It is perhaps worth noting that what Wordsworth is here saying in poetic terms is put philosophically in P. F. Strawson, *Individuals*, Part I, iii.

[4] *Phenomenology of Perception*, pp. 412 and 369.

[5] Ibid., p. 369.

or texture that older authors focus on. He seems to be suggesting, by such techniques, not only that the geometry of objects is somehow 'objective' but that we can observe and describe it without reference to our own bodily movements or sensations.* But Merleau-Ponty is surely right to say that 'just as the localisation of objects in space . . . is not merely a mental operation but one which utilises the body's motility . . . so the geometer, who generally speaking, studies the objective laws of location, knows the relationships with which he is concerned only by describing them, at least potentially, with his body.'[6] Yet in *Towards a New Novel* Robbe-Grillet nowhere takes any account of the fact that my body is an object. Of course, it is an object for you in a way that it can never be wholly an object for me; yet it is the same body in both cases, and in some sense therefore it is the same object. This fact must surely be at the root of the whole problem of narrative 'point of view' in fiction. Without some bodily being, some transaction with the physical environment as we know it in real life, the narrative voice must either turn into the voice of God, who sees all things from all angles at once, or into a disembodied human consciousness as contradictory as the faceless grin of Lewis Carroll's cheshire cat. The narrative voices that bring their obsessions to our attention in Robbe-Grillet's novels finally reveal themselves as just such contradictory abstractions.

I should not like it to be thought from the preceding discussion that I am wholly unsympathetic to Robbe-Grillet's aims. Much of this diagnosis (though not his cure) is undoubtedly very apt. There is a good deal of sense in his objection to the Romantic picture of the artist as a kind of madman, unaware of the true source of his inspiration, who produces his masterpieces by a kind of miraculous accident:

> Far from being the result of an honest study of the question, this attitude betrays its metaphysical origin. These pages which the writer is supposed to give birth to in spite of himself, these un-organised marvels, these random words, reveal the existence of superior force that has dictated them. In this interpretation the nove-list, instead of being a creator in the proper sense, would be no more than a mediator between the common herd and some obscure power, something beyond humanity, an eternal spirit, a god . . . (*Snapshots*, p. 46)

[6] Ibid., pp. 386–7.

Furthermore, as I have said, Robbe-Grillet's detestation of metaphor is extremely discerning. He realises that you cannot have metaphor without metaphysical commitments; that is to say without those analogical counterparts which lead at once to the two-dimensional, potentially religious world-view. The question, however, is whether it is in fact possible to eliminate such elements from language without falling into nonsense, or ceasing to be able to communicate at all. To answer this question fully is beyond the scope of the present chapter. I can only say at this point that a careful examination of the results of trying to do so does, I think, show the impossibility of the enterprise. I have argued this elsewhere, in the case of one of Robbe-Grillet's own novels (*In the Labyrinth*) and can only refer the reader to this work for further discussion of the point.[7]

---

[7] See Gregor and Stein, *The Prose for God*, Chap. 8.

Mailer and the Big Plot being hatched by Nature

When we compare Mailer's novels with those of Waugh, Beckett or Robbe-Grillet, we notice an immediate difference of style which reflects a difference of 'world' also. We may say of the three novelists previously considered that they tend to see the novel as relatively self-justifying and autonomous, preoccupied with itself. But when we come to Mailer we seem to be once more in the company of a writer who sees the novel as a vehicle for ideas, for a prophetic vision. In order to understand Mailer properly perhaps we need to begin, therefore by returning to the prophetic work of Lawrence, and in particular *St Mawr* and the evil vision which confronts Lou Witt as she rides off to get help for the stricken Rico during the excursion into the Welsh Hills. There are two significant points to be made about this vision. First, it is a vision of a coming chaos described metaphorically in terms of an irresistible flood: 'Like an ocean to whose surface she had risen, she saw the dark-grey waves of evil rearing in a great tide . . . all the nations, the white, the brown, the black, the yellow, all were immersed in the strange tide of evil that was subtly, irresistibly rising'. Secondly, this flood is coming from the core of Asia, 'as from some strange pole, and slowly was drowning the earth . . . there it was in socialism and bolshevism: the same evil' (pp. 76–7). It is primarily from the old world and its chaotic politics that the subtle tide of rising corruption flows. It is inevitable therefore that Lou should turn to the American continent for some alternative, some place of escape, some desert in which to retreat in order to fight. But the flood of evil is not merely political: it is metaphysical, a threat to the whole rhythm of life itself. In its natural state, Lawrence insists, creation only destroys the past, the obsolete growths, in order to make way for new more advanced forms. There may be terrible pain in this process but we cannot call it evil, for it is a necessary part of the balance of Nature. Evil occurs only when mankind, with its 'ideals' interferes with this natural process. 'Ideal mankind would abolish death, multiply itself million upon million, rear up city upon city, save every parasite alive, until the accumulation of mere existence is swollen to a horror' (p. 78).

It may be that Lawrence's prophetic vision of evil as mysterious and irresistible came out of the shabbiest side of his mind: but its relevance today would hardly be denied. 'Ideal mankind' has released forces within the natural environment, from hydrogen bombs to penicillin and DDT, the defoliants and the plants of the green revolution, which taken together do seem to threaten the world with tragic fecundities and an uncontrollable proliferation of destructive powers. It is not surprising to find that in the face of such awesome facts and dilemmas, writers should turn to scrutinising the heavens once more for signs of unseen presences, demons and occult powers, gods or devils, in order to explain the course that civilisation seems to have taken. Nor is it surprising to find them turning to every device of art and style and plot to set up centres of resistance, whether individual heroic characters, actions or symbolic gestures, to defy the encroaching, seemingly irresistible flood of coming chaos. Yet it is necessary to look critically at the way writers handle what they sometimes seem to regard as 'evidence of a Manichean demon at work in the land'[1] in order to decide for ourselves how far this is a healthy development of an imaginative response to a global crisis, and how far it is simply an expression of the shabbiest aspects of a dying culture.

Tony Tanner, in his study of post-war American fiction, concentrates a whole chapter on the theme of the universe 'running down'.[2] He notes the presence of this theme as a major preoccupation of Norman Mailer, Saul Bellow, John Updike, John Barth, Walker Percy, Stanley Elkin, Donald Barthelme, Thomas Pynchon, Susan Sontag, William Burroughs, James Purdy and others—not to mention Scott Fitzgerald[3] and Henry Adams, whose work in an earlier generation prompted much of this feeling. One paragraph of Tanner's chapter is worth quoting in full as providing a context for the following remarks:

The obsession with plots, agents, codes, often accompanied by a general uncertainty of who is working for whom or towards what ends, which is I think a discernible characteristic of much of the

---

[1] Tanner, *City of Words*, p. 148.   [2] Ibid., pp. 141–25.
[3] The 'waste-land' imagery of *The Great Gatsby*, Chap. 2 is a notable example.

fiction we are considering, is not only a measure of the paranoia induced by American life. It is also, I think, connected to a larger uncertainty about the big plot being hatched out by nature. Final information on this matter is of course unavailable to any of us, but it seems to press far more insistently on the consciousness and imagination of the American writer. Demons and conspiracies are to the fore. The work of, for example, Burroughs, Mailer and Pynchon suggests that entropy may be seen as evidence of a Manichean demon at work in the land.[4]

If demons and conspiracies are to the fore, what is certainly not to the fore is any feeling that the attitudes of the enlightenment and the traditional structures of American society are of much value in stemming the tide. Credulity, it might be said, has filled the vacuum left by the loss of credibility. But to put it this way is perhaps to underestimate the value of the fiction that has come out of this obsession with the big plot being hatched out by nature, and also to ignore the continuity that may be discerned between the new American fiction and that of an earlier generation. In illustration of this point, the work of Norman Mailer may be taken as representative.

That Mailer may be seen as representative of the contemporary American scene as a whole can be inferred from the fact that he was offered $400,000 for a semi-official writer's reaction to the first manned landing on the moon. The resulting book *A Fire on the Moon* is perhaps Mailer's most energetic and mind-boggling attempt to comprehend the universe in metaphor rather than in measure. It might even be argued that the book contains a surfeit of metaphors just as Robbe-Grillet's novels starve for the lack of them. Mailer rejoices in the 'metaphysical pacts' he makes with Nature and the bridges he tries to throw over the 'heart-breaking schisms' he sees between himself and the external world.[5] Thus in *A Fire on the Moon* the question of whether the moon is 'dead' or not—a question Robbe-Grillet would have ruled out from the start—leads him into the following reflections:

> If dead, the death was with dimension. It was a heavenly body which gave every evidence of having perished in some anguish of the

---

[4] *City of Words*, p. 148. Tanner also points to the resurgence of interest in astrology, magic and occultism in America in recent years, and their presence in fiction (p. 348).

[5] The phrase is Robbe-Grillet's (*Snapshots*, p. 92).

cosmos, some agony of apocalypse—a face so cruelly pitted with an
acne would have showed a man whose skin had died to keep his
soul alive . . . The moon spoke of holes and torture pots and scars
and weals and welds of molten magna . . . (p. 230)

Yet in trying to comprehend the universe in metaphor, and to pick the
lock of its mystery, Mailer suggests that he and the rest of us, all alike
dull and unresponsive inhabitants of technology and 'corporation-land',
may simply be walking towards the brink of some final catastrophe:

In this hour they landed on the moon, America was applauding
Armstrong and Aldrin, and the world would cheer America for a
day, but something was lacking, some joy, some outrageous sense
of adventure. Strong men did not weep in the street nor ladies
copulate with strangers. Any armistice to any petty war had occa-
sioned wilder celebrations. It was almost as if a sense of woe sat in
the centre of the heart. For the shot to the moon was a mirror to our
condition—most terrifying mirror: one looked into it and saw
intimations of a final disease . . . (p. 313)

Now this disease is most clearly manifested, according to Mailer,
in the one-dimensional, unmetaphorical language used in 'corporation-
land'. Contrary to what Robbe-Grillet says, Mailer believes that
science and technology have penetrated the modern mind so completely
that 'voyages into space [have] become the last way to investigate the
metaphysical pits of that world of technique which choke(s) the pores
of modern consciousness', and that perhaps we will have to continue
to explore what Pascal called our 'little dungeon—I mean the universe'
until 'the breadth and mystery of new discovery [forces] us to comprehend the world again as poets, comprehend it as savages who knew
that if the universe was a lock, its key was a metaphor rather than
measure' (pp. 379–80).

If Mailer is right in suggesting that we can only understand the
mind-boggling mysteries unearthed by modern science and technology
by employing a language of primitive metaphorical richness, surely it
is equally true that the laconic factuality of the gigantically tall stories
science has to tell us seems to prompt exactly the opposite conclusion:
namely that what we need is a prose of unprecedented ordinariness,
with clear and distinct words for clear and distinct ideas, to head off
the spiralling rhetoric that the very tallness of the stories we have to

tell seems to require and encourage. Mailer, I suspect, was commissioned to describe the first manned moon-shot, not just because he was so representatively American,[6] not just because, as people kept telling him, he was the best journalist in America, but because he had already confessed to being entranced by the moon's lure as if by the American Dream itself[7] and had already made himself the master of the metaphorical revels necessary to celebrate the dream's coming true. This 'rather ruffianly Jew' already comprehended the world as a savage, if not quite as a poet: and if the whole space-adventure was expressive of corporation-land's most presumptuous madness, it was also, for Mailer, a profoundly poetic madness. Yet, in the end he had to admit that the riot of metaphor with which he had tried to capture the mystery of the moon was quelled by a single, little inviolable fact: a piece of the moon itself. Standing before the precious trophy of man's longest journey, Mailer was baffled into silence. Poetry could not save him. His metaphors were defeated by the moon's measures (*Fire on the Moon*, p. 380).

Mailer's problem, of finding a rhetoric adequate to the tallness of the true stories he had to tell, is a problem that faces all story-tellers in our age. If the present time has so many stories to tell that it cannot tell them properly; if it is so poetic an age that it dare not to take itself poetically; may this not be because it actually prefers the helpless fumbling understatements of scientists or reporters to the grandiose rhetoric of poets or visionaries? Is there not a certain honest humility about the astronaut's 'measures', when we compare them with the metaphors of the 'historian' who is also a 'novelist'?[8] When Mailer describes the moon as having perished, we begin to wonder whether he is not trying to shift the whole burden of man's tragic predicament, his own guilts and corruptions, his cruelties and his crimes, on to the face of the moon: to sign some metaphysical pact with the universe on our behalf, whether we like it or not. Is it really the moon he is talking about, or ourselves?—our own acnes, weals and eviscerations? Is he not

[6] As Philip Toynbee said in *The Observer*, London, 29 October 1970: 'Did it occur to anyone in N.A.S.A. that the untidy, rather ruffianly Jew who had come to study them was the inescapable ghost at their glistening and hygienic feast? Mailer *was* the America they said they were.'

[7] See Rojack's balancing-act on the parapet, when he is almost lured by the moon to jump into her embrace, in *An American Dream*, Chap. 1.

[8] See *The Armies of the Night*, which is subtitled 'History as a Novel, the Novel as History'.

simply projecting our problems on to the innocent moon, a victim that cannot defend itself? And when he likes to flirt with the idea that perhaps the moon is alive after all, and may sometime take a terrible revenge upon us for our crimes against it, is not this a piece of rhetorical fancy dreamt up to justify the rape itself, to make it seem less brutal?[9] However that may be, it is certain that Mailer's metaphor-laden moon is not that of the prosaic astronauts:

> zooming in now on a crater called Schubert N . . . very conical inside wall . . . coming up on the Bombing Sea . . . Alpha 1 . . . a great bright crater. It is not a large one but an extremely bright one. It looks like a very recent and I would guess impact crater with rays streaming out in all directions . . . coming back towards the bottom of the screen into the left, you can see a series of depressions. It is this type of connective craters that give us most interest . . . (pp. 249–50)

In many ways, the astronauts' dislocated syntax and their lack of metaphorical involvement seem more honest than Mailer's rhetoric. They are, we feel, more *interested* in the moon than Mailer is: and certainly less interested in themselves. They are looking at the moon with the alert and innocent eyes of scientific observers, trying to tell the truth of what lies before them, not reading its mysteries with the eyes of guilt-ridden 'Nijinskys of ambivalence' (p. 381). It is not the astronauts but Mailer himself who is caught in the intolerable paradox that when our metaphors bind us so tightly to things that we cannot get away from them, the world becomes just a rubbish dump for our own spiritual garbage. It is not the astronauts who are worried by the absurdity of the fact that, as liberators of modern consciousness, which is how Mailer chooses to see them, these modern explorers have to be imprisoned in a little mobile dungeon, ironically bound and gagged with 'life-support systems', in order to explore that other 'little dungeon' (pp. 145–50). It is Mailer who puts himself into this prison of paradox. The astronauts seem to be blithely unaware of their predicament.

Mailer would like to persuade us that it is only by way of metaphor that the modern story-teller can take the measure of contemporary

---

[9] 'It is one thing to shatter a taboo, it is another to escape the retribution which follows the sacrilege' (p. 337). This is said à propos of the fear that the astronauts might never succeed in getting off the surface of the moon.

facts. But I think Wallace Stevens was equally persuasive when he remarked, in his off-handedly far-sighted way, that 'reality is a cliché from which we escape by metaphor'.[10] Robbe-Grillet makes the same point when he says that metaphor is never 'an innocent figure of speech' because 'in practically all our contemporary literature . . . anthropomorphic analogies are too insistently, too coherently repeated, not to reveal a whole metaphysical system'.[11] If Mailer believes that it is only by metaphor that we can liberate modern consciousness from the constricting prison of the contingent and the arbitrary, clearly Robbe-Grillet believes just the opposite: 'Man looks at the world, but the world doesn't look back at him. Man sees things, and he notices, now, that he can escape the metaphysical pact that other men made for him in days gone by, and that by the same token he can escape slavery and fear . . .'[12] Rejoicing in his new-found liberty from the tyranny of metaphors and meanings, the modern story-teller will see to it that in future novels 'gestures and objects will be *there*, before they are *something*; and they will still be there afterwards, hard, unalterable, ever-present . . . indifferent to their own meaning'.[13]

The same will go for the hero of the new kind of story:

> Whereas the traditional hero is always being got at, cornered, destroyed, by the author's suggested intepretations, for ever being pushed into an intangible and unstable elsewhere, which gets more and more vague and remote, the future hero will on the contrary remain *there* . . . When the hero's presence is indisputable [authorial comment] will seem useless, superfluous, and even dishonest.[14]

In Robbe-Grillet's own case the result of this liberation from metaphors and meanings is a descriptive language which is extraordinarily like that of the astronauts. His notorious description of a tomato segment lying on a plate reads exactly like a space-man's report of a hitherto unnoticed species of rock picked up from the surface of the moon:

> A quarter of tomato that is quite faultless, cut up by the machine into a perfectly symmetrical fruit. The peripheral flesh, compact, homogeneous, and a splendid chemical red, is of an even thickness between a strip of gleaming skin and the hollow where the yellow,

---

[10] *Opus Posthumous*, p. 179 (*Adagia*).   [11] *Snapshots*, p. 78.
[12] Ibid., p. 82.   [13] Ibid., pp. 54–5.   [14] Ibid.

graduated seeds appear in a row, kept in place by a thin layer of greenish jelly along a swelling of the heart. This heart, of a slightly grainy, faint pink, begins—towards the inner hollow—with a cluster of white veins, one of which extends towards the seeds—somewhat uncertainly.[15]

Yet Robbe-Grillet's tomato is, quite simply, a tomato and nothing else, whereas Mailer's moon rock, as he stares at it in wonder and awe, instantly takes on a personal identity:

He saw the lunar piece through not one glass but two, rock in a hermetically tight glass bell . . . she was not two feet away from him, this rock to which he instinctively gave gender as she—and *she* was gray . . . as a dark cinder . . . with craters the size of a pin and craters the size of a pencil point, and even craters large as a ladybug and rays ran out from the craters, fine white lines, fine as the wrinkles in an old lady's face . . . (*Fire in the Moon*, p. 380)

It seems clear from a personifying passage such as this that Mailer has affinities with Lawrence—the Lawrence who would like to know the stars as the Chaldeans knew them.* What may seem a good deal less obvious is his affinity with a dandyish writer like Evelyn Waugh. Yet when we look at a book like *An American Dream*, or better still *The Armies of the Night*, the connections do seem worth noting. Mailer's left-conservative mixture of radicalism and reaction, his continuous performance of a public balancing act on a parapet over vast metaphysical abysses,* his concern to define this poise by the creation of an apparently outrageous and irresponsible style (perhaps most notable in *Why Are We In Vietnam?*): all these serve to establish a certain sympathetic link with the world of Waugh. An 'untidy rather ruffianly Jew' can hardly be a dandy: yet Mailer at times comes close to an inner dandyism which serves a protection against the ravages of reality:

Mailer was a snob of the worst sort . . . Like most snobs he professed to believe in the aristocracy of achieved quality—'Just give me a novel with a few young artists, bright-eyed and bold'—in fact, a party lacked flavour for him unless someone very rich or social was present. An evening without a wicked lady in the room was like an opera company without a large voice. (*Armies of the Night*, p. 24)

[15] *The Erasers*, pp. 129–30.

The dandyism here lies not so much in the snobbery or the taste for wicked ladies as in the mixture or ironic detachment and flippancy of tone which he directs against himself. (With the dandy 'flippant tone authenticates the seriousness of his remarks'[16]) This is a tone that is constantly present in *The Armies of the Night*, constituting a dandyish refusal to take with full seriousness the tragic implications of the events that Mailer is both publicly involved in, as character in his own non-fictional novel, and detached from as their 'historian'. What prevents him from having more than an oblique resemblance to Waugh, however, is just this public involvement. With Mailer, the public and the private personalities are hardly distinguishable. Everything that, in another time or place, would have remained secret, here becomes material for the public advertisement of the self.[17] Waugh's private personality, on the other hand, remained a closely-guarded secret to be kept in quite a separate compartment from the public personality of the narrator of the novels. That this strategy did not always succeed is shown, of course, in *The Ordeal of Gilbert Pinfold*, where the method of self-projection is not so very different from that of Mailer, though the invention of a different name is significant as a sign of an ultimate reserve which Mailer seems to lack. But there is a deeper difference as well, which is that the action of Waugh's self-revelatory novel is itself a private affair: the story of one individual's struggle with 'with his aeons',[18] whereas Mailer's self-revelatory novels are parts of a public action, a kind of self-advertising campaign in fact. For example in *The Armies of the Night* Mailer seeks to understand the march on the Pentagon as a kind of collective American tragedy on the grand scale, with himself at the centre of it. Yet he is also pictured as a clown within the tragic action, detached like the still centre of the whirling world. (Just as Shakespeare drops the fool in *King Lear* when the tragedy comes to its consummation, so Mailer disappears from the stage when the 'novel' becomes 'history' in order to work out its own final meaning.)[19]

[16] Gregor, op. cit., p. 504.

[17] For example, Mailer introduces the breakdown of his own marriage into *A Fire on the Moon*.

[18] The phrase is William Golding's (*Pincher Martin*, pp. 50–53 etc.).

[19] 'The fool is withdrawn from the pressures and tensions and dislocations of the play just as these arrive at their fullness. Laughter remains latent within the play, but pity and terror have finally disarmed it. Tragedy, pushed to a point where it violently presses upon the absurd, without itself collapsing, thus establishes its sovereignty over humour.' Stein, *Criticism as Dialogue*, pp. 86–7.

The tragic tone, with its consequent repression of humour, comes out most clearly at the end of the book, in which Mailer tries to give some kind of quasi-Shakespearean hope to an otherwise tragic action by evoking the picture of a few dedicated Quakers, naked in jail, the remnants of the long march, still holding out against the tide of evil around them by fasting and prayer. Mailer writes their prayer as he imagines it:

> O Lord, forgive our people for they do not know, O Lord, find a little forgiveness for America in the puny reaches of our small suffering, O Lord, let these hours count on the scale as some small penance for the sins of the nation, let this great nation crying in the flame of its own gangrene be absolved for one tithe of its great sins by the penance of these minutes, O Lord, bring more suffering upon me that the sins of our soldiers in Vietnam be not utterly unforgiven—they are too young to be damned for ever.

Then the author comments:

> If the end of the March took place in the isolation in which these last pacifists suffered naked in freezing cells, and gave up prayers for penance, then who was to say that they were not saints? And who is to say that the sins of America were not by their witness a tithe remitted? (p. 319)

In addition to the felt need to reclaim the structure of belief implied in that hieratic Christian language (belief without which the words can only signify a gesture of reluctant but forced resignation to the encroaching 'gangrene') the most notable thing about this ending is the absence of Mailer, the representative American from the scene. Of course Mailer sees himself as part of the guilty nation. But though he had made his protest, he himself had not gone so far as to be kept naked, like poor Tom, in the 'hole'. Yet he was supposed to be the centre of the novel's attraction, the clown whose antics held the entire structure together. Why is Mailer missing at this crucial juncture of the story?

We may explain the fact by reference to Mailer's 'Nijinsky-like ambivalence' so publicly and wittily acknowledged throughout the book. Mailer hovers between the need to sin and the need to repent; and as he describes himself in this predicament he valuably articulates a general feeling. But surely this personal ambivalence rests on a deeper ambiguity, between the language of sin and the language of sickness, both of which seem to be necessary to Mailer if he is to describe America's problems. Within the space of a few lines he speaks both of the nation's 'sins' and the nation's 'gangrene'. Now, visions of a nation's— indeed the whole world's—sickness are, of course, part of the sense of the entropic decay which fascinates and yet appals so many contemporary writers. The nation's 'gangrene' is an organic calamity, alive and growing as the visible manifestation of an invisible demonic power, a 'principality' within the world order. But there is a conflict between the language of sickness and that of sin. The one implies personal responsibility, while the other does not. One of the damaging things about talk of a cosmic entropic sickness is that it suggests that no individuals are finally more guilty than any others. In the end nobody can do anything much about the problem, except to adopt a dandyish personal style as a protest against it. Yet Mailer's style at the end of *The Armies of the Night* is interesting because, instead of taking that way out, he chooses to combine, quite seriously, the language of disease and the language of sin. The result seems to me to be fatal to his valuable self-consciously clownish pose.

Of course, today the nation's gangrene is just as likely to come to our notice in the form of a technological 'cancer' as under the metaphor of an organic disease. It is therefore not surprising to find that both kinds of imagery abound in Mailer's work. The mingling of biological and mechanical language to describe the disorder is something that we have already noticed in Evelyn Waugh: Silenus and Grimes are ancestors of Mailer's demonic pantheon. In *Why Are We In Vietnam?* we find a confrontation between on the one hand guns, helicopters and deep-freezes for the storage of dead Alaskan game (described, at times, with a technical pedantry that reminds one of Joyce) and on the other, bears, wolves and caribou described in a language reminiscent of Conrad or Lawrence at their most lush. In *The Armies of the Night* we find a similar mixing of the demonic metaphors:

The air was violent, yet full of amusement, out of focus . . . There was a hint of hurricane calm, then wind-bursts, gut-roars from the hogs. If the novelist had never heard of Hell's Angels or motorcycle gangs, he would still have predicted, no rather *invented* motorcycle orgies, because the orgy and technology seemed to come together in the sound of 1200 cc's on two wheels, that exacerbation of flesh, torsion of lust, rhythm in the pistons, stink of gasoline, yeah, oil as the last excrement of putrefactions buried a million years in Mother Earth, yes indeed, that funky redolence of gasoline was not derived from nothing, no, doubtless it was the stench of the river Styx (a punning metaphor appropriate to John Updike no doubt) but Mailer, weak in Greek, had nonetheless some passing cloudy unresolved image now of man as Charon on that river of gasoline Styx wandering between earth and the holy mills of that machine. Like most cloudy metaphors, this served to get him home—there is nothing like the search for a clear figure of speech to induce gyroscopic intensity sufficient for the compass to work. (pp. 97–8)

That paragraph is not only wholly typical in its mixing of the mechanical and biological in evoking the sense of metaphysical powers at work in the nation's system (a sense that 'politics had become mysterious again, had begun to partake of Mystery; that gave life to a thought' that the gods were back in human affairs' (p. 103):[20] it is also typical in its subterranean deflation of itself, and of Mailer as its author. But as I have said, the trouble with the mixing of these metaphors is that it tends to discourage just that sense of personal guilt and responsibility on which Mailer's 'tragedy' has hitherto relied. When Lawrence was calling for a kind of tragedy that went beyond the 'merely human', which would encompass the 'stir' of natural forces as in Hardy's Egdon Heath, which would be war to the death between man and the 'fretful elements', he was seeking to redress a lost balance, to go beyond the pathetic fallacy to a new (which would also be an old) pathetic truth. But to see the problem in terms of a general sickness[21] seems not only to absolve men of their vile offences but also to render them politically impotent. (As Greene's whisky priest knew, if everyone is sick, it seems pointless to pray for forgiveness.)

However, the conflict between the two ways of describing the general condition does not necessarily have to be fatal. Within the metaphysical reach of a tradition such as the Christian one to which the jailed Quakers belonged, a structure exists whereby the two *are*

---

[20] Mailer notes (*Fire*, p. 377) that nowadays he carries Frazer's *The Golden Bough* on his trips by plane.

[21] This is Lucas-Dockery, the prison governor's view, in *Decline and Fall*, p. 178.

reconciled in one historic moment: the moment when the language of healing and the language of forgiveness come together in a single man's words:

'To prove to you that the Son of Man has authority on earth to forgive sins', he said to the paralytic, 'I order you: get up, pick up your stretcher and go off home.' (Mark 2:10–11)

Mailer's ending to his novel is an open one: and it is open in particular to the possibility that this man's historic words have a universal application, an application directly relevant to the nation's sins as well as to its gangrene. But Mailer does not go so far as to embrace that commitment for himself, even though he seems to admit that only through some such commitment can America obtain both the healing and the forgiveness that she needs.

Forgiveness involves a structure of beliefs: in a heaven which can send down visible spirits to tame our vile offences, and an earth which is such that it can accept these spirits and make them fruitful. A concept, in short, of unseen presences within Nature. But can such a concept be recovered? Is it to be found anywhere within our ravaged planet? I do not think that modern fiction in its present state has any coherent answer to give to that question: and yet the modern world that is shaped by its stories awaits one with increasing impatience. Therein lies the dilemma of a story-shaped world.

Notes to Part Two

p. 121. See *Stephen Hero*, Chap. XIX: 'The romantic temper, so often and so grievously misinterpreted and not more by others than by its own, is an insecure, unsatisfied, impatient temper which sees no fit above here for its ideals and chooses therefore to build them under insensible figures. As a result of this choice it comes to disregard certain limitations. Its figures are blown to wild adventures, lacking the gravity of solid bodies, and the mind that has conceived them ends by disowning them. The classical temper on the other hand, ever mindful of limitations, chooses rather to bend upon these present things and so to work upon them and fashion them that the quick intelligence may go beyond them to their meaning which is still unuttered. In this method the sane and joyful spirit issues forth and achieves imperishable perfection, nature assisting with her goodwill and thanks.'

p. 124 The thoughts are Lou Witt's, as she meditates on the coming flood of evil in the world: 'The dead will have to bury their dead, while the earth stinks of corpses. The individual can but depart from the mass, and try to cleanse himself. Try to hold fast to the living thing, which destroys as it goes, but remains sweet. And in his soul fight, fight, fight to preserve that which is life in him from the ghastly kisses and poison-bites of the myriad evil ones. Retreat to the desert, and fight' (p. 79). Of course this theme is not pursued in a wholly unrelenting way in Lawrence's work. At times, in *Lady Chatterley's Lover*, in some of the last stories, in the second part of *The Man Who Died*, even in a sense in *The Ship of Death*, the individual returns home to the familiar world, to personal relationships, to the search for human love. The New England woman who preceded Lou on the Mexican ranch, in *St Mawr*, is one of these. 'She was glad to go down from the ranch, when November came with snows. She was glad to come to a more human home, her house in the village' (*St Mawr*, p. 159). But always in these last works there is the counter movement, the search for a cleansing retreat in the desert where the individual is not touched or polluted by relationship to others. Lou takes over from the New England woman in the end, to face the 'fretful elements' alone. *The Woman Who Rode Away* does not come back, but continues her 'retreat' to the point of death. *The Man Who Died* commands those among whom he comes not to touch him, and the boat he takes in order to get away is only another version of the little Ship of Death itself.

p. 125. For Lawrence, the horse St Mawr is a mixture of the 'dead' domesticated horses seen in London ('over here the horse has died . . . oh, London is so awful: so dark, so damp, so yellow-grey, so mouldering piece-meal') and of the dragon symbols he had seen in Mexico everywhere, staring out on him from old ruins, jaws gaping to hold doorways and gleaming here and there wherever he might be. It was a god there, a god he admired . . . ' (see F. W. Carter, reminiscence in *D. H. Lawrence: A Composite Biography*, Maidson 1958, vol. 2, p. 314, and also letter to Willard Johnson in *Collected Letters of D. H. Lawrence*, ed. Harry T. Moore, London 1962, vol. 2, pp. 767ff). Lawrence was of course much taken up with the symbolism of the dragon at the time of writing *St Mawr*. He had received the MS of Frederick Carter's *The Dragon of the Apocalypse* at Chapala in 1923 before making the journey to England from which *St Mawr* finally emerged. The conversation in the story between Cartwright (= Carter) and the others helps to give metaphysical depth to the meaning of St Mawr himself (*St Mawr*, pp. 60–4). Cartwright's goat-like appearance starts a conversation on the subject of the great god Pan. Cartwright believes that the figure of the goaty satyr is a debased version of a pre-Greek conception in which the god was hidden, dangerous but powerful, in everything. 'In those days you saw the thing, you never saw the god in it: I mean in the tree or the fountain or the animal. If you ever saw the god instead of the thing, you died.' This Ruskin-like theory leads Lou on to ask whether she might see Pan in a horse, and Cartwright gives her a knowing look. What Lawrence does not allow us to know is whether, in the ranch, Lou ever did see the god directly, with the naked eye, and whether the experience had the fatal outcome that Cartwright predicts. It is as though Lawrence is not really prepared to go through with his tragic conception to the bitter end in *St Mawr*. See also Frank Kermode, 'Lawrence and the Apocalyptic Types' in *Critical Quarterly*, 10 (Spring and Summer 1968), pp. 14–38.

p. 130. Consider what the effect would be if the 'should' and the 'would' of the penultimate paragraph were changed into straightforward past tense verbs. In place of 'In absolute motionlessness he watched till the red sun should send his ray through the column of ice. Then the old man would strike, and strike home, accomplish the sacrifice and achieve the power', we would have the far more definite and 'final' sentence: 'In absolute motionlessness he watched till the red sun sent his ray through the column of ice. Then the old man struck, and struck home, accomplished the sacrifice and achieved the power'. But Lawrence does not want to be committed to all the implications of so positive an ending, so strong a 'sense of an ending'.

p. 132. Donald MacKinnon has pointed out the importance, for a theology of the atonement, of seeing Christ's death as a tragic death: see 'Subjective and Objective Conceptions of the Atonement'; in *Prospects for Theology*, essays presented to H. H. Farmer, London (Nisbet), 1967, pp. 167–82; 'Theology and Tragedy' in *Religious Studies*, 2 (April 1967), pp. 163–70; and 'Atonement and Tragedy' in *Borderlands of Theology*, London (Lutterworth Press), 1968, pp. 97–104.

p. 135. Of course this does not imply that Birkin and Ursula are not, like Gerald and Gudrun, both parts of a world that is finished. They will never themselves inherit the new world Birkin dreams of. Exile from the world that is finished is all they can expect, at best; at worst they must expect to go down with it. On this see John Goode in *The Twentieth Century* (ed. Bernard Bergonzi), Vol. 7 of the *Sphere History of Literature in the English Language*, London (Sphere Books), 1970, pp. 106–52, especially pp. 137–9.

p. 137. Mann's own *alter ego* Gustav Aschenbach, in *Death in Venice*, exhibits just such a tendency. Mann's commentary upon Aschenbach's work is revealing. Insofar as 'tout comprendre c'est tout pardonner' is a life-affirming principle, Aschenbach's rejection of it in favour of moral austerity and aesthetic detachment, his dedication to 'an almost exaggerated sense of beauty, a lofty purity, symmetry, and simplicity . . . [a] conscious and deliberate mastery' is a rejection of life. As Mann suggests, such an attitude results in a 'dangerous simplification' in Aschenbach's work. Yet the artistic discipline required to maintain it is what Aschenbach possesses above all other artistic gifts. Hence his role as 'the poet spokesman of all those who labour at the edge of exhaustion; of the over-burdened, of those who are already worn out. . .' Thomas Mann, *Stories and Episodes*, London (Everyman's Library), pp. 79–81, and also D. H. Lawrence, *Thomas Mann*, originally published in *Phoenix*.

p. 146. Admittedly Bloom's most sublime aesthetic experiences are even here couched in banal overwritten phrases: but this is a calculated dramatic placing of Bloom's response, vulgar but full of genuine appreciation. Furthermore, the song from *Martha* inevitably has kinetic implications for Bloom, who has constantly in mind his flirtation with Martha Clifford and his wife's infidelity. These in fact have a good deal to do with his vulnerability to the beauties of this particular song, sung at this particular juncture.

p. 156. See *Decline and Fall*, p. 121: 'How loathsome and beyond words boring all the thoughts and self-approval of this biological by-product! this half-formed, ill-conditioned body! this erratic, maladjusted mechanism of his soul! on the one side the harmonious instincts and balanced responses of the animal, on the other the inflexible purpose of the engine, and between them man, equally alien from the *being* of Nature and the *doing* of the machine, the vile *becoming*!' The really modern people, like Margot Beste-Chetwynde, are themselves little more than machines; Silenus decides, quite logically from his point of view, not to marry Margot simply because, as he puts it, she will be 'worn out' in ten years (pp. 126–7).

p. 157. *A World on the Wane* is the English title of Lévi-Strauss's *Tristes Tropiques*, a study of the declining cultures of certain South American tribes. Lévi-Strauss ends his book with the speculation that it is of the very nature of civilisation itself to level out differences and thus to contribute to the increasing entropy of the world (see pp. 397–8). Waugh's most eloquent endorsement of this idea is to be found in the fate of Tony Last, in *A Handful of Dust*, viz. a monstrous living death in the South American jungle 'Du Côté de Chez Todd'. In Lévi-Strauss's words, 'Taken as a whole . . . civilisation can be described as a prodigiously complicated mechanism: tempting as it would be to regard it as a universe's best hope of survival, its true function is to produce what physicists call entropy: inertia, that is to say. Every scrap of civilisation, every line set up in type, establishes a communication between two inter-locutors, levelling what had previously existed on two different planes and had had, for that reason, a greater degree of organisation. "Entropology", not anthropology, should be the word for the discipline that devotes itself to the study of this process of disintegration in its most highly evolved forms' (p. 397).

p. 176. In fact *The Unnamable* (in common with a good deal else of Beckett) presents itself as simultaneously a ratification and a caricature of the world-view which insists that the good of existence is always to be preferred to the evil of outright annihilation, however painful the form of existence in question may be. Beckett's work may be understood as a grim dramatisation of the consequences of the view, expressed for example by St Augustine, that it is a greater good to exist and be miserable than not to exist at all. Aquinas, in his commentary on the *Sentences* of Peter Lombard, discusses the consequences of this idea for the problem of God's justice in damning sinners to eternal punishment. Two of his answers seem peculiarly appropriate to the Beckettian vision. The first is the reply to an objection that seems to follow from Augustine's principle, namely that since sheer existence is the greatest of all goods, from which all other goods stem, it is impossible for the damned to wish their own annihilation. Aquinas argues that, though it is impossible to wish one's own annihilation *per se*, it is still possible to do so *per accidens* in the sense that it is possible to wish for an end to misery even if this can only be had by an end of existence itself. It follows, of course, that the fact that this wish cannot, in justice, be granted by God—since to grant it would be to prefer the lesser good (an end of misery) to the greater good of existence—adds a further twist to the misery of the damned, in the form of frustration of their dearest wish. But Aquinas has yet another ingredient to add to the argument. Surely, he wonders, the sin of ingratitude deserves the loss of commensurate benefits. Hence ingratitude for the benefit of existence itself must surely in justice deserve the loss of that very benefit. Now, mortal sin against God, the author of existence, is always a kind of ingratitude for the gift of existence: it is a flinging of existence on the creator's terms back in the face of the creator. Hence justice itself must entail the utter annihilation of the mortally ungrateful sinner. But this would imply a denial of the eternity of Hell. Aquinas's answer is a piece of reasoning that is surely 'unbridled' in Whitehead's sense of the term. A punishment is fitted to the enormity of the sin, not to the dignity of the person sinned against. (If this were not so, any sin, being a sin against the infinite God, would merit infinite punishment—and this would certainly mean the loss of existence itself.) Now no sin is great enough to deserve the loss of existence: for to lose that would be to lose the very benefit on which the whole business of justly assessing a man's deserts rests. Such a punishment would make it impossible to do justice to the sinner, since he would cease to exist as a subject to whom justice can be done. Thus both justice and mercy entail that the damned man continues to exist, even if that existence can only be in an eternal Hell. Such reasoning has a truly Beckettian ring. (See Aquinas, *In Sent.*, 4, Dist. 50, q. 2, art. 1; and Dist. 46 q. 1, art. 3)

p. 185. John Sturrock has put the main point of Robbe-Grillet's novels well, in a review of the most recent of them (*Project for a Revolution in New York*) printed in *The Observer*, London, 28 January 1973: 'What the novel is really about, though it can never admit it openly, is the imagination's overheated and generally ludicrous efforts to get the better of an indifferent reality and insinuate its emotions into it. The characters—who scarcely qualify for the term—are all caught up in this ontological romp either as culprits or victims. But in the end, after umpteen transformations, of scene and identity, and much obviously cod-sado-erotic endeavour, the whole thing founders in contradiction. Reality, after all, is inviolate.'

212 · Part Two: Critical

p. 191. In this sense perhaps Goldmann is right to see Robbe-Grillet as simply expressing the reification of things characteristic of modern capitalism, rather than (as Robbe-Grillet himself claims) expressing man's hopes of liberation from the dominion of things. See Goldmann, *Pour Une Sociologie du Roman*, Paris 1964, and the discussion by Miriam Glucksmann in *New Left Review* 56.

p. 193. Robbe-Grillet upbraids Sartre for the use of metaphorical language because of its 'visceral' basis in bodily experience. Sartre is wrong, we are told, to make Roquentin conclude, in describing a cardboard box that contains his ink bottle, that geometry is completely useless; and that to say that the box is a parallelopiped is to say nothing about it. See *Snapshots*, p. 89.

p. 202. See D. H. Lawrence, Introduction to Frederick Carter's *The Dragon of the Apocalypse*. A more recent attempt to mingle Biblical and scientific ideas about the stars is to be found in the following note by Olivier Messiaen concerning his work *Et Expecto Resurrectionem Mortuorum*: 'In our times of scientific precision, at the very moment of the theories on the expansion of the universe, we perceive that the Bible has always told the truth: that the stars really are "numberless"— and also that the stars "sing" . . . indeed certain stars are gaseous, behave like organ pipes, and we can observe their vibrations'. Messiaen is here referring to 1 Cor. 15: 45; Rev. 2:17; Job, 30:7 (see sleeve note on EMI recording, ASD 246). Another expression of Lawrence's feeling, roughly contemporary with his own, is, of course, Holst's orchestral suite *The Planets*, written during the 1914–18 war.

p. 202. Tony Tanner has drawn attention to the importance of the parapet-walking episode in *An American Dream* as a symbol of the predicament facing the hero: how to walk safely on the edge between conflicting imperious demands: the demands made upon him by 'corporation-land' with its applause for the astronauts and all they stand for, and on the other side, the sinister, possibly demonic but humanly fascinating call of the moon, 'princess of the dead' asking for his allegiance to the truth that (as Lawrence put it) 'in astronomical space, one can only *move*, one cannot be . . . [whereas] in the ancient zodiacal heavens, the whole man is set free, once the imagination crosses the border'. Of course, the moon-image in *Women in Love* ('Moony') has just the opposite connotations: that is why Birkin tries to destroy it.

Conclusion

I began this book by insisting on the connections that exist, or ought to exist between the study of literature and the philosophy of religion. I end it by asking whether any progress has been made towards establishing those connections. I can only answer this question by reasserting two of the assumptions on which my enquiry has been conducted.

The first is that I regard as valuable and profitable the modern movement in the literary criticism of fiction which may be said to date from the era of Henry James and which is usefully described—to use Wayne Booth's famous designation—as the study of its 'rhetoric'. By 'rhetoric' here, Booth meant the whole technique of communicating what the author wants to say to the reader; the marshalling of the resources available to the story-teller as he tries, consciously or unconsciously, to impose his fictional world upon us.[1] But as Mark Schorer has reminded us, in another well-turned phrase, technique is also discovery. To find a new way of doing something—such as telling a story—is always to find something new to do: a new kind of story to tell. And in so far as the kind of stories that a society tells are symptomatic of that society's common world-view, the study of the ever changing rhetoric of story-telling in a particular society is *ipso facto* the study of how that ever-changing world-view is communicated.

Secondly, I take as basic to my enquiry the view that wherever the content of a religious belief-system such as that of Christianity is under examination, a *metaphysic* of some sort is also necessarily in question. In other words I regard as fundamentally correct the intuitions of post-Humean empiricists, Vienna Circle positivists and neo-Thomist scholastics, that to pose the question of religious belief is to pose at the same time the question of the possibility of metaphysics. However

[1] *The Rhetoric of Fiction*, Preface.

different may be the answers given by philosophers in this century to that question, in recognising that the question itself is crucial, at any rate to theistic religion, they are at one. In saying this I am dissociating myself, of course, from that tendency in twentieth-century Christian theology which stems from the work of Barth. However necessary Barth's fundamental hostility to philosophical theology may have been as a corrective, I have here taken it as granted that it will not do as a full account of Christian belief. There is no way of avoiding metaphysics once the question of God has been raised: and there is no way of responding to the challenge of the New Testament without raising the question of God.

Thus two of my most basic assumptions have been that in the study of stories, the matter of narrative rhetoric is crucial to a disciplined criticism, and that in the study of religious belief the matter of the adequacy of metaphysical foundations is equally crucial. But a third, linking assumption has been that, in the nature of the case, religious belief is founded upon stories. Hence, bringing these seemingly quite distinct areas of study into some kind of mutual connection must involve relating the matter of narrative rhetoric and the matter of religious metaphysics. How is this to be accomplished? The burden of my answer has been this: that if we readily admit a rhetoric of fiction and a metaphysics of belief, it is equally important to recognise that there is a rhetoric of belief and a metaphysics of narrative.

But a belief-system such as Christianity is not only founded upon stories; its articulation at any particular moment of a society's history, the flesh and blood of its living reality (or indeed, the overt lack of it) largely depends upon that society's ability to tell itself the appropriate kinds of story. We have therefore to consider not only the rhetoric of the founding narratives, we must also consider the rhetoric of today's fictions.

In the case of the latter I have tried to show that the study of fiction using the equipment of the linguist and the anthropologist reveals metaphysical implications—what I have called an 'analogical dimension'. That is to say, literary criticism which is to do justice to narrative material must include a recognition of the complementary dimensions of metaphor and analogy (to use the traditional metaphysical terminology) or—to use the language of modern linguistics— of the paradigmatic and the syntagmatic dimensions not only of language but of 'story' as a specialised use of language. If my argument is in any sense right, I would regard it as one of its most useful by-products that the metaphysics of Aquinas should be recognised as playing a crucial role within the world of Saussure and Lévi-Strauss.

But if it is useful to draw attention to the metaphysical implications of stories, it is perhaps even more important to recognise the rhetorical element in religious belief. If linguists and critics have recently shown little interest in metaphysics, students of religious stories (Biblical critics for example) have often shown equally little interest in the rhetoric of the narratives they study. Yet if the literary critics are right then it is just as crucial to understanding e.g. what a Biblical narrator wishes to say, that we should appreciate his rhetorical 'technique' as it is to study his sources or his language, or his 'genre'. If one implication of my argument has been to say that the 'anthropological linguistic' and the 'literary critical' approaches to narrative texts are not incompatible but complementary, it has equally been my object to show that the historical and linguistic study of the stories which offer the basic data of religious belief is not enough. We need a literary criticism in the humane if inexact tradition of Jamesian criticism, a study of religious rhetoric in narrative, to complement the linguistic, anthropological and historical studies that we have hitherto been confronted with.

In the first part of this book I attempted to discuss the 'rhetoric' of belief in terms of some very elementary study of Biblical narratives. But in the second I have tried to show what the 'metaphysics of fiction' implies for contemporary belief by the consideration of a few selected modern examples. But I am aware that to do this with extended and complex works such as the novels discussed in Part 2 is an extremely delicate business. This is why I have tried to avoid any simple mechanical application of my theoretical conclusions to particular cases of fictional narrative. It is one thing to expound, say, the paradigmatic/syntagmatic structure of a sonnet: quite another, without doing radical injustice to the complex reality which is a major novel, to attempt the same for, say, Waugh's trilogy, or Beckett's. This is why, having indicated at the outset which aspect of the theoretical enquiry I am mainly putting to the test in each particular instance, I have left the discussion of each author's 'rhetoric' to speak for itself, in the hope that the implications of the theory will make themselves more or less apparent from the treatment of each example. But, to reiterate very briefly what I have attempted to do in the critical part of this book, it may be worth noting that what I have said about Waugh, Beckett,

Robbe-Grillet and Mailer all stems from what I see as a basic dichotomy which is best exposed in the differing endeavours of Lawrence and Joyce. These two great figures of the modern period in fiction seem to me increasingly representative of the two main tendencies of narrative. In a multiplicity of ways, Lawrence seems to stand for the 'vertical' dimension and its recovery in fiction: in his search for the 'unseen presences' that he feels above and below him in the natural world, in his sense of the narrator's presence in and moral responsibility for interpreting his own vision to us, in his radically metaphorical language, in his immersion in (rather than detachment from) what Stephen Daedalus called 'desire and loathing'. Joyce, equally increasingly, seems to stand for the opposite qualities, the 'horizontal' qualities, for an art in which the narrator is impersonalised out of both desire and loathing. I have sought to show in the subsequent discussion how some particular aspect of this dichotomy is embodied in each of the authors I have chosen to discuss. In the case of Waugh, I have emphasised the ambiguous and perilous relation between teller and tale in his fiction, the substitution of what I have called narrative 'dandyism' for a commitment either to Joycean impersonality or to its Lawrentian opposite as a narrative ideal. In the case of Beckett, I have tried to trace the consequences that follow when neither dandyism nor narrative commitment seems a possible option, and instead the narrator as a distinct voice is simply obliterated or totally absorbed into what is being told. But naturally, these different responses to the fundamental problem of narrative 'rhetoric' have consequences elsewhere—for example in the sort of language that the narrator finds it possible to use, and especially in the degree to which a coherent framework of metaphor is available in it or not. In the cases of Robbe-Grillet and Mailer I have used just this approach, beginning with the question of metaphorical language and its availability or non-availability, and ending with some consideration of the effects this has in each case upon the 'metaphysics' or 'anti-metaphysics' of the author's fiction.

Inevitably, such an enterprise, even in so tentative form as is to be found in this book, is fraught with problems both of method and content. Most of these I must leave unsolved, or allow to lie fallow for further cultivation. There is however, one further point to be made about the kind of 'inter-disciplinary' study which has here been attempted. It is obviously subject to all the shortcomings of ignorance, obsolescence and misunderstanding attendant upon trying to work in several fields at once: fields which are themselves each too vast to be properly mastered in a lifetime. But it is equally obvious to me, from a consideration of the principles involved and from practical experience, that there is no truly 'interdisciplinary' work except that which goes on inside the brain of a single individual. To knock together in a single course of study the heads of persons variously engaged in (say) literary, theological, philosophical and linguistic studies may produce, with luck, a fairly exciting, even explosive mixture. But it will seldom produce a permanently valuable new compound. For new compounds can only be produced within a single vessel where the necessary reaction takes place: and similarly, new intellectual relationships can only be brought into being by some single and no doubt very fallible intelligence. This is the root problem of all systematic attempts to cross the boundaries of established disciplines. I am sure I have not solved it: my only justification is that I have tried.

Bibliography of Books Cited

Aquinas, St Thomas, *Summa Theologiae*, Latin Text and English translation in 60 volumes, London (Eyre and Spottiswoode) 1963—, New York (McGraw Hill) 1963—.

—, *In Metaphysics*, ed. M. R. Cathala and R. M. Spiazzi, Rome (Marietti) 1950.

Armstrong, A. H., *An Introduction to Ancient Philosophy*, 3rd edn. London (Methuen) 1968.

Ashby, W. Ross, *Introduction to Cybernetics*, London (Chapman and Hall) 1958.

Augustine, Saint, *Confessions*, trans. E. B. Pusey, London (J. M. Dent and Sons) 1957.

Aylen, Leo, *Greek Tragedy and the Modern World*, London (Methuen) 1964.

Barnard, G. C., *Samuel Beckett: A New Approach*, London (J. M. Dent and Sons) 1970.

Bayley, John, *The Characters of Love*, London (Constable) 1960.

Beckett, Samuel, *No's Knife: Collected Shorter Prose*, London (Calder and Boyars) 1967.

—, *Murphy*, first published 1938: London (Calder and Boyars), New York (Grove Press).

—, *Watt*, first published 1953; London (John Calder), New York (Grove Press).

—, *Molloy*, first published in French 1951; in English 1955.

—, *Malone Dies*, first published in French 1951; in English 1956.

—, *The Unnamable*, first published in French 1953; in English 1958.

—, The above three works published in a single volume, London (Calder and Boyars), New York (Grove Press), referred to in notes as 'Trilogy'.

—, *Not I*, London (Faber and Faber) 1973.

—, *Waiting for Godot*, first published in French 1952; London (Faber and Faber), New York (Grove Press).

—, *How It Is*, first published in French 1961; London (John Calder), New York (Grove Press).

—, *The Lost Ones*, first published in French 1971; London (Calder and Boyars), New York (Grove Press).

—, *Lessness*, first published in French 1969; London (Calder and Boyars).

—, *Happy Days*, first published in English 1961; London (Faber and Faber, New York (Grove Press).

—, *Endgame*, first published in French 1957; London (Faber and Faber), New York (Grove Press).

Bergonzi, Bernard, *The Situation of the Novel*, London (Macmillan) 1970.

—, (ed.), *The Twentieth Century*, London (Sphere Books) 1970 (Volume 7 of *Sphere History of Literature in the English Language*).

Black, Max, *Models and Metaphors*, Ithaca (Cornell University Press) 1962.

Booth, Wayne, *The Rhetoric of Fiction*, Chicago and London (University of Chicago Press) 1961.

Boyle, Robert, *Metaphor in Hopkins*, Chapel Hill (University of N. Carolina Press) 1960.

Bradbury, Malcolm, *Evelyn Waugh*, Edinburgh and London (Oliver and Boyd) 1964.

Brooke-Rose, Christine, *A Grammar of Metaphor*, London (Secker and Warburg) 1958.

Burrell, David, *Analogy and Philosophical Language*, London and New-haven (Yale University Press) 1973.

Caird, G. B., *Principalities and Powers*, Oxford (Clarendon Press) 1956.

Cameron, J. M., *The Night Battle*, London (Burns Oates and Washbourne) 1962.

Camus, A., *Selected Essays and Notebooks*, ed. Philip Thody, Harmondsworth (Penguin Books) 1970.

Carson, Rachael, *Silent Spring*, Harmondsworth (Penguin Books) 1965.

Chardin, Teilhard de, *Le Milieu Divin*, London (Fontana Books) 1964.

Chesterton, G. K., *Orthodoxy*, London (The Bodley Head) 1927.

Chomsky, Noam, *Aspects of the Theory of Syntax*, Cambridge, Mass. (M. I. T. Press) 1965.

Coleridge, S. T., *Coleridge's Shakespeare Criticism*, ed. T. M. Raysor, London (Constable) 1930.

—, *Collected Letters*, ed. E. L. Griggs, Oxford (Clarendon Press) 1956.

Conrad, Joseph, *The Nigger of the Narcissus*, Harmondsworth (Penguin Books) 1963.

Copleston, F., *A History of Philosophy*, 8 vols, London (Burns Oates and Washbourne) 1946–66.

Coe, Richard, *Beckett*, Edinburgh and London (Oliver and Boyd) 1964.

Cox, Harvey, *The Secular City*, London (S.C.M. Press) 1965.

Crystal, David, *Linguistics*, Harmondsworth (Penguin Books) 1971.

Dante, *Letters*, ed. Paget Toynbee, Oxford (Clarendon Press) 1920.

Dewart, Leslie, *The Future of Belief*, London (Sheed and Ward) 1967, New York (Herder and Herder) 1966.

Dewart, Leslie, *The Foundations of Belief*, London (Search Press) 1969, New York (Herder and Herder) 1970.

Donoghue, Denis, *Yeats*, London (Fontana Books) 1971.

Durrant, Michael, *The Logical Status of 'God'*, London (Macmillan) 1972.

Eliade, Mircea, *The Myth of the Eternal Return*, trans. W. R. Trask, London (Routledge and Kegan Paul) 1954.

Ellmann, Richard, *James Joyce*, London (Oxford University Press) 1959.

Ford, Boris, (ed.). *From Dryden to Johnson*, Harmondsworth (Penguin Books) 1965.

—, *The Modern Age*, Harmondsworth (Penguin Books) 1961.

Forster, E. M., *Aspects of the Novel*, Harmondsworth (Penguin Books) 1962.

Fletcher, John, *The Novels of Samuel Beckett*, London (Chatto and Windus) 1964.

Flew, A. and MacIntyre, A., *New Essays in Philosophical Theology*, London (S.C.M. Press) 1955.

Fuller, R. H., *The Formation of the Resurrection Narratives*, London (S.P.C.K.) 1972.

Gardner, W. H., *Gerard Manley Hopkins*, London (Secker and Warburg), Vol. I 1944; Vol. II 1949.

Geach, P.T., *God and the Soul*, London (Routledge and Kegan Paul) 1969.

—, *Three Philosophers* (with G. E. M. Anscombe), Oxford (Basil Blackwell) 1961.

Gilson, Etienne, *The Spirit of Mediaeval Philosophy*, trans. A. H. Downes, London (Sheed and Ward) 1950.

Goldberg, S. L., *The Classical Temper*, London (Chatto and Windus) 1963.

Golding, William, *Pincher Martin*, London (Faber and Faber) 1960.

Goldmann, Lucien, *The Hidden God*, trans. Philip Thody, London (Routledge and Kegan Paul) 1964.

Goldsmith, Edward, (ed.), *Blueprint for Survival*, Harmondsworth (Penguin Books) 1972.

Goulder, M. D., *Midrash and Lection in Matthew*, London (S.P.C.K.) 1974.

Gregor, I. and Stein, W., (eds.), *The Prose for God*, London (Sheed and Ward) 1973.

Gross, John, *Joyce*, London (Fontana Books) 1971.

Hartshorne, Charles, *The Divine Relativity*, New Haven (Yale University Press) 1964.

—, *A Natural Theology for our Time*, La Salle (Open Court Publishing Co.) 1967.

Hawkes, Terence, *Metaphor*, London (Methuen) 1972.

Healey, F. G., (ed.), *Prospects for Theology*, London (Nisbet) 1967.

Hick, John, (ed.), *The Existence of God*, New York (Macmillan) 1967.

Hopkins, Gerard Manley, *Collected Poems*, ed. W. H. Gardner, 3rd edn. London (Oxford University Press) 1948.

—, *Notebooks and Papers*, ed. Humphrey House, London (Oxford University Press) 1937.

Hough, Graham, *The Dark Sun*, Harmondsworth (Penguin Books) 1961.

Hume, David, *Treatise of Human Nature*, 2 vols, London (J. M. Dent and Sons) 1949.

Jakobson, Roman and Halle, Morris, *Fundamentals of Language*, The Hague (Mounton and Co.) 1956.

Josipovici, Gabriel, *The World and the Book*, London (Macmillan) 1971.

Joyce, James, *A Portrait of the Artist as a Young Man*, first published 1916: in *The Essential James Joyce*, ed. H. Levin, Harmondsworth (Penguin Books), New York (Viking Press, as *The Portable James Joyce*).

—, *Stephen Hero*, first published 1944: London (Four Square Books), New York (New Directions).

—, *Dubliners*, first published 1914: in *The Essential James Joyce*.

—, *Ulysses*, first published 1922: London (The Bodley Head) 1960, New York (Random House).

Kaufman, Gordon, *God the Problem*, Cambridge, Mass. (Harvard University Press) 1972.

Kenny, Anthony, *Descartes: A Study of His Philosophy*, New York (Random House) 1968.

—, (ed.), *Aquinas: A Collection of Critical Essays*, London (Macmillan) 1969.

Kermode, Frank, *The Sense of an Ending*, London (Oxford University Press) 1967.

—, *Shakespeare, Spenser and Donne*, London (Routledge and Kegan Paul) 1971.

Larkin, Philip, *The Less Deceived*, London (The Marvell Press) 1955.

Lawrence, D. H., *Study of Thomas Hardy*, first published in *Phoenix*, 1936: also in *D. H. Lawrence: Selected Literary Criticism*, ed. Anthony Beal, London (Heinemann) 1961.

—, *Birds, Beasts and Flowers*, first published 1923: in *Complete Poems* 2 vols. London (Heinemann), New York (Viking Press).

—, *Lady Chatterley's Lover*, first published 1929: Harmondsworth (Penguin Books), New York (New American Library).

—, *Introduction to the Dragon of the Apocalypse*, in *Phoenix*, London (Heinemann), New York (Viking Press).

—, *Women in Love*, first published in 1921: Harmondsworth (Penguin Books), New York (Viking Press).

—, *St Mawr*, first published 1925: Harmondsworth (Penguin Books), New York (Random House).

Lawrence, D. H., *The Woman Who Rode Away*, first published 1928: Harmondsworth (Penguin Books), New York (Viking Press).

—, *The Man Who Died*, first published 1931: in *The Short Novels of D. H. Lawrence*, Vol. 2, London (Heinemann), New York (Random House).

Leach, Edmund, *Lévi-Strauss*, London (Fontana Books) 1970.

Leavis, F. R., *D. H. Lawrence, Novelist*, London (Chatto and Windus) 1955.

Lévi-Strauss, *Le Totemisme aujourd'hui*, Paris 1962, trans. as *Totemism*, Rodney Needham, Harmondsworth (Penguin Books) 1969.

—, *Tristes Tropiques*, Paris 1955, trans. as *A World on the Wane*, John Russell, London (Hutchinson) 1961.

Lodge, David, *The Novelist at the Crossroads*, London (Routledge and Kegan Paul) 1971.

Lovejoy, A. O., *The Great Chain of Being*, Cambridge, Mass. (Harvard University Press) 1936.

MacKinnon, Donald, *Borderlands of Theology*, London (Lutterworth Press) 1968.

Maddox, John, *The Doomsday Syndrome*, London (Macmillan) 1972.

Mailer, Norman, *A Fire on the Moon*, London (Weidenfeld and Nicolson), Boston (Little Brown) 1970.

—, *An American Dream*, London (Mayflower Paperback), New York (Dial Press) 1965.

—, *The Armies of the Night*, Harmondsworth (Penguin Books), New York (Signet Books) 1968.

—, *Why Are We in Vietnam?* London (Panther Books), New York (Putnam) 1967.

Mann, Thomas, *Stories and Episodes*, London (J. M. Dent and Sons) 1947.

Mascall, E. L., *The Openess of Being*, London (Darton, Longman and Todd) 1971.

Masterson, Patrick, *Atheism and Alienation*, Dublin (Gill and Macmillan) 1971.

Merleau-Ponty, M., *Phenomenology of Perception*, trans. Colin Smith, London (Routledge and Kegan Paul) 1962.

Meynell, Hugo, *God and the World*, London (S.P.C.K.) 1971.

Mill, J. S., *System of Logic*, London (Longmans, Green, Reader and Dyer) 9th edn., 1875.

Monod, Jacques, *Chance and Necessity*, trans. Austryn Wainhouse, London (Collins) 1972.

Mooney, C., *Teilhard de Chardin and the Mystery of Christ*, London (Collins) 1966.

Moore, Harry T., (ed.), *Collected Letters of D. H. Lawrence*, London (Heinemann) 1962.

Newman, J. H., *Parochial and Plain Sermons*, 8 vols, London (Rivingtons) 1868.

—, *An Essay in Aid of a Grammar of Assent*, London (Longmans, Green and Co.) 1898.

—, *The Development of Christian Doctrine*, London and New York (Sheed and Ward) 1960.

Orwell, George, *Collected Essays, Letters and Journalism*, 4 vols, London (Secker and Warburg) 1968.

Pascal, B., *Pensees*, trans, A. J. Krailshcimer, Harmondsworth (Penguin Books) 1966.

Rad, G. H. von, *Genesis*, trans. John H. Marks, London (S.C.M. Press) 1961.

Richards, I. A., *The Philosophy of Rhetoric*, London (Oxford University Press) 1936.

Robbe-Grillet, Alain, *Snapshots and Towards a New Novel*, trans. Barbara Wright, London (Calder and Boyars), New York (Grove Press) 1965.

—, *The House of Assignation*, trans. A. M. Sheridan Smith, London (Calder and Boyars), trans. Richard Howard, New York (Grove Press) 1966.

—, *The Erasers*, trans. Richard Howard, London (Calder and Boyars), New York (Grove Press) 1964.

—, *The Voyeur*, (1958), trans. Richard Howard, London (Calder and Boyars), New York (Grove Press) 1958.

—, *Jealousy*, (1965), trans. Richard Howard, London (Calder and Boyars), New York (Grove Press) 1965.

—, *In The Labyrinth*, trans. Christine Brooke-Rose, London (Calder and Boyars), New York (Grove Press) 1965.

—, *Project for a Revolution in New York*, trans. Richard Howard, London (John Calder), New York (Grove Press) 1972.

Roszak, Theodore, *The Making of a Counter Culture*, London (Faber and Faber) 1970.

Rousseau, J. J., *Confessions*, trans. J. M. Cohen, Harmondsworth (Penguin Books) 1953.

Ruskin, John, *Modern Painters*, 5 vols, Orpington and London (George Allen), 1897.

Sayers, Dorothy, *The Mind of the Maker*, London (Methuen) 1941.

—, (transl.) *The Divine Comedy*, Vol. III ('Paradise'), Harmondsworth (Penguin Books) 1962.

Schlier, Heinrich, *Principalities and Powers in the New Testament*, Freiburg and London (Herder and Collins) 1961.

Scholes, Robert and Kellogg, Robert, *The Nature of Narrative*, New York (Oxford University Press) 1966.

Sewell, Elizabeth, *The Orphic Voice*, London (Routledge and Kegan Paul) 1960.

Snow, C. P., *The Two Cultures and the Scientific Revolution*, Cambridge (Cambridge University Press) 1959.

Stanford, W. B., *Greek Metaphor*, Oxford (Basil Blackwell) 1936.

Stein, Walter, *Criticism as Dialogue*, Cambridge (Cambridge University Press) 1969.

Stevens, Wallace, *Opus Posthumous*, ed. S. F. Morse, London (Faber and Faber) 1959.

Strawson, P. F., *Individuals*, London (Methuen) 1959.

Stopp, Frederick, *Evelyn Waugh: Portrait of an Artist*, London (Chapman and Hall) 1958.

Tanner, Tony, *City of Words: American Fiction from 1950–1970*, London (Jonathan Cape) 1971.

Tate, Allen, (ed.), *The Language of Poetry*, Princeton, 1942.

Taylor, G. Rattray, *The Doomsday Book*, London (Panther Books) 1970.

Usborne, Richard, *Wodehouse at Work*, London (Herbert Jenkins) 1961.

Van Buren, Paul, *The Secular Meaning of the Gospel*, London (S.C.M. Press) 1963.

—, *The Edges of Language*, London (S.C.M. Press) 1972.

Vaux, Roland de, *Genèse*, Paris (Editions du Cerf) 1951.

Vawter, Bruce, *A Path Through Genesis*, London (Sheed and Ward) 1957.

Ward, Barbara and Dubos, René, *Only One Earth*, Harmondsworth (Penguin Books) 1972.

Waugh, Evelyn, *Scoop*, first published 1938: Harmondsworth (Penguin Books), New York (Dell).

—, *Decline and Fall*, first published 1928: Harmondsworth (Penguin Books), New York (Dell).

—, *The Ordeal of Gilbert Pinfold*, first published 1957: Harmondsworth (Penguin Books), Boston (Little Brown).

—, *Vile Bodies*, first published 1932: Harmondsworth (Penguin Books), New York (Dell).

—, *A Handful of Dust*, first published 1934: Harmondsworth (Penguin Books), New York (Dell).

—, *Brideshead Revisited*, first published 1945: Harmondsworth (Penguin Books), New York (Dell).

Waugh, Evelyn, *Men at Arms*, first published 1952: Harmondsworth (Penguin Books), Boston (Little Brown).

—, *Officers and Gentlemen*, first published 1955; Harmondsworth (Penguin Books), Boston (Little Brown).

—, *Unconditional Surrender*, first published 1961; Harmondsworth (Penguin Books), Boston (Little Brown).

Wheelwright, Philip, *The Burning Fountain*, Bloomington (Indiana University Press) 1968.

Whitehead, A. N., *Process and Reality*, Cambridge (Cambridge University Press) 1929.

Wiener, Norbert, *The Human Use of Human Beings*, London (Sphere Books) 1968.

Williams, Raymond, *Modern Tragedy*, London (Chatto and Windus) 1966.

Wisdom, John, *Philosophy and Psycho-Analysis*, Oxford (Basil Blackwell) 1953.

Wittgenstein, L., *Tractatus Logico-Philosophious*, trans. D. F. Pears and B. F. Guinness, London (Routledge and Kegan Paul) 1961.

Index